# UNIVERSO-i

The 7-Day Path to Overcoming
Anxiety and Fear and Living
the Life of Your Dreams

Brian Frederiksen

Inspired by my life story

**Book Title:** UNIVERSO-i
**Sub-Title:** The 7-Day Path to Overcoming Anxiety and Fear and Living the Life of Your Dreams
**Author:** Brian Frederiksen

Publishing and Marketing Consultant: Lama Jabr
xanapublishingandmarketing.com
Sydney, Australia

Cover design by Pamela Mastro

First Edition

ISBN: 978-1-63649-008-3



A CIP catalogue record for this title is available from the British Library.

# About the Author

**BRIAN FREDERIKSEN** holds a Master's Degree in Engineering and a Master's in Business Administration and is considered one of the world's leading change agents for Artificial Intelligence innovations disrupting Healthcare.

A serial entrepreneur and a Senior Advisor on Artificial Intelligence to European governments, as a Fortune 500 Executive he devised the largest and most disruptive AI Healthcare deals in the world.

A Global Business Development Executive, Brian promotes a culture of experimentation, generosity, kindness, and courage to take the path less traveled. Brian runs a business accelerator for early stage companies promoting bright minds on saving and improving the lives of others and the planet.

# Claim Your Free eBook

Feeling uncertain about the future? Anxious about pursuing your dreams? Reluctant to get out of an unhealthy relationship? Less inclined to start your own business or to move to the location you always dreamed of?

Do you know why?

For most people there are usually one or two reasons.

1. The first reason is that now more than ever in history, there's enormous power and money at stake for organizations that can make you forget you were born with God-like powers to shape your life and instead keep you in a constant state of anxiety to distract you from what's really important, trading your freedom for free shipping of things you don't need.

2. The second reason is that, perhaps at some point in your life, someone told you things intended to lower your self-worth and doubt your potential: things such as: 'stop dreaming' or someone pressured you into a life that you didn't want.

In the end, your escape from a life based on anxiety and fear to one of purpose, peace and prosperity depends on who is in control of your life—you, or someone else?

*If you're ready to free yourself and achieve everything you want from life, no matter what anyone ever told you or whatever your current circumstance is, then Download my free book, and I will show you how to escape and take back control of your life.*

https://brianfrederiksen.com/free-book

# Dedication

*For my beloved wife and son.*

*The…*

*Kray family, thank you for always being my port in the storm when I needed you the most. You're the best and most dependable of friends a person could ever wish to meet in a lifetime.*

*And…*

*All the brave and powerful women in our lives. Our mothers, grand-mothers and great-grandmothers, who, early in their lives were left alone to raise and support their children. Generation after generation, these strong women never complained. They overcame the most grueling obstacles and sacrificed their lives to ensure a safer and more prosperous path for generations to come.*

# Author's Note

We say children are special. Children's minds give birth to dreams; those dreams give birth to wings, the instrument needed to achieve dreams.

As children grow older, society tries to strip away those wings, one feather at a time. If they listen, those children of dreams slowly begin doubting themselves and the sense of direction in their lives.

They drown out the voices of their ancestors and stop conversing with the rivers and the swaying trees. Slowly but surely, they lose their ability to remember the magic inherent in all creation.

Over time, these children with wings—you and I—become anxiety-riddled adults. In that state, our minds clouded by stress, confusion, fear, and anger, we forget our immense power and instead become easy targets for manipulation.

When fearful, we're willing to hand over control of our lives to those we believe can offer us safety. In our state of passivity and fear, we stick to our jobs, pay our bills, vote for people who claim they can protect us, and push away our dreams for a later time.

A time that may never come.

However, it wasn't always like this.

Human civilization started around 12,000 years ago. We went from zero to the Declaration of Human Rights, Michelangelo's Pietà, Shakespeare and Mozart, to modern advancements like the telephone, flight, moon landings, gene-editing, artificial intelligence, and quantum computers…in less than 500 generations.

That progress is astounding, but it didn't happen by chance. Generation after generation, every soul born had to conquer their fears of failure, the unknown and of disappointing others.

But those who overcame fear unleashed powers granted to everyone at birth; greatness with unimaginable potential to shape their lives and control their destiny, leaving a path for others to follow.

This book is an inside story of fear, told by one of those children, born of wings and dreams, who crossed oceans and land to rediscover the magic he'd lost on his journey through life.

Should the following story give you a lesson to learn about how to overcome fear to live the life you were always meant to lead, dear reader, then it has achieved that dream.

I hope that by sharing my life story, you too will find the courage to overcome anxiety, fear, and oppression and begin living the life of your dreams.

With all my prayers and blessings for your journey and the adventures that lie ahead…

Yours sincerely,

*Brian Frederiksen*
*July 11, 2020*

**F-E-A-R**

*has two meanings:*

*"Forget Everything and Run" or" Face Everything and Rise."*

*The choice is yours.*

— *ZIG ZIGLAR*

*"The conscious and intelligent manipulation of the organized habits and opinions of the masses is an essential element in a democratic society. Those who manipulate this unseen mechanism of society constitute an invisible government, which is the true ruling power of our country.*

*We are governed, our minds are moulded, our tastes formed, our ideas suggested, largely by men we have never heard of. This is a logical result of the way in which our democratic society is organized. Vast numbers of human beings must cooperate in this manner if they are to live together as a smoothly functioning society.*

*In almost every act of our daily lives, whether in the sphere of politics or business, in our social conduct or our ethical thinking, we are dominated by the relatively small number of persons...who understand the mental processes and social patterns of the masses.*

*It is they who pull the wires which control the public mind..."*

—EDWARD BERNAYS,
THE FATHER OF PR AND COUSIN OF SIGMUND FREUD,
PUBLISHED IN 1928

## LIVE THE LIFE OF YOUR DREAMS
## THE 7-DAY PATH TO OVERCOMING ANXIETY AND FEAR

What if I show you how to overcome anxiety and fear - how to discover your real purpose - enabling you to unleash God-like powers granted to you from birth - giving you incredible potential to shape your life and control your destiny, making you feel more effective, successful and peaceful than you could ever imagine?

Would you want it?

I am willing to share the secrets with you and I promise you the story I'm about to tell is unlike any you have experienced.

I wrote this book for you, to help your transition away from a life of uncertainty, anxiety and fear. Although my life story will hopefully inspire you to make the necessary changes, the key to transforming your future is to reflect deeply on past events and people in your own life and on how they influenced important decisions that you've made - who are today the people you surrounded yourself with, your relationships, your home and choice of occupation.

To assist you, I have structured the book in 7 parts. Each represents major events in most people's lives, including mine.

1. Childhood (Learning and Unlearning)
2. Growth to Young Adulthood
3. Money, Power and Temptations
4. Searching for a Balance - a Spiritual Path
5. Corporate Growth - and Betrayals
6. The Puppet Masters - Escaping the Matrix
7. Love and Family

At the end of the book you will find important questions for each of life's pathways. Over the next 7 days I encourage you to focus on the 7 parts of your life, one day at a time.

You'll want to have a notepad at hand to write down all the thoughts that come to mind for each of these critical parts of your life.

If one of these seven parts or aspects of your life takes more than a day to reflect on, then don't worry. It is important to take the time you need to identify the past experiences that obstruct your life in the present. This helps you to discover the life you really should be leading and come up with a concrete plan to change your life in that direction.

Remember, in the end, your escape from a life based on anxiety and fear into a life of purpose, prosperity and peace depends on who is in control of your life - you, or someone else?

So, choose to take control of your life and your thoughts. Don't give others power over your life through things they did or said to you in the past, or try to control you with in the present.

Everything you need for your new journey, you already have. Be brave, take risks, experiment, be curious, be bold and challenge the status quo in your life.

Now let's begin. Remember you're not alone. I am going to be right there with you, to make sure you too find the life you dream of.

# Contents

# UNIVERSO-i

I am **THE UNIVERSE** is me

# Prologue

"Tell me about your dream again," said the Bruja.

The man hesitated. He stared into the flames of the crackling fire, filled with a terrible sense of dread. He could feel the eyes of the witch on him, the stone cave walls surrounding them. He shivered in the damp chill, the answer to her question frozen in his throat.

The Bruja waited, tapping her finger on her bony chest. The man could feel his own chest was in agony. He tried to fill his lungs with air. *Oh, God, it hurt.* He rotated his head and stared at the subterranean wall streaked with stiletto-shaped shafts of moonlight. As he turned, his tattered shirt fell off from his upper torso, exposing the makeshift bandages on his chest. Baffled, he levelled his eyes at the old witch.

"My dream?" he said.

The Bruja and her witchcraft had led him here like a sleepwalker, to a Native American cave thousands of feet up a mountainside, somewhere in New Mexico. His last real memory was of a crash. Darkness. Then immense pain. The man narrowed his eyebrows in concentration. Had he told her about his dream?

The witch stayed silent, her eyes in a squint. The man gazed around the dark stone chamber, the smoke-scarred walls surrounding them, fighting his fear. *How long have I been here?* he wondered, stroking his chin, feeling four to five days of beard stubble. Outside he heard the wind stop. Cold fear raced through him. His bowels turned to water.

The man had been warned about the witch. As a boy, the man had been frightened of monsters and witches. This one, the Bruja, looked about 60, with raven-black hair, sun-wrinkled brown skin and glittering white teeth, and moonlit eyes that watched the man coldly. The man trembled, trying to reassure himself, yet fear filled his gut as his mind returned to the dream.

"It's a dream from my childhood," he whispered, eyes fixed on the fire, his mind fading back into the haze again. "I'm in the desert, the sun beating down on me. I hear fearful voices by the millions cry out in agony. Then, in the distance, like an oasis mirage, I see the blurry outline of a figure coming towards me. A woman I believe, though I can't see her face from the faceless white mask. She suddenly stops, kneels, and with her finger draws a symbol in the sand. I want to move closer to see what it is, but my legs won't let me." The man paused, staring, more in-depth into the fire. "Suddenly, a massive sandstorm approaches, like a towering tsunami. It erases the symbol in the sand and envelops me…"

He paused again, emptying his lungs of air, his mind suddenly adrift.

"Go on," said the witch.

Apprehensively the man looked at her. His lungs went back to the work of breathing. He gulped air, cleared his throat, and continued. "The voices crying out are suddenly drowned by the sounds of ancient horns being blown, announcing the beginning of a battle for the end of the world. I see seven angels with seven trumpets and hear the battle commencing, but I am blinded by the dust and sand. Then I wake up. Each time the same."

The Bruja remained silent. The man felt his nerves becoming frayed.

"What does it mean?" he asked, his throat tightening, his voice cracking.

The witch's eyes glittered at the man. Suddenly he felt himself struggling to breathe. In a panic, he choked. Far off, he swore he could hear the Bruja's laughter, sharp as icicles. Could this crazy older woman read his mind?

*"Answer my question!"* the man blurted out, a sharp bolt of agony stabbing his temples.

The words floated in the air, sizzled into the crackling bonfire. The night wind picked up again and whipped through the cave. The man felt an icy chill envelop him, sucking the breath out of his lungs, twisting him in circles. His legs buckled. His numbed hands lashed out for anything they could grasp, as he felt himself plummeting downward, into darkness, into an abyss again.

The Bruja heard the breath go out of the man. She offered him a grotesque smile.

"Why should I?" she asked. "How do I know that you are worthy of my time?" Anticipation flashed in her moonlit eyes. "Instead, tell me about your worst fear."

The man clawed at the air, feeling the ground beneath him vanish, his mind swallowed in panic.

"My worst fear…" he said, struggling to breathe. Sweat rolled down his face, stinging his eyes. He tried to push the sensation of plunging out of his mind. "When the time comes for the present to slip away, that I have failed my Creator, and did not fulfil the potential of the life and opportunities I was offered." *Oh God!* he thought, his pin-wheeling arms finding nothing to grab, trying to brace himself from falling. "Dying," he continued, "without having done enough to bring joy, love, and light into the lives of others. I fear that more than the ghost of those who dwell in the darkness of the valley of death."

"We will see about that." The older woman's smile widened.

Suddenly the man felt an overwhelming sense of pain and the most profound sadness; it was the pain of all the people in his life who had suffered because of his selfish choices. Voices swirled around him. A feeling of hopelessness and defeat pounded his brain. Would he ever be able to make amends?

*How do I overcome fear to live the life I want?* he shouted at her from the depth of his pain and anxiety.

For a heartbeat, he dared to look across the bonfire into the Bruja's eyes. Her face looked twisted, her eyes sunk in deep brown circles.

"The answer is as important as the question. Do you think you have the strength to face the truth," the Bruja snorted, still smiling, "and overcome your deepest fears?"

The man stared across at the Bruja, eyes streaming tears of angst. With all his strength, he tried to nod his head, to say *yes*, but the pain was overwhelming.

"Would you like the pain to stop?" whispered the Bruja. "I can awaken you in a warm bed, remembering nothing. Or do you want to learn about your dream, and how to overcome your fear, so you can become the man you were meant to be?"

The man struggled. His knees buckled. *I must know!* his mind pleaded. *I'll take the pain and suffering, no matter how immense. I can't face life, avoiding my worst fears.*

Hearing these thoughts, the Bruja smiled. Suddenly the man's heart stopped in his chest. He found it impossible to tear his eyes away from her. A tangle of sweat trickled down to his collar. Is this what death looks like? Did this older woman have a pact with the devil? He clawed at the air to stand, his legs weak and wobbly. He found himself struggling to breathe. His chest tightened even more, and he gasped, clutching his heart in fear and with some sense of relief that finally, this life was over.

"I have *another* question for you," said the witch, interrupting his thoughts. Her lips wriggled away from her teeth in a horrible smile. Her eyes flashed. The man trembled.

"Why shouldn't I kill you?" she said.

* * *

# Path / Day One

## Childhood

# One

As far back as the boy could remember, he'd experienced the fear that someone was watching him. Not just now and then, but all the time.

It began when he was only seven years old.

It was a warm summer day in Vanløse, the boy's little hometown on the outskirts of Copenhagen.

There on a street corner, he stood, outside the family home, selling beautiful wildflowers he'd plucked from a big forest of lilac trees in full bloom in the community gardens, placing them in little plastic cups and setting them out on a tiny, rickety table.

The colors of the flowers reminded the boy of the stories of compassion and mercy he'd heard from his mother and grandmother. Gazing at the rainbow of colors put him into a state of utter calmness, of deep and serene peace. The boy was born an introvert, so standing on a corner trying to convince people to buy flowers took much courage.

His tiny, frail legs were tired from standing. The boy's mother, selling flowers there also, nudged him. "Stand up straight."

The boy sighed. He avoided the eyes of his mother. He would've preferred to be alone yet needed to do something to make money because he came from a divorced family and his mother, a beautiful psychiatric nurse, already worked three shifts, so they needed the cash.

Poverty went as far back as the boy's baptism, where it was up to mom to find and borrow the money for him to be christened.

As a child, however, he never noticed poverty. Such is the beauty and innocence of childhood.

"You have an extraordinary boy," the older, brown-skinned man with a limp said in a foreign accent, as he approached the boy and his mother that day.

In confusion the boy crouched behind his mother, sighting from around her skirt the strange man. "I didn't mean to frighten you," the man said, politely tipping his hat. With a furrowed brow the boy plucked up a bouquet then offered it to the man, then looked to his mother, noticing the brown-skinned man was barely taller than he.

"Thank you," his mother said. She smiled proudly at her son and then turned back to the limping stranger. But like a ghost in the wind, he had gone.

* * *

Later that afternoon, the boy went inside his house for some water. Gulping a drink from the sink he splashed water on his face. His mother was on the phone in the hall and didn't see or hear him.

"Confirm my identity? Why? Who is this?"

She was annoyed, the boy noticed. *I'll ask her what's wrong,* he thought. He didn't know who was on the phone and really didn't want to ask, fearing it was another bill collector.

"My financial interest? What does that mean, Mr. Swanson?"

*Mr. Swanson?* The boy wondered. He'd never heard the name before. His mouth went dry with fear. His mother listened, and suddenly, her body language changed, and she looked both intrigued and wary.

"So, who is this supposed rich guy?" she said.

Now, she sounded sarcastic. This troubled the small child. Instantly he wanted to climb into his mother's lap.

"Okay, okay, international man of mystery," his mother sniggered, and suddenly looked at the boy and winked. "Listen, you're probably some scammer, so…"

The caller spoke again, and his mother's demeanor changed dramatically.

"*How* much?" Her eyes widened. "My *God…*"

The boy's heart pounded, as he watched his mother slump into a chair, hair all over her amazed face.

"He…he needs to do *what?* Prove his capabilities?"

She gave the boy a gaze and turned away, whispering into the phone conspiratorially.

"He's a little young..." The boy listened closer, hearing a man's voice that sounded important and American like the boy had heard in the movies.

His mother listened for a minute, then said, "Alright, just to meet him, nothing more. He's just a boy."

She made an appointment with the man, then hung up, deep in thought.

The boy's flesh stood out in bumps. "Who was that, mom?" he asked, drawing closer to his mother.

She turned slowly to face him, forcing a smile.

"Brian, darling..."

"Who's a little young?" the boy asked, curious.

"You, Brian. That was an attorney. He wants to come from New York to meet you." She ruffled the boy's hair. He hunched his shoulders protectively, his young brain grinding to understand his mother's words.

"What's a...*attorney*?"

"Well," explained his mother, squatting down to the boy's eye level, "he's a legal person, and he'd like to meet you to discuss your inheritance, and..."

The boy had heard enough. "I'm thirsty," he said and ran to the kitchen, not taking in what his mother had said.

The mother watched him, tears coming to her eyes. A minute later, she joined him. Before the boy could say anything, she squatted before him, stroking his ruffled hair to make it straight, then handing him a white pebble with strange symbols carved on it.

"What is this symbol, mom?"

"It is the Algiz rune, son. It aligns your life with a divine plan and gives you protection on your journey. Besides, Algiz is a protective teaching force, the power which great teachers and mentors transfer to students or seekers."

The boy stared, curious.

"Promise me you'll keep this, Brian," she said, looking very anxious.

"OK, mom?" the boy mumbled, drinking milk.

The boy shrugged, shoved the pebble in his pocket, put his glass in the sink, and ran outside to play.

Little did he know that his destiny had begun unfolding, and plans were made for him before he was even born.

* * *

Days passed. The boy forgot all about the mysterious phone call his mother had received. One Saturday, as he was in the backyard talking to the neighbour's Labrador, his mother called him inside, saying the attorney from America was at the door.

Finishing his conversation with the dog, the boy raced in the house. His mother led him to the living room, wherein their best chair—strategically covered in a blanket to hide the rips—sat a well-dressed older man.

"Hello, Brian."

Upon hearing the man's hoarse and wheezing voice, the boy's stomach suddenly knotted up. The man, frail and stooped, had the most peculiar eyes—one blue and one brown—a grey hat and slick black clothes that looked very expensive, and sat perched on the edge of his chair, like a bird.

Reluctantly the boy sat down on the couch in front of him.

Without saying a word, the older man cocked his head and looked straight at the child. His one blue eye rotated slowly as if it were made of stone.

"We've been watching you, Brian," he said, this time in perfect Danish.

Immediately the boy wanted to get away. He sat still, out of respect, flinching as his mother with a shuddering motion hitched her red shawl more snugly around her shoulders. Carefully he looked at the older man, his heart thumping, then at his mother who seemed as confused.

"I came all this way to meet you," said the man, gazing down the length of his beak-looking nose at the boy. "I hear that you're quite the entrepreneur," he said. "Know what that means, Brian?"

The boy shook his head.

"It means you know how to spot opportunities others don't see and make money from it."

The boy sat up straight. Fear burned in the middle of his belly. The older man narrowed his single blue eye.

"How much did you make selling flowers?" he asked.

*How did he know about me selling flowers?* thought the boy. The muscles in his back suddenly ached. He felt the gaze of that single blue eye fastened on him.

"Thirty kroner," he replied, "on my best day."

The older man looked at him, blankly. He nodded his crooked head like a bird and said, "How'd you like to make thirty *million*, or more?"

The boy's mother who was eating cheese with bread coughed, choked and nearly fainted.

"That's a lot of flowers," the boy said, and the man laughed.

"You know what inheritance is, Brian?"

"No."

The man's mouth twitched in a smile. "It's the practice of passing on property, rights, and titles, upon the death of an individual."

The boy studied the older man's face, "Who died?"

A grim cast came to the man's blue eye. "That's a secret, for now, Brian."

The boy heard the older man's breath go out in a long hiss. He gazed at his mother, looking for answers, but she was as bewildered as him.

"For now," the old man continued, "you have to keep doing what you do; making money. But, you're heir..."

*Air?* The boy frowned. "What's that?" he asked.

"...you're *in line* to inherit..."

"...inherit?"

"Brian, let the man finish!" his mother interrupted.

"You're going to inherit a big financial empire," the old man explained, "but it comes with certain conditions. The most important one is that you need to prove you're capable of handling great responsibility. Which means you need to demonstrate first that without help from anyone, you can make your fortune."

The boy looked at his mother for guidance, but she just stared at the man.

"And that means continuing to make money. Lots and lots of money."

"I like money," the boy answered, and for the first time, beamed a wide smile.

"Good boy," the older man muttered, his knobby fingers tightening around the arm of the chair like a wolf trap. "Let me give you three golden rules. Number one: Keep being an entrepreneur. Number two: Remember, charity is for fools. And number three: Focus on making money. Lots of money, as if money is the only thing that matters."

The older man smiled so hard that his teeth rattled. His fingers tightened their grip around the chair. As he wiped the sweat away from his upper lip the boy felt his whole body go numb.

"It is you against the world, Brian," the old man said, squinting his gleaming blue eye at the boy, "and others won't hesitate to take what's rightfully yours if you give them a chance."

The boy nodded. The man stood.

"I'll be in touch."

Shaking the boy's hand, he shuffled to the door.

"Do you have a business card, please?" his mother cried out, leaping wildly from the couch.

"Sorry, I ran out of them," the old man replied and left.

The boy's mother stood in the doorway for a moment, afraid to speak. A shadow fell across her face.

"I'm going to soccer practice," the boy said as if none of this ever happened.

"What an intriguing man," the mother said, but she looked like she'd been struck by lightning.

* * *

# Two

Like all children, the boy experienced fear.

Fear shook him into wakefulness at night. Fear drove him to worry about his grades in school, to be embarrassed about his lack of cognitive skills, his heart skipping a beat whenever a teacher asked him to explain Latin grammar or math. At times, fear made the boy so ashamed he wanted to cry. He didn't understand these feelings, or where they came from.

His first memory of fear was lying in bed with his older brother, in the tiny ground-floor bedroom they shared. It was a single bed with a drawer underneath that could be pulled out. The boy slept in the drawer, his eyes turned to the ceiling as if heaven itself was perched there, floating above his bedroom in the dark shadows of night.

One night, the boy jerked awake. Upon waking he heard his brother talking about scary things. Both brothers had vivid imaginations. Suddenly, the bedroom window blew open, the light went out, and the room turned pitch black.

*Holy shit!* His brother leapt up and raced to their parent's bedroom, screaming. The boy had the brilliant idea of hiding under the covers until he realized he was now alone in the room. Leaping up, he dove into his parents' bed for cover, hiding behind his mother.

The boys convinced their Dad that some strange man had come in and switched the light off, planning to murder them. Bravely marching into their room with a chair in front of him, their father found the light bulb had blown out, the night winds causing the window to open. Tugging on his father's nightshirt, the boy was cradled back to his little drawer bed, where he lay dreaming and perspiring the whole night.

The boy's second memory of being fearful occurred when he was six.

It was the first bitter weeks of winter; time to buy fireworks to celebrate the upcoming New Year. Unfortunately, firecrackers were forbidden in Denmark, though not in Sweden. With the proximity between Copenhagen and Malmö being by ferry, the boy and his brother decided they could sneak into Sweden to buy firecrackers. There was only one problem. To re-enter Copenhagen, one had to go through customs. The brothers came up with the ingenious idea of convincing their 70-year-old, purple-haired grandmother, to help them smuggle in the fireworks.

The moment came for the trio to go through customs. Guilt was written all over the boys' faces, their hearts pounding out of their chests as two customs officers singled them out, approached and asked to see their bags. Fear choked the boy; he almost started crying, certain it was the end of his life. To his shock, when the officers emptied their bags on the counter, there was nothing. A few minutes later they were out of the terminal, now more puzzled than scared. *What happened?* they asked their grandmother. Grandma smiled and pointed downwards; the boys couldn't believe what they saw. Thinking quickly, grandma knew no one would ever dream to check the winter boots of a 70-year-old Danish pensioner, so she had stuffed them with all the firecrackers. Coming back home, she emptied her boots on the dining table. Knowing they'd dodged a bullet, they had one hell of a New Year's Eve that year, thanks to their fearless grandma.

The next time was not so fun. His parents were divorcing, and they sat the boy down and asked him, "So…do you want to live with Mom or Dad?"

The child stretched his neck to squint at both parents. For a moment, he felt the eyes of love shining down on him from both. Then he noticed his father looking angry, sucking the air in over his teeth. "Mom, please," the boy quickly answered. As he scurried in fear from the room he heard his parents begin arguing.

The boy's last and most vivid memory of fear was when he was barely ten. His mom had repeatedly seen the ghost of a woman in their little apartment but never told him. One night, she hurried into his room and picked him out of his bed, as he shrieked and pointed, *"She's there! She's under my bed!"* She hugged the child tight, clasping him to her breast and rocking him, singing quiet lullabyes and assuring him it was just a dream and that there were no ghosts under his bed. His mom figured it was the fastest way for her to get the boy out of the apartment without the ghost knowing she'd seen her again.

* * *

Fear continued to hound and stalk the boy. As he grew, he abandoned the imaginary friends that had once tugged at his heart. At age 11, the problem became the neighbourhood bullies.

They laughed and jeered when they saw the boy riding a Long John cargo bike for the local grocery store, delivering groceries and petroleum for heating. Then they noticed he was making money. That annoyed them. One day, the whole gang ambushed him, shoved him off the bike, scattering all the groceries he was supposed to deliver to an elderly lady as they wandered off.

The next day, they surrounded the boy outside the grocery store where he worked. The gang leader, a fat, pimply-faced bully named Bjørn, took all the boy's money. As they mocked him, the boy felt fearful, humiliated, and powerless.

Next day was the final straw. The boy had taken a different route. All day, he'd been visited by the neighbourhood dog, a lovely mongrel named Aksel who would run behind his bike.

The gang came again—the boy became fearful. Only this time, instead of laughing, they giggled about the Scandinavian law of *janteloven:* a set of social codes relating to being overly ambitious, of disdaining individual achievement. *Never think you're better than anyone else*, was the saying.

Fat Bjørn jabbed his finger in the boy's bony chest and accused him, saying, "You think you're something special, don't you, you little dumbfuck?"

"Everyone can be special," the boy replied. That set the gang off laughing at him again.

Bjørn snarled, then reared back, and punched the boy hard in the face. The boy collapsed in a heap on the ground. He curled up, trying to protect himself, as the gang started kicking his head and body.

As he lay groaning and pleading in a fetal position, Bjørn walked up and viciously kicked Aksel, the dog. He kept booting and assaulting the dog, shaking his head, violently back and forth. "Scram! Beat it!" Bjørn screamed, plunging his foot into the dog's chest. "And don't ever come back!"

Aksel raced off, tail between his legs, in fright. The boy lay there, in agony, watching the dog flee. He never saw him again.

*That* was the last straw.

Things had to change.

* * *

A year later, the boy had grown and filled out. Being young, he'd forgotten all about the old attorney with the peculiar eyes. He'd discovered girls, Bruce Lee, and rock n' roll. And he'd discovered boxing.

He joined Club IK99, the oldest and by far the best boxing club in all of Denmark and based in Østerbro, not far away.

Boxing took away the boy's fear. Before each fight, and up until the moment the bell rang, his mind was battered by fear so loud he couldn't breathe—yet once the match started, instinct took over, and he conquered his doubts, fighting to win. He trained hard, though he was still young, feeling like he was in a fight for his life, without a second to think about fear.

His coaches said he was a natural. He won his first fight, hurling a sturdy left hook which decked his bigger opponent. His coaches liked what they saw. He was a fighter with grit, a fighter with tenacity, a fighter with heart.

Years passed. The boy became proficient at boxing. Knockout after knockout after knockout. Then came the day he was forced to use his training outside the ring.

One day, as he was carrying a sack of groceries home to his mother, the boy came across the bully, Bjørn and his gang in the street. Not wanting a fight, he crossed the street to avoid them.

They spotted him. Followed the boy. And surrounded him.

The boy was prepared this time. He stuck his hand in his pocket, feeling around for the strange pebble his mother had once given him. *There it is.* He rubbed it. As he did, he felt a steel dagger of strength possess him, as if the pebble ignited immense power through his whole body. In the past, he'd felt tense and anxious. Now, he was fearless. He remembered the dog, Aksel, with love. And he remembered the torture the poor animal had suffered at the hands of these goons that day.

Getting right in his face, Bjørn spat into the air and laughed, jabbing the boy's newly muscled chest.

The boy's breath caught in his throat. *Back off,* he thought. Then his thoughts burned again with the torture of Aksel. He turned. Bjørn must have thought he was walking away.

But today, it was Bjørn's time to learn a lesson; what you seek, is seeking you.

The boy slammed his fist hard into Bjørn's fat stomach, knocking the bully off-balance and down.

"That's for Aksel, you asshole," the boy whispered.

Bjørn gasped in pain and surprise. As he staggered to his knees, the boy raised his fist and slammed his best uppercut into Bjørn's chubby jaw. Bjørn crashed to the ground, coughing and gasping, his lip spurting blood.

"And that's for the damn *janteloven,*" the boy said, looming over him.

The rest of his gang stared speechlessly. The boy started grabbing for Bjørn's collar—but was taken by surprise when the group pounced on him like a pack of hyenas.

There was no time for thinking, just fight. Twice he was kicked in the ribs. A knee slammed into his back, and blood from another punch smeared his face. He was taking a terrible beating, worse than any fight he'd ever been in.

Out of nowhere, the boy heard a demonic shriek. Suddenly, the bullies were tossed aside, crying out in pain. The boy lay there, as they howled and scattered.

He was dizzy, only half-conscious, face smashed and bleeding, when he looked up and saw, moving with incredible speed and no sign of a limp, the strange little man from the flower stand.

Then he blacked out.

* * *

# THREE

When the boy regained consciousness, he had crawled away to a park bench. A hand was gently dabbing his bloodied face with water. The bullies were gone. Still, he could feel the heat of anger and rage coursing through him.

"Calm down, son. Everything's okay," whispered a voice from somewhere overhead.

The boy lay there, dizzy. Squinting one eye, he saw a little brown-skinned man with a wise face looming over him. *The limping flower man*, he realized.

The boy gasped, trying to get up on all fours, then collapsed and rolled over again. The man's gentle hand stroked his head. The man's soft touch cut through the fog of rage, soothing him.

"Thank you," the boy mumbled, running his tongue along his swollen, blood-smeared lips. The limping man smiled down like a kind father.

"Such a terrible thing," the man whispered, "to happen to a child."

"Who are you?" The boy gasped.

The man smiled, patting the boy's hair back into place. "Please, call me Gurung. Friends have called me that for a very long time. "

*Gurung?* The boy stared up at him, as though hypnotized by this kind, hovering face. Slowly the boy nodded. He found himself replaying the fight in his mind, every single blow, wanting just to land one more good punch. Then his squinting eye noticed the glint of a dangerous-looking blade hidden inside the limping man's coat pocket.

"Why do you carry that knife?"

Gently the man took the boy's head and dabbed it. "It's a Kukri."

The man took his hands away, then pulled out his long knife, exposing the curved blade. It looked fearsome.

"All Gurkha warriors carry this knife into battle."

"You're a warrior?" the boy asked, his eyes half-closing.

Gurung smiled at the boy. "And much more, my little friend."

* * *

They walked. The boy dabbed at his bloodied eyebrow, which was stinging. Confusion pounded his brain. The man was small, with black curls over his ears, his dark suit streaked with dust from their battle. At this moment, the boy liked him, without hesitation. He listened attentively to everything this strange man named Gurung had to say.

"Against multiple opponents, you need multiple weapons," Gurung explained.

"Is that how you moved so fast and beat them all up when you're so tiny?"

Gurung looked at the boy and smiled.

"What if…I told you that our bodies, houses, cars and everything in our incredible vast Universe," he said, pointing to the clear blue sky, "are almost empty space? 99.9999% of your body is space."

"Does that include my brain?" the boy said with a grin, almost forgetting the pain.

Gurung smiled. "Yes, especially *your* brain. Your body and everyone else's are empty space, on an empty planet, in an empty universe. Nothing is solid."

He reached to the ground and said, "In fact, there's so much space, that if the nucleus or core of an atom was the size of a pebble," he picked a pebble up and continued, "the outer shell of the atom itself, would be about the size of a football stadium."

"American football, or soccer?"

Gurung laughed, the black curls over his ears bobbing merrily. "Both. And if we lost all the dead space between the core and the outer shell of our human atoms, we would each be able to fit into a particle of dust."

"That's…tiny."

"And, the entire human species would fit into the volume of a dice.

"So maybe God does play dice after all," the boy said and smiled.

The man laughed out loud. "A very clever observation," he remarked. The boy saw a burst of love shining in his eyes.

All at once a burning question in the child's heart found its voice. "Wait...," muttered the boy, scratching his head, "it looked pretty solid when you threw those bullies around."

"What they were feeling was the electromagnetic force of my electrons moving fast around the atoms on my fists—in this instance, pushing away the electrons on their chins when I punched them. So you see, Brian, size doesn't matter. There is almost no physical mass, just a lot of kinetic energy and electrons bouncing off each other, making things feel solid."

"So, it's all about moving the energy most efficiently?"

"Exactly."

The boy's eyes fell back on Gurung's dangerous-looking curved knife. The blade both worried and empowered him.

"Even if you say everything is energy, does it make you more confident and less fearful, carrying that wicked knife?"

Again with kindness, the strange man looked at the boy. "Yes, Brian. However, fear allows me always to be vigilant and sense when I need to be ready. In many ways, fear protects me by alerting me of danger."

Gurung continued. "Sometimes though, fear can get out of hand and be irrational and only live in our minds tormenting us by creating scenarios of defeat, loss, humiliation, and pain that will never occur since they only exist as a figment in our minds. They seem so real, we can smell and feel them, and so they can have a great effect on our physical and mental health, even though they are pure fiction."

"That seems very strange to me."

Gurung smiled. "Well, you may look at the bigger bully and think of all the ways he is going to hurt you and almost feel the pain before it happens. Then, as you fight him and realize you're faster than him, suddenly he is afraid of you, and he runs away. Reality rarely plays out the way our mind fictionalizes it. Or you may be afraid of entering a dark room thinking you heard something, imagining all the scary things it could be, only to realize it was just the wind when you turn on the lights."

"That makes sense. Both things happened to me."

"Good!" Gurung clapped him on the back, ruffling the boy's hair. "Your mind is powerful, Brian. It can help you materialize anything you want in life, but also everything you *don't* want. It takes discipline to control your thoughts and make your mind work for you, not against you."

For a moment, the boy's face went grim. He stared into Gurung's clear, serene eyes. "Gurung, I have had difficult times, and there are so many things I'm afraid of. So how do I overcome all my fears and live a good life, preferably far away from here?"

Gurung thought for a second, searching for an answer the boy would understand. The child had listened to everything, carefully and respectfully. When he spoke, there was deep affection in his words.

"With regards to difficult times, you need to understand that without them, you will learn nothing. Every single challenge you'll encounter in your life is perfectly designed to prepare you for obstacles that are ahead for you. When life is easy, no one digs deep—why should we, it's easy! Comfort truly is the enemy of progress, so we should all pray for a job and life full of challenges, so we learn and grow to become the person we were born to be. So yes, Brian, you'll have to view adversity as a good friend that will hone your skills."

The boy stared hard. He struggled to comprehend, wanting to understand more than anything he'd ever wanted. His face grew hot with confusion. Still, he looked up at the man and smiled. "Even though it is not what I wanted to hear, Gurung, it makes perfect sense."

"Remember this quote by Peter Marshall every time life challenges you, and you will look at it as a blessing instead. '*When we long for a life without difficulties, we must remember that oaks grow strong in contrary winds and diamonds are made under pressure.*'"

The boy stared, all ears now. He smiled a little. "Thank you," he said.

"Now, Brian, to your second point about how you can overcome fear to live the life you want. First, you have to accept that it will always be with you. Everyone has fear in their lives. So, the question is not,

'Are you fearful?' The only question is, 'What are you planning to do about it so that it doesn't control your life?"

"I don't know Gurung, that's the problem. I don't know what to do about it."

"There is no other way past fear than through it. It's as simple as that," Gurung said. "When fear makes you compromise on your life by following others, and then fail, it hurts a thousand times more than having some momentary setbacks in pursuit of your incredible dreams."

"I'm not sure I understand," the boy said.

Gurung leaned back. "Brian, you have to face it head-on no matter how scared you are and how many times you fall."

"Like Churchill said, '*If you're going through hell, keep going,*'" the boy added.

Gurung was impressed. "Indeed, never to stop, always keep moving forward during good or bad times. As you begin the next phase of your life, you will realize that your most important learnings begin at the end of your comfort zones. However, there will be very tall fences around your zones…fear.

"Some will look manageable to get over; however, others will be mighty tall with warning signs, dogs, sirens, and guards shouting at you to turn back and follow the road everyone else took.

"When you learn to trust yourself, even if looking up at the fence makes you slightly nervous, the only way around fear is to throw caution to the wind in exchange for the opportunity to change your life—and at times, the lives of others."

The boy smiled at Gurung, "You mean like, 'Screw it, I'm just going to do it' and go for it with everything I got."

A loving smile touched the old man's lips. "Exactly, Brian, I couldn't have said it any better myself. Sometimes, you'll only make it halfway up the fence, but interestingly enough, suddenly all the other fences in your life will look surprisingly easy to climb."

The boy grinned from ear to ear. "Gurung, I am starting to think that for me, the alternative of doing nothing and not overcoming fear to discover the magic in my life, will always be scarier."

"I truly hope so, Brian. When you learn to use fear as motivation to transform your life, you control your destiny. Most importantly, trust that God is always conspiring to help you live the life you dream of, but you have to take the first step."

"And then what happens after the first step, Gurung?"

"Your single focus in life becomes to make sure that regret is no longer your constant companion. To never give up on your dreams no matter how long it takes to accomplish them and no matter how many times you fail. Last but not least, you never, ever—I mean *ever*—let anyone tell you that there is something that you can't do."

For a moment the boy stared perplexed. "Gurung, how come everyone is not already doing this?" he asked naively.

"Because it takes tremendous courage to search for the answer to what will make you feel useful, peaceful, and happy. You see the answer to the key question, *how to overcome fear to live the life you want*, comes cloaked as your worst fears, and not everyone has the strength to face them, and so they refrain from living the life they were meant to live and instead follow others. But you do."

"You think I do? Really?" the boy smiled.

"I believe in you."

At that moment the man's words healed something inside the boy, something he didn't even know was broken. They walked on, in silence. Five minutes later, they stood outside an old factory building. The boy looked up, blinking at the new sign on the wall, smiling through his cut lip.

It was a karate club.

Beckoning with his hand, Gurung took the boy inside. They spoke to the instructor, a big-shouldered Japanese, who bowed respectfully, smiled at Gurung, and then looked at the boy.

"You've boxed, so you'll be a natural," the instructor said to him.

*Will I?* the boy asked himself. *Like the already mythical Bruce Lee?*

Suddenly a rash of goose bumps rose up on his skin. Karate would change him. Oh yes. Oh, yes…

What it would transform him into didn't matter. He wanted it enough, so he started karate that day. He was 14.

The boy looked for Gurung to thank him again.

But he'd disappeared.

* * *

The karate school, Frederiksberg Karate Club and Viking Kickboxing, was in an old, freezing factory building in Frederiksberg, only five minutes away by bicycle.

At first, the boy's training was tough, yet he was determined to learn to stand up for himself, and to defend himself from future bullies, so he attended classes six nights a week.

The dojo was a classic old-school. Seemingly endless repetitive stretching, abdominal crunches with a medicine ball pounded into the boy's guts, push-ups on knuckles, push-ups on two fingers, no padding on the floor.

The path to physical transformation wasn't easy. The boy often stumbled in his training, his mind struggling to understand the bigger picture, and sometimes he went to bed weeping in pain. In the summer heat, they trained in the alley. In winter, the dark hardwood floors bitterly cold, the boy trained even harder just to keep warm, especially the mornings they trained outside in the freezing snow.

Years passed. The boy trained. He worked hard, exhausting himself each day. He seemed to be a natural at martial arts.

Still, he had that gnawing sensation that someone was watching him—perhaps it was Gurung. *Or maybe the American attorney,* he thought, though the boy never saw him again, only hearing his mother talk to the man on the phone now and then.

As time passed, he wondered if Gurung was still alive. In his heart, he felt an empty place for this odd little man and hoped for his return. He approached the dojo each day, praying Gurung would be standing there within its walls.

Sometimes there were guest instructors at the karate club. One night, the boy was delighted to see him again; Gurung, his old friend. It took great effort for the boy not to silently weep for his mentor's return.

"I'm going to guide you now," Gurung said. "Tomorrow, meet me here, before dawn."

The boy's real training then began. Gurung taught him many intricate moves, including defensive weapon techniques, using that wicked-looking Kukri.

Through karate, the boy had studied Zen Buddhism. Gurung took his education to a deeper level, making the boy read *The I Ching, The Tibetan Book of the Dead* and the *Bhagavad Gita.* They practiced meditation, how to calm the mind, and how to track someone in the jungle.

Where Gurung had received his wisdom, the boy could not guess. He began to realize the Universe had a plan in mind for him. It sounded strange to the boy, but he trusted in Gurung.

He began training against bigger opponents—more experienced fighters, both men and women—getting the lumps, bumps, cuts, bruises, smashed ribs and cracked shins, screaming muscles and broken fingers Gurung said he needed.

The boy loved every second. It was a gruelling training, but eventually, the boy became stronger, more fit, more used to the pain. He used his wounds to spur himself on.

* * *

At 18, the boy received his black belt—and a call from the American attorney, congratulating him.

Inside, the boy panicked. Old fears rose up, burning brightly. With effort he quelled them. The attorney kept inquiring what the boy was doing to make something of himself. The boy never mentioned fighting. *He means making money,* the boy thought.

Those old doubts swirled in his head, but now the boy had a method to tune them out. Meanwhile, he kept training. Learning how to fight gave him a way to carry himself.

That and his confident approach to people and life meant no one ever again mistook him for an easy target. Those who tried got the fight they'd hoped to avoid.

By now, he was beginning to feel superhuman. Capable of anything. He had no idea just how genuinely incapable he was. He still had very much to learn.

Unknown to the boy, his most important quest in life had begun. There would be many other vital journeys and questions he needed to be answered to defeat his enemies, but only one had the potential to show him the path to free himself and others of all fears to live the life that he, and those he would influence, had always dreamed of.

* * *

# FOUR

A bitter cold afternoon in March. The Damhus Lake on the western outskirts of Copenhagen. The lake seems deserted. Ducks and swans gathered around the only opening in the ice, as a man stands with a bag of breadcrumbs, throwing it by handfuls into the icy waterhole.

Each time the bread lands in the water, it's a frenzy. The man, Azazel, watches the ducks and swans fight. He looks to be in his mid-fifties, about one metre, eighty-two centimetres in height with an athletic build. If he is a Dane, then he is unusually well-dressed in a long black cashmere coat, leather gloves, and shiny polished shoes, his noble-looking head covered in a grey Borsalino hat with a black silk band. Danes usually dress according to what is practical.

Not this man.

Azazel tosses more bread to the ducks. Gently. Watching the peaceful way their feathers move in the wind. Suddenly, a large yelp erupts from fifty metres further down the pathway. He stops throwing bread in the water, turning his attention to a thick-necked, burly man, in a long winter coat, and holding on to the leash of his dog while kicking and screaming at it. From the sound of it, the dog—a large and beautiful female Rottweiler—has been trying to eat some of the bread laid out for the ducks.

"Get away, you stupid, stupid bitch!"

*Bitch.* Azazel registers the word. It burns in his ears but he tilts his head back to the ducks at his feet.

As he does, the man kicks the dog — the Rottweiler yelps. Azazel feels the kick in his gut and winces. He turns his attention back to the swans and ducks and continues to feed them. Yet something in his brain is suddenly on fire.

Almost before his next crumbs hit the water, the dog is screaming again. Azazel turns and stares at the bigger man. He releases another handful of crumbs. *Stay calm,* he tells himself. *Wait.* The swans glide toward him, while Azazel scrunches up his face, thinking.

Azazel can tell by the faint crunch of footsteps in the snow that the man is coming his way. Out of the corner of his eye, he gets a better look at the dog. She has a slight limp, perhaps from this last beating or from a previous one. The owner has a red face, probably more from his morning drink than from the bitter cold. The man approaches, muttering curses. *Not yet,* Azazel's brain tells him.

Again, the female dog lunges for the bread. The owner launches his foot savagely into the dog's throat. "You fucking *bitch,* I told you to leave it alone!" He continues to yank on the leash and kick the dog in the side, producing more yelps of agony and distress.

Azazel clenches his fists. Winces. A vein in his temple pulses. He waits.

The man is twenty metres away. Then ten metres. Now five.

Now the man is two metres away, coming straight at him and expecting him to move out of the way like everyone else when a big man with a Rottweiler comes straight at them.

Azazel calmly empties the bag of bread. Rubs his fine leather gloves together to remove the last crumbs.

He turns around facing the dog owner and the animal, as they are barely a metre from him. The burly man condescendingly eyes him, annoyed that his dog is not in the least intimidating this man.

"What the fuck do you want?"

"What a beautiful dog you have," Azazel says with a foreign accent and looks calmly at the owner with his intense dark eyes.

"You better get out of the way," the owner snarls, "or the bitch will bite you."

"I'm sure it will be fine," Azazel says and takes one step closer, looking straight at the dog. He peels off one leather glove to allow the dog to sniff the back of his hand.

"What do you think, girl? I'm not dangerous, right?" he says, completely ignoring the owner, speaking serenely to the dog.

The dog nuzzles Azazel's hand as he cradles its nose. The owner is growing annoyed that the dog is not vicious and that the man is ignoring him.

Without asking permission, Azazel inspects the dog's chest. "I see you have an injury, girl," he says to the dog, patting her lovingly, stroking her short coarse coat.

He leans down, pressing an ear to her chest, listening to the dog pant, each laboured breath wheezing in and out.

Azazel pats the dog gently, his face troubled. He moves to the dog's side and gently slides his right hand across its chest. "My guess is you have a pulmonary contusion," he says, narrowing his brow. "And a fractured rib."

"What are you, some kind of doctor?" the owner snaps mockingly.

Azazel gives the dog a gentle stroke, then smiles. "Something like that," he responds, still probing the dog for further injuries.

Finally, he finishes, bends in close and tells the dog, "Hey girl, I'm going to need you to listen very carefully to what I say. I need you to sit down and no matter what happens, *stay*."

The dog tilts its head to one side and sits, as Azazel unlocks the animal's heavy chain collar, and releases the leash.

The owner cries with dismay. "What the *fuck,* buddy! This is not your fucking dog!"

The men look at each other uneasily. A sudden silence descends over the lake. Without warning and with tremendous speed and force, Azazel slams the owner with a savage kick in the groin, doubling the man over in pain.

In a split second, Azazel wraps his hands around the animal owner's head, and smashes his right knee in two quick upward movements into the man's ruddy face, instantly breaking his nose and all his front teeth into a bloody pulp.

The dog watches. Eyes fixed on Azazel. Not moving an inch.

Azazel stares at the stream of blood erupting from the man's nostrils. Without releasing his grip around the man's bloody head, he grips the leash and tightens it around the dog owner's neck, dragging him like a sack of potatoes over his shoulder towards the frozen lake.

The owner gasps for air and wheezes, as blood flows from his nose and mouth. Tears flow from his pleading eyes, but no words escape his throat.

Tighter and tighter Azazel squeezes the leash. He squeezes until the man's face is turning blue. Then with brutal force, he hurls him onto the ice facedown. He kneels and smashes the blood-soaked face five times so viciously hard into the frozen lake that his face breaks through the thick ice.

The Rottweiler tilts its head, regarding the men. With both hands, Azazel holds the other man's head under the freezing water, the man's legs kicking and struggling as the last bit of life is drained out of him.

Within a minute, the dog's owner gives up and stops moving.

Azazel tosses the man's body aside. As though nothing has happened, he stands up and brushes himself off. He adjusts his Borsalino hat and replaces the missing glove snugly. For a brief moment, his shoulder holster concealing a 3D-printed ghost gun is visible, as he walks to the slight incline to the road.

Ducks quack. Calm has already returned to the water hole.

The Rottweiler is still sitting when he approaches and gives her a last pat on the head. As he walks off, Azazel hears the dog whimper.

Moments later, he hears the crackle of crunching snow behind him. Azazel turns.

The Rottweiler is following him.

Azazel's heart breaks. His eyes travel back to the dog, who is trotting along at his heels, whimpering for attention. "Sit, girl!" Azazel commands. The dog obeys, gazing lovingly up at him. But the minute Azazel begins walking again, she follows behind.

Azazel's eyes move over the lake, to the shattered bloody hole in the ice. His phone rings. He answers, looking across the water towards a frozen meadow, where a young man is practicing karate moves with an older, shorter brown-skinned man, both of them barefoot in the snow.

Azazel focuses his gaze on the young man. "Yes, I'm here," he says into the phone, adjusting his gloves. "Quiet day, so far."

Rays of sunlight burst through the clouds, spotlighting the boy on the meadow.

"Yes, I see him. He's about to get his butt kicked."

Azazel watches. The older man throws the young man around, then forces him to do push-ups, face down in the snow. No expression crosses Azazel's face. "Naturally," he interrupts the voice on the phone, "I'll continue to keep an eye on him."

The other voice doesn't reply, and Azazel ends the call. Behind him, he hears a slow exhale of breath from the dog.

Azazel stays at a distance, observing the young man practice and fight in the snow, with the Rottweiler loyally standing beside her new master.

* * *

Gurung and the boy continued their training.

That winter, every day after school, Gurung made the boy continue to run barefoot in his karate Gi through the snow, from his mom's house to the local meadow. After teaching the boy to ignore the pain of bitter cold and push away the fear of becoming sick and staying focused while training in a foot of snow, the boy sprinted back to his house again. Not a single blister, no frostbite, not a runny nose, not even a cold that winter.

His mom watched from the window, shaking her head in disbelief.

Soon, Gurung had him competing in tournaments. One day, the boy woke up to find himself entered in the W.A.K.O. World Kickboxing Championship, held in Munich. Here he was, competing in semi-contact at the highest level in the martial arts world. Unbelievable.

The boy kissed his mother goodbye and joyfully climbed into the team minivan. As they drove off, he twirled in his seat, watching his home slowly disappear. Without realizing it, he felt remorse for leaving his mother, and silent tears flowed from his eyes.

On his way to the tournament, the boy was tired and decided to lay down in the back of the van, on top of all the team bags. For some reason, he mysteriously woke up. He looked ahead, only to see that the driver was nodding, the car veering to the right, towards death and destruction. He shouted at the driver to wake him up. The driver cursed and steered the van back on the road.

The boy didn't sleep for the rest of the trip, from Copenhagen to Munich. Again, he felt someone was watching over him.

* * *

At the tournament, there were 290 competitors from 29 countries, with 11,000 spectators packed in the arena.

The boy sat in the dressing room. His eyes shut tight. He was preparing himself. In his mind he pictured his mother's caring face. As he strode out to the ring, he was nervous to see Gurung seated in the stands.

For the first time in years, fear hit him. A few rows above Gurung, a man in a Borsalino hat and gloves sat, all by himself, watching the competitors. He appeared to be sizing the fighters up.

As he climbed in the ring, the boy felt his heart pounding. *I'm scared,* he thought. He wondered if his opponent felt the same. His muscles trembled with anticipation, and his lungs ached for breath, but his focus was on one thing; the opponent right in front of him.

The first fighter was from South Africa. The boy, trained as a southpaw by Gurung, fought with his right foot forward. He was good at sweeping his opponent's feet when they come too close. Whenever the South African fighter got in tight, with his left leg close to the boy's right leg, the boy would sweep his opponent's foot with the inside of his right foot. In less than a second, the South African's foot was off the mat. In that split second, the boy slammed the outside of his foot, tumbling the other fighter to the ground. He continued to slam the South African, hard. His boxing skills had made him agile. His hands were strong, firm, and lightning fast.

With a strong sidekick, the boy ended the fight, winning on points.

He glanced up at the loudspeakers and into the stands as he limped back to the dressing room. There was no sign of Gurung. He looked for the mysterious man in the stands, but he'd disappeared.

The second fight was with a guy from Hungary.

Before entering the ring, another fighter had warned the boy that the Hungarian was very flexible and excelled at high kicks. It turns out the boy should have paid more attention. As they battled, the Hungarian moved his right leg outside the boy's peripheral vision, high above his head, then came down heel first, slamming the boy's skull. The boy never saw it coming. He breathed in sharply, the pain bringing him to his senses. Too late, he began punching and kicking furiously but was defeated on points.

He was out of the tournament.

Limping away in tears, the boy tried to blink away his pain and disappointment. The fight had ended so quickly. He was not prepared for the strength and cunningness of the Hungarian and still had so much to learn.

Through the dressing room tunnel, he saw Gurung moving toward him. For a moment, the boy felt like fleeing. Instead, he limped up to his old trainer.

The boy lowered his head as if to receive a blow.

Instead, Gurung let the boy sag against him, caressing him in a bearhug, then quietly led him outside the arena.

Atop the battered hood of a Trabant they sat. Gurung said nothing. He stared out at the horizon. Gazing, the boy thought as if something were coming.

His head against Gurung's shoulder, the boy closed his eyes. Sweat poured off his face. Disappointed with himself, he felt his life had fallen apart. Gurung placed his hand on the boy's bruised shoulder. He touched the bruise on the boy's cheek. He sensed the boy's humiliation, the tears he was holding back.

"You have now learned enough, Brian. It's time."

Tears burst from the boy's weary eyes, splattering his Gi. He felt immensely relieved. The knot in his stomach brought a new tension. "Time? For what?" he asked Gurung. "For the next phase of training?"

A breeze began to blow. The wind whipped around the boy and touched his bruised face. Gurung continued to gaze off at the horizon, eyeing the figure in the Borsalino hat, watching the figure slowly vanish into the night. Out of worry for the boy he drew him close, one hand caressing his tear-stained face.

"For the quest life has prepared you for," was his chilling answer. "A quest to save many innocent lives—or end yours early, long before it has even begun."

* * *

ROLLINGSTONE MAGAZINE
OCTOBER 6, 2016

THIS IS THE SAFEST TIME IN HUMAN HISTORY.
SO WHY ARE WE ALL SO AFRAID?

Around the globe, household wealth, longevity, and education are on the rise, while violent crime and extreme poverty are down. As reported in The Atlantic, 2015 was "the best year in history for the average human being."

So how is it possible to be living in the safest time in human history, at the same time to be so scared?

Because we are living in the most fear-mongering time in human history. And the main reason for this is that there's a lot of power and money available to individuals and organizations who can perpetuate these fears.

In the wrong hands, this is a playbook that can be used for mass manipulation and power…

WIRED.COM/SCIENCE
MARCH 29, 2019

CRISPR GENE EDITING COULD ONE DAY CUT AWAY FEAR, ANXIETY, AND HUMAN PAIN.

A 71-year-old Scottish woman recounted to The New York Times Earlier this week that she has lived a life virtually free of pain, fear, and anxiety, thanks to a missing stretch of DNA.

After years of investigating, a never-before-seen mutation is believed to be responsible for her almost supernatural pain tolerance.

Super-soldiers might just be a twinkle in authoritarians' eyes for now, but they're one reason the former US spy chief, James Clapper, called out gene editing as a potential weapon of mass destruction in his 2016 national safety threat report. The intelligence assessment specifically pointed out the possibility of using the technology to edit the DNA of human embryos...

# Path / Day Two

## Growth to Young Adulthood

*We can easily forgive a child who is afraid of the dark;*
*The real tragedy of life is when men are afraid of the light.*

— PLATO

# FIVE

I can see by the red morning sky, without taking my eyes off the surf waves crashing against the shore, that a storm is approaching. We're on the beach, behind my home in the Hamptons, New York. I am standing on the sand overlooking the surging sea, holding my one-year-old son's hand, as we watch the birds flying overhead.

In the wind are seagulls, soaring down through the marshlands. The air is hot and humid. I have seen these marshlands a thousand times, in dreams and in the flesh; my son has not. To him, the smell of the beach, the squalling flock of seagulls, the crashing waves, the hot sand beneath our bare feet, are all brand new.

When I take my son outside, he barely says a word, but instead stands with big and curious eye, observing life in action. The storm cloud bank is larger now on the horizon, but it's not moving in fast. *That's good,* I think, as I take my son's hand, and together we stroll down the beach.

I'm happy to be back home. Here in the Hamptons, anxieties are gone. Instead of meditating on old fear, I spend my time meditating on the innocence of childhood. Where children's innocence and faith that whatever they need would always be provided, as a wise man in my childhood once said.

Playing in the blazing sun, my son swats his tiny fingers up at the squawking gulls. He looks back at me and smiles. We have the entire ocean to ourselves. The beach is clean and white and fresh. Here, my son and I are free—free to walk this beach, to feel the ocean spray on our faces, free of the scars of the past I still carry. I keep wishing there was some way to tell him about the danger out there, beyond the horizon. His world won't always be safe.

For me, our time together is all mixed up with memories. Memories I cherish; memories I would gladly erase. Sometimes a whole day from the past will replay in my head, for no reason. The first time I recalled the winter snows falling in Denmark—a beauty I never recognized until it was gone—I wept. When my son is old enough to have memories like these, I pray that he will have dreams strong enough to pull him through.

As I watch the waves crashing against one another, my mind's eye is plunged back into that dark place again, until it feels like my head will burst. I thrust my hand in my pocket, feeling around for the strange pebble my mother once gave me. *There it is.* Relief and strength flash through me, and without warning, I feel a tear forming in my eye.

At some point, I need to unlock the past, to overcome the darkest of my demons.

I watch my son in the surf, the warm ocean water enveloping him, swallowing him. My son falls, and I see the flick of fear in his eyes. I pluck him up, by his little hand, before the water sucks him under.

The scream of gulls pierces the sounds of the sea. For a moment, I feel my son's panic, that explosion of fear surging through him. Feeling his angst takes me back to the kickboxing ring, to that night in Munich. That night, many years ago, when I was a boy too…

* * *

It was hours later when Gurung and I returned to the kickboxing arena. The bleachers were abandoned at this hour. We wandered through the vacant seats, glumly carrying my black belt and fighting gear in silence, finally taking two folding chairs ringside. I stared at the empty ring, home of my humiliation, my defeat.

My brain still pounded with the thousands of voices echoing through the immense sports complex. Gurung had told me the design of the Olympic Hall was considered revolutionary when it was built. As I gazed up at the sweeping canopies of glass and steel, I felt small, as insignificant as an ant to an elephant.

Still with a heart heavy from my defeat, I groaned. Sensing my deep grief, Gurung patted my head, then took my black belt in his hand as he smiled with understanding.

"Remember what your fellow Dane, Søren Kierkegaard, said," he advised, gently caressing the belt. "*'Life is not a problem to be solved, but a reality to be experienced.'*"

I looked at the fight ring and nodded my head, not ready for Gurung's wisdom right now, though his words tugged at my heart. Luckily, my mentor saw through this.

"Remember, Brian," he said patiently, "few who crouch at the starting line of life are fighters. Fewer still are *innovators* like you. Moments from crossing the starting line, they take a different direction from anyone else to the barren deserts, the arctic, lush jungles, and the devil's canyon. They climb mountains, wander forests and see the most beautiful things on earth. But beware, this path is not what it seems. Along the way, people hand them water to quench their thirst, but it is vinegar. Others appear on the peak and reach down to give them a hand up, only to let go the minute they trust them. On this path, there are charming but venomous snakes, mosquitos the size of bats sucking their blood, and greedy raccoons attracted to anything of theirs that glitters."

I stared at Gurung, his way with words mesmerizing. Sensing he had my attention he placed the belt back in my hands, drawing my fists over it.

"Food is offered, but only if they give up something dear to them. It is a lonely road that offers the best and worst of this world. On this path, there's a temptation to leave friends behind so that they get all the water and food. They will be tempted to forget promises made to them and use them to get themselves ahead faster. Giving in to these smaller temptations will make them run in circles, unable to progress until they've learned their lesson. Failing the larger seductions, trust and greed…will immediately put them back at the starting line. Some fall off a cliff, never to be seen again and others—especially the gentle souls—will be so tormented, exhausted and disillusioned that they take their own lives."

As he spoke, I wanted to scream *Stop!* I averted my eyes, wanting to understand but having trouble switching my thoughts from my defeat.

"If they reach the finish line, there will be a time of reckoning. Rucksacks will be inspected to see if the extra food, medicine, and the water given to them were shared with others less fortunate on their way, or if they kept it all for themselves until the end."

I dropped my eyes shut, feeling something inside of me crack open. I didn't want to be a person like that and wondered if I had been in the past or would become one in the future.

Gurung's next words were spoken with conviction. "Brian, such is the path for the *entrepreneur.* You carry the heaviest burden, but if you're strong in your faith, have discipline and a generous heart, then this is the road that will give you a life like no other."

"I feel like I have the heart of an entrepreneur," I whispered.

"I know, Brian. Remember I saw you selling flowers when you were barely seven years old."

"I remember Gurung. But even if I take the difficult path, how do I find peace? Right now, I feel the most unhappy I can ever remember."

Gurung squinted. He could see I was still a blithering, emotional mess, running away from my pain, when what I needed was to forge a new path ahead. "Brian, there is a Japanese concept known as *Ikigai.* It is like *janteloven*, impossible to describe with one word. However, its purpose is to guide you in life on how to choose the things that will bring you happiness."

I nodded. Gurung sensed my fear and was probing its cause.

"As you begin the next phase of your life, your focus will be on what you're good at, and what you can get paid for. That is both your *vocation* and your *profession.*"

"I don't know what any of them are."

"Yes, but you will. And soon, you will discover that those will not give you peace. You need to discover your *passion,* what you truly love doing. All of those things will *still* not bring you satisfaction until you discover your true life-mission."

"My life-mission?"

"What the world needs Brian, and how you can contribute to that by making yourself useful to others and the world."

I narrowed my eyes. Gurung hardly seemed to be breathing.

"You will discover that what the world needs is…*you.* To reveal to them how to overcome fear and begin living the lives they were meant to live. Just as you must learn this."

"Me?" I scoffed. "How?"

"You'll know when your insights and magic are strong enough."

"What magic?"

"The magic people have forgotten. You will have to rediscover that and overcome many battles, then walk through the valley of death before you become the man and protector you were born to be."

"That sounds...scary."

"Because it *is*, Brian."

I shook my head, thinking about my defeat at the fight, checking my bruises and now this, wondering what it all meant.

"I can only teach and tell you so much, Brian. At some point, you will need to find the Bruja, the Curandera."

His eyes were on mine, calmly guiding me to collect myself. "The Curandera? What's that?"

"It's not what, Brian, it's *who*. And *she* will teach you the last skills that you will need to finally overcome the adversaries that are a thousand times stronger and more cunning than Bjørn and your opponents today."

I sat quietly, shrinking down in my seat, my head bowed, arms dangling. Sensing my confusion, Gurung leaned closer.

"A Curandera is a healer, and a Bruja is a witch who practices magic. It is a healing system, blending Native American and Hispanic techniques involving herbs, prayers to catholic saints and the Virgin Mary, tarot cards, spiritual medicine, psychic healing, and magic since it presumes that illnesses have both natural and supernatural sources such as evil spirits."

Once again, I was bewildered, "So which is she, a healer or a witch?"

"It is complicated, Brian. She is both good and bad, depending on who she believes you to be. When you find her, be very careful what you ask of her and if she offers you something to drink before you've developed trust, politely refuse."

*She sounds interesting,* I thought, both good and bad, like all of us.

"She will test you and make you endure things that will make your training so far pale in comparison. If you survive her trials, she may make you her apprentice and teach you everything you need to know.

If you don't, she will put you into a deep trance sleep such that you will never wake up again. That will be the end of you, Brian. Not even I will be able to save you then. The last person that came to her went insane and is still locked in an asylum, where his cell is covered in strange signs he scratches with his nails into the cement walls."

I sighed. "Can't wait to meet her, Gurung," I muttered, trying to force a smile but failing miserably.

Gurung smiled back, sensing my heart was torn in two. "Now you know why I could never make it easy on you."

I lifted my eyebrows, eyes huge with anticipation. "But why do I need to do all of this, why *me?*"

"Because Brian…it is your destiny." As I stared at him, Gurung looked down silently with a frown. "That's all the guidance I can give you for now."

I exhaled slowly, gazing at Gurung, and shivered. Once again, I felt the hand of fate on my shoulder, guiding me. I had the feeling I would be meeting this Bruja and must be prepared for whatever fate and anything else this witch had in store for me.

Gurung smiled. He stood, shook my hand warmly, and said, "I'll be watching, Brian." Gently placing my gear in my hands, our eyes met, and I could see in his face the same sad yearning I'd seen in my mother. Hopping backward, he jabbed his fists at an imaginary opponent, his black curls flying, his nimble feet defying gravity. Then he gave his invisible prey a little finger wave, clasped his hands behind his back, and elbows jutting out moved silently through the arena to the rear stairs. And was gone.

* * *

# Six

The next phase of my life began when I was twenty. As I ended my teens, life took a hard turn. I had no way of contacting Gurung but believed him when he said he'd be watching over me, and I felt safe.

I had no idea what he or this Bruja or Curandera had in store for me, but I did know one thing.

I was going to become an engineer.

The thought of this new path brought as much fear as joy. I knew I was taking a huge risk. I found myself experiencing panic attacks, thinking back to the moment I went down in the ring against the Hungarian, my jaw flopping when his foot slammed into me. Anything physical didn't scare me anymore, but my lack of cognitive skills filled me with insecurity. To others I looked confident; yet inside I nurtured a darkness no man should carry.

The engineering school I'd chosen, Københavns Teknikum, was world-renowned and prestigious. I pored over the school's entrance exam, studying with a mania to pass. All the effort I'd put into karate I now threw into my studies. Against all the odds, I was accepted.

This impressed no one in my family.

"Why don't you get a real job, like becoming a plumber or some sort of craftsman?" suggested my grandmother.

I tried to explain that engineers get paid better, but she was from the country and would hear nothing of it.

"Get a *real* job, boy," she said.

I sighed. The Brian she knew was no longer my authentic self, the Brian I yearned to become.

Days later, I arrived at Københavns Teknikum. I was twenty years old and ready to devote myself to my first year of studies, so I pushed karate to the back, giving my new career precedence.

I had big dreams. Big plans. And big fears. My all-consuming determination to succeed made me work extra hard at engineering, for the simple reason that I was terrible at it. My mind simply was not prepared for maths, physics, and chemistry. I was always more emotionally intelligent. If someone asked me to find a way to cure a disease, go to Mars or solve a world problem, I would get excited and believe I could make it happen. If the same person in the same breath said, "If it takes three men 2 hours to dig a hole, how long will it take one man?" my heart would race out of my chest in fear. I just couldn't get my head around that shit.

In our talks, Gurung had taught me to hone my unique abilities. "Each of us is born with abilities and skills that make us great in some areas, and not so good in others," he'd say.

Life and the education system seemed to teach everyone using the same method, even though we all learn differently. My intelligence lay in my physical, emotional, and natural-world abilities. Whenever I failed in my cognitive logic abilities, Gurung would see my head hung down.

"Don't feel bad about it," he'd say, putting a gentle arm around my shoulder. "Remember, Brian; you're a unique and beautiful person in other ways. More importantly, trust me when I say that a high IQ alone won't make you stand out. People want to do business with someone honest, generous and has leadership skills. So you see, life is not just about getting the highest grades—it's sometimes the little things, being polite, giving credit where credit is due, being trustworthy, showing humility, offering to help others, being respectful and being willing to admit that you made mistakes. Those characteristics are much more likely to determine if you become a successful professional than your cognitive abilities."

In childhood, my mom and Gurung had shaped who I would be in manhood. Over and over, I faced humiliation. It took me right until the end of each term before I managed to catch up and receive just average grades.

Year One passed. Then Year Two. The school was about five kilometres from my home. For five long years, I'd leave behind the warm and cozy house of my mother, waving to her in the kitchen window as I rode my bike every morning to school, no matter the season. In winter when it snowed, and the snow was too deep for me to ride my bike, I'd sling a pack on my back containing my books and race through the icy-cold road to school, arriving with my fingers so frozen stiff that it took minutes before I was able to write with a pencil in my hand.

At that time, no one owned a personal computer or a printer. Each time I needed to use one for projects—especially for my final thesis—I'd have to ride a bike to the school campus to use one.

In-between classes, I'd stay late after the other students left to catch up on my lessons. My math instructor begged me to rest. "Take a break, like your classmates," he insisted—but I couldn't. I needed the extra time to understand what was taught. My stamina from karate made it possible for me to keep going, day after day, year after year, over and over again.

Obstacle after obstacle stood in my way. It seemed unlikely I would graduate. I flunked physics twice and had to sit with classes below me, which humiliated and shamed me. Had I failed a third time, they'd have kicked me out of engineering school.

I passed the final time, getting an A, third time lucky.

As my schooling progressed, and I began getting excellent grades in computer coding, math, and physics, I picked up speed and proficiency in my subjects.

By Year Five, I was ready to graduate.

Suddenly realizing what I was now facing—my first test of adulthood—I felt shaken. All during my five years at Københavns Teknikum, I'd experienced nightmares. Fear burned in me, that knowledge of my old failures, that shame. It dripped like a poison into my belly. Witnessing this, my mother took my face in her hands, a mix of worry and love in her eyes. "Oh, Brian," she said, searching my face. "It'll be all right. You are not a weak man." Her soothing voice comforted me, and turned my fragile faith into blocks of granite. Yet on the eve of my graduation, I was haunted by surreal dreams of my professors saying it was all a terrible mistake, that I hadn't graduated and they wanted my diploma back.

As I crossed the stage to receive my Master's Degree the next day, I felt fearful, yet immensely proud of myself. I hoped and prayed that

Gurung would appear at my graduation like he did at my big fight. I looked into the crowd of graduates and family, scanning. No Gurung.

I drifted silently back to my seat, disappointed. I hadn't heard from him in years and had no way of reaching him. He said he would be watching, so maybe he was there in the shadows or perhaps right in front of me. I just couldn't see him.

As I sat and listened to the graduation speeches, a second wave of fear assaulted me. Suddenly I couldn't breathe. I felt as if I would faint. I looked around for my mother's calming face, needing to feel her strength, her clearheadedness, wanting to dash outside and find someplace dark and cavelike to hide, beads of sweat exploding across my brow. But it wasn't from the heat in the packed auditorium. It was from the unnerving realization of what lay next.

Finally graduating, I found my mind asking, *Now what, Mr. Engineer?*

In a whisper I heard the voice in my head. *Paris,* my mind answered. My face crinkled, and I nodded several times. *Yes. That ties everything together.* In my blood I felt a deep certainty, a sense of things falling into place. Allowing a wide grin to break across my face, I decided to move to Paris on my quest to discover more about life.

* * *

# SEVEN

It was a beautiful morning, and I was out walking along the glistening Seine River, looking at *Ile de la Cite* with awe and admiration, hunting for somewhere to have a nice lunch.

Milling around I saw only a few people. The crowds and noise would come later; at the moment it was a nice view, peaceful, quiet. I walked past a tiny wooden booth where a woman with a kind face sat, looking like the tiny clairvoyant from the horror film *Poltergeist*—a psychic, reading tarot cards to a man.

I never gave it a second's thought and walked on, feeling hungry.

The morning sun was bright, filtering through the trees. I had just seated myself outside a lovely street café on the river when there was a tap on my shoulder — *tap, tap.* I looked up and squinted, as the sun was right in my face. When I eventually saw who it was, I was surprised.

It was her. The psychic.

She gave me a strange look, then uninvited, sat down beside me and stared deep into my eyes.

"Forgive my intrusion," she said, her voice a whisper with a German accent.

"Can I help you?" I asked bewildered.

"I saw you walking past me."

I must have given her the oddest look because she tried to smile.

"I left a customer to find you."

"Maybe you should go back to him."

"Him."

"Sorry, I'm a bit confused…"

"You said *him*. That means you noticed."

"Well yes, but only in passing."

The hum of the river drowned out my thoughts. The woman edged her way closer to me. "My customer," she whispered. "A man in a Borsalino hat and gloves. Sadness, death, and violence were all the cards kept telling me. But strangely he seemed little concerned because he was looking for someone."

I shrugged. "OK, who was he looking for, and what does all of this have to do with me?"

"He was looking for *you,* Brian!"

*Brian?* I stared at this tiny woman. "How do you know my name?" I gasped in shock and surprise, a hollow pain knotting my stomach. "What's going on here?"

The woman leaned in, evidently not puzzled by my reaction. "Your name…how is not important. I predict things, especially when people are going to die," she said out of nowhere.

"Am *I* going to die?" I asked half-joking.

"Yes," she said, staring at me intensely.

My heart stopped. Suddenly the world around me went silent. Had this woman suddenly lost connection with her sanity?

"If that man finds you, I fear that you will not live," she said as she turned around pointing, looking, eyes scanning…but the man was gone.

I furrowed my brow. This was making no sense. "What does he want from me? Why does he want to kill me?"

"I can't tell you. But I saw your destinies entwined."

She pulled out her tarot cards and began reading them.

"You see?" She pointed. "It is your…fate."

I paused to catch my breath, the sunlight suddenly burning my eyes. The woman stared at me, her look unwavering. "Look, I'm hungry, a little tired and weirded by all of this, so…"

"Your path is clear," she continued, studying the cards. "You'll make your fortune, then travel the world on a journey of discovery, a pathway, a…*quest.*"

By now, I'd had enough of this woman and gestured to the waiter.

"Thanks, but I'm happy with life as it is."

Suddenly the woman moved closer, and the sunlight was gone. "You will do something astonishing, but the journey is tough and fraught with danger, not only from this man. Beware of the Bruja and her witchcraft. She can be the greatest ally on your journey or your deadliest foe. No one can release you from her spells."

I almost choked. Fear pounded my brain. *Bruja?* "Wait...d'you know a man called Gurung?"

She just gave me the strangest look, one that said maybe but didn't reply.

"You must be guarded. You must be careful, very careful..." and an expression of concern and fear spread across her face. "We...*watch* you."

I felt sweat breaking out on my forehead. "Who watches me?"

She just stared.

"What's your name?" I demanded, becoming enraged.

"That's not important, Brian. But *you* are."

"You've been talking to Gurung!" I screamed. "Give me his phone number. I need to..."

Suddenly, the woman seemed startled. She stared around the restaurant and the street, teeming with people.

"I have to leave. They have eyes everywhere."

"Who does? What is all this about?!"

"Be careful, Brian."

"Tell me what the hell is happening?!"

"We are few; they are many."

"Who is *we*? Who —"

"Brian, the universe is always there to guide us, but people don't pay attention to the signs all around them and especially to themselves and their inner voice and instinct. That's why we're in this mess, and very few are fighting back."

What mess was she talking about? All at once my body felt hot and cold, my sanity pushed to the threshold.

"Remember, stay safe and always heed your sixth sense. It tells you who to avoid, even if you don't understand why. Good people often risk their lives because they worry about offending another person. They stay when someone sits next to them at a bar and makes them uncomfortable. They walk towards a person asking for advice, in spite of knowing that they should instead turn around and run. Or, they stay in an elevator and let the doors close, in spite of some creep who entered and gave them goosebumps. Everything tells them to get away, yet due to social etiquette, not wanting to offend someone or correctness, like lambs to the slaughter, they stay."

"What is this about? Tell me, please!"

The woman sat forward, then leaned in, lowering her voice to a whisper. "Me, Gurung, the Bruja, and a few others. We battle them in a shadow war."

I tried to force a laugh, but it came out like a choke of terror. "Who?"

"An extremely powerful group of people."

"Who are they?"

"We made a pact to fight them till our last breath to keep you safe, Brian. Humanity is running out of time. You must intensify your training and be ready for the final battle that will reveal who truly is behind all the evil."

Sweat ran down my face. I collapsed back in my chair, not believing what I was hearing.

"We will protect and guide you on your journey. Be alert to our messages."

"Pact? Protect me from these powerful people? Why? And how will I know when you've sent me a message?"

"This is dangerous for both of us. I must go," she said, looking around furtively. With that, she stood, gave me a last look of awe, took my hand, and smiled.

"It is my honour and privilege to meet you. If you're still alive, let's meet again someday," she said casually. Then off she went.

*Still alive? What the hell, how could she say that?*

Random, baffled thoughts rattled through my mind. The waiter came, and I waved him away, trying desperately to take in everything the psychic said. *What on earth could she mean? Why did she single me out? And who are these powerful people?*

My insane reverie was broken by laughter from the next table. A beefy man was tickling his daughter with his beard stubble. She giggled and put a hand over her mouth. Disoriented, I went into the restaurant to use the restroom.

On my left, I saw the sign for the phone. As I turned the corner, my blood froze to ice.

Inside the phone booth was the man in the Borsalino hat and gloves the psychic described, his back to me. In a flash, it hit me. It was him—the man from the Munich boxing arena, sitting a few rows above Gurung.

For what seemed like an eternity, I just stood there, frozen. As I listened, the man's voice leaked out of the booth.

"We just missed her. She left, but I didn't see where she went since I had to keep an eye on Brian."

*Keep an eye on Brian?* I shuddered. It was surreal to hear a stranger speak my name. He kept his back to me and grunted.

"No, I couldn't hear what they said, but she read him tarot cards."

*This man has been watching me!* The thought brought on a claustrophobic terror, beyond fear, beyond panic. I slowly glanced to my right and saw a big silver candelabra. I picked it up and held it firmly in my right hand, ready to pounce.

"What do you want me to do with him?" The man in the Borsalino hat listened, then nodded. "OK, consider it done. I've been waiting for this moment for a long time."

I hesitated, gripping the candelabra tight. Squaring my shoulders I took a step forward. Suddenly a couple of young guys came around the corner heading to the restroom. In a split second, I decided it was my chance to get out, still pretending to myself that it was all a big mistake and it was someone else this guy was talking about.

I quickly exited the restaurant and turned the corner and ran as fast I as I could, down the cobblestone streets of Paris, gasping for air, not knowing where I was going or what to do next.

I bumped into other pedestrians, jostling them, zig-zagging down the street like a madman. I couldn't help wondering if Mr. Swanson and the inheritance had anything to do with all of this. Why would Swanson have me killed if he wanted me to inherit? It didn't make any sense—

except perhaps if there was someone else not wanting me to succeed. But who? I didn't know anyone except for a few old friends, my brother, and my parents.

Down one street I raced, then down another. I ran blindly, letting out a guttural cry. Suddenly I yearned to be back home, in the safe arms of my mother. I knew I couldn't stay where I was. My life had taken a dangerous turn. It was now no longer about a joyful pursuit of happiness; it was a matter of survival.

I ran until my vision was blurred, and I could run no longer. Two hundred yards in the distance, I spied a shuttle bus terminal, and a sign reading CHARLES DE GAULLE AEROPORT. Resolutely I ran that way, drenched with unease. Paris had brought me a sentence of death. I could conceive of no other way to save myself. And so my strange and twisting journey led me back home, to Denmark, to the place I wanted to escape from since I was a boy.

* * *

# EIGHT

Returning to Denmark, that cold and snowless November, answered a desperate hope. Leaving Paris, not knowing what would happen next, I decided to take the road less travelled—partly to continue building my life towards proving I was worth receiving my inheritance, and secretly hoping to crush out the inevitable doom.

Out of nowhere the CEO of an IT company that I had once met briefly in the past for a job interview called me. He had a new opportunity he wanted to discuss.

Intrigued and flattered that he remembered me, I agreed to an interview at their glitzy skyscraper offices in downtown Copenhagen.

I rode the elevator to the sixteenth floor. The CEO kept his eyes fastened on me while the HR lady kept smiling at me. Sitting before them was like being in hypnosis.

However, Gustav, the sales director, took an instant disliking to me. Whenever I spoke, he let out a deep-throated laugh.

For some reason, this agitated me. Fear and instinct exploded throughout my body. I flashed back to myself in the boxing ring, backed into a corner by my opponent. My head was thudding, pulses of pain blasting deep in my brain.

Sucking up my fear, I concentrated my efforts into winning Gustav over. I'd seen guys like him before of course; corporate men and women, towing the company line all their lives, always obeying the rules, somehow scratching and clawing up the career ladder, devoid of original ideas and ever critical of those who produced them.

My eyes crawled sideways, watching him. He gave me a steady look, trying to conceal his thoughts. *We'll never get on in a million years,* I realized.

Instead of focusing on Gustav, I leaned forward, and studied the CEO's eyes. The package the CEO presented was extremely tempting, and the position and responsibility were high, major significant steps up the corporate ladder for me.

For some weird reason, the conversation with the psychic came to mind.

And of course, the American attorney.

In the back of my mind, I remembered that so far, life had rewarded me for taking chances; for overcoming fear and just doing things that generally would make me hesitate.

Working for Motorola back in Paris made me realize that the American way of doing business was a perfect fit for me. I was good at sales, had much stamina, and the entrepreneurial gene; an instinct for business that should never be underestimated.

I talked. Everyone in the room listened. As I gave my pitch, the CEO straightened up. Without missing a beat, I jerked my eyes over to Gustav. Red spots of rage glowed slowly on his cheeks.

At that moment, Gurung's training came into play. I saw my opponent sweating. What was he nervous about? Was Gustav also filled with fear, living a lie? Worried his job could vanish in the blink of an eye?

Gurung's message about street-fighting exploded in my mind, making my eyes water. I blinked, gathered up my courage, and then sat forward in my seat. I grabbed the initiative.

"You should consider opening an office in America," I said, watching Gustav's expression turn pale, then sat back and sipped my lukewarm tea.

I felt a slight tremble in my hand while pretending to be super confident in my suggestion. In my heart I was anything but confident.

The CEO looked at Gustav, then the HR girl, then smiled at me.

"How did you know?" he said, a big grin on his ruddy old face.

I glanced over at him, trying to keep the desperation out of my voice. "Know what?"

"That we were thinking about that? It's a secret hardly anyone knows."

I was dumbfounded. Another round of pain shot through my brain. Yet I stayed calm. "I research important meetings like this. The time is right for you. Your market is saturated in Europe."

The CEO nodded his big head and looked at Gustav, who looked like he'd been sucking lemons.

"And I'll run it," I said.

It was all bluff. I never researched them, had never run a business, and had only ever been to America vacationing as a teenager, surfing and skateboarding with long hair and not a care in the world.

I was flying on fumes of pure instinct, another thing to which I had become increasingly alert.

I smiled at the CEO and held his gaze, like a professional Las Vegas poker player.

Across from me I could hear Gustav groan. Suddenly the CEO stood. I thought the interview was over, that he was leaving and I was out of my mind. But he just pressed an intercom button and said, "Lars, could you join us, please?" then sat back in his chair.

Nobody said a word for a minute, the atmosphere loaded, Gustav swallowing hard and shaking his head.

For a long moment the room was cloaked in silence. Then the door opened, and a man I assumed was Lars stepped in, a big bear of a man in an expensive blue suit.

"Brian, this is Lars, our Chairman. He is also CEO of NESAN A/S, Denmark's largest utility company," and the man shook my hand warmly, then sat beside the CEO.

"Brian wants to run the new American office," the CEO said. Lars nodded and smiled.

Again, I heard Gustav groan. The HR girl was rocking in her chair, arms crossed. I needed to take the initiative and spoke up.

"I'll need ten thousand a month salary," I said with an outer calm, but inside, my heart beat like a drum. *Where the hell did I get that crazy and exorbitant figure from?* I thought, trying to keep eye contact with Lars.

The CEO smiled at Lars, and then looked me right in the eye.

"Danish kroner," he said.

The HR girl shifted her weight. I gulped. "US dollars," I replied, knowing the currency rate was one US dollar equaling ten Danish Kroner.

Gustav nearly choked on his coffee, and the CEO started to object, but the Chairman interrupted, saying, "It's greedy, a big uplift on your present salary." He smirked, and I wondered how he could know that.

"But I like a man who's comfortable at negotiating preferential financial terms."

*Whoa. Really?* "Meaning I'll be good at building the company," I quickly interjected. Struggling to overcome my amazement at the words pouring out of my mouth, I managed to find a new wave of confidence and added, "And 25% ownership of the new subsidiary."

The threesome growled at me, Gustav groaned again, then suddenly the CEO burst into loud laughter, and the Chairman chuckled.

"How about the keys to my car and my house?" the Chairman said.

"Not at the moment, but we'll discuss that at a later point," I said with a smile.

The room fell into a hush. Gustav sat there with his mouth hung open. All anxiety was gone. I stayed nonchalant and casual, feeling a rush of pure adrenaline. I was back in the ring, in the thick of the fight, all fear gone, and there was no other place in the world I wanted to be than right here in this moment, winning.

"You know anyone there?" Gustav piped up, thinking my answer would be no.

"An attorney," I answered to my surprise. "A very powerful attorney who can open all the doors for us."

Gustav growled. That cinched it. The CEO stood, came over to me, shook my hand warmly and smiled, then said, "Welcome to my company, Brian. And good luck in the USA."

That was it. The negotiations were over. I stood and pumped his hand, more than a little amazed.

"HR will discuss the contract and relocation terms with you. Goodbye, Brian. Great to meet you." And with that, he nodded and left with the Chairman, Gustav trotting obediently behind.

I imagine I was standing there with my mouth hanging open now, trying to figure out how all this had happened. In a daze I rode the elevator sixteen floors down. Carefully, heart still pounding, I stepped outside into the cold November morning. What had I gotten myself into? As I looked up at the sky, a voice whispered in my head.

*You did it, Brian. You passed your first test. You killed them!*

* * *

Outside the flashy offices, I felt like celebrating, so I ducked into a stylish bar in virtual darkness, full of models and advertising suits.

I ordered rye and dry and gulped it down, thinking of Gustav's preening cockiness and the incredulous look in his eyes. This gave me a broad grin. I began to realize that so much of how life turns out for us is based on the choices we make. If we overcome our hesitation to just ask for a discount, we just may get one; if we ask for a better room, we may get a junior suite; and if we ask for an upgrade, we may end up in business class.

Last but not least, if we ask for the salary we dream of, we just may get it!

I sipped another drink and leaned back in my chair, gazing at the ceiling. Gurung and the fortune-tellers' predictions for my life, the man who was searching for me and my personal quest, had given me a new sense of time, an urgency that didn't allow me to live a single moment of my life full of regret at being underpaid and sitting in the back of the bus.

Lost in my thoughts, my cell phone sitting on the bar suddenly rang, the caller-ID reading ANONYMOUS.

I sat up and sighed. I don't usually pick up calls without ID but picked it up and answered.

"Brian, many congratulations on your new position," a smarmy American accent drawled.

My heart thudded. I placed my drink down on the table. *How stupid I'd been! The attorney.* And he sounded very pleased.

"The sales director had already been tentatively promised the position to lead their new US subsidiary. I guess you didn't know that. But the calmness with which you offered to build a new company in America of all places, your experience of working for Motorola and your suggestion that a powerful attorney, me, would be helpful, convinced the Chairman that you could do it far better than their sales director."

Leaning back, I locked eyes on the ceiling again, while a calm voice whispered inside of me. "Mr. Swanson. Thanks, but how did you know?"

"I know *everything,* especially about you, Brian. But also understand that you will receive no help from me in your new endeavour. I will stack the cards against you to see what you're made of. The arrogance you showed in that meeting will not get you past day one in the USA. They will eat you alive and then I will know that you aren't fit for the inheritance. In fact, I can't wait to tell the other trustees that you failed and you went back to your mom. Enjoy your drink! I hope they didn't add too much ginger ale, ruining the whisky."

And with that, he hung up.

* * *

I pressed a hand to my forehead and shut my eyes. For the briefest of moments, I nearly burst out laughing. *How did he know? Am I being watched?* My hand tightened around my forehead, no answer rising in my throat. I was in shock, and as my inner laughter died, a paralyzing sense of panic came over me.

I felt like a cheap conman who had just been caught counting cards at a Vegas casino, being dragged off my chair to a backroom by two musclebound goons with orders to break my fingers to teach me a lesson.

If the attorney was working on me to fail, how in the world would I ever succeed?

More importantly; how the hell did he know about my new job?

How did he know about everything that happened at the meeting? Where did he get my number? And how did he know I was in a bar, drinking rye and dry?

I gazed across the bar into the mirror, wondering if there were hidden cameras. *Don't be paranoid!* I thought. Then I looked at the ceiling above the cash register and spotted one.

My mind froze. My breathing halted. Everything was getting weirder and weirder.

Across the room, a woman coughed. I whirled to see her staring at me, behind a cigarette. Beside her a short man raised a smartphone to his lips. Then the woman puffed a whirl of smoke and watched it float up.

Neither of them seemed to care that I was watching them. I felt my head swaying. The man on the phone nodded, gulping air. At the next table, a plump little man leered, eyeballing me over his empty glass.

*I* am *being watched!*

I whirled around, in a sweat, and suddenly I felt everyone was staring at me. An obese waiter dropped his tray of shot glasses, his gaze fixed on me, perspiration glistening on his chin.

Turning away, I forced my eyes to focus on the exit door. I had to get out. *Get out of Denmark!* My mind shrieked.

Desperately I threw back my chair, and raced out of the bar, plunging into traffic. I spied an empty taxi on the street corner. Clutching my phone, I ran towards it. The traffic policeman in the street also seemed to be watching me, as he dropped his arms from directing traffic, and started waving them at me.

"Taxi! Taxi!!" I screamed. My mind was dizzy, losing focus. Leaping in the cab, I grabbed the driver by the collar, watching as the cop raced over.

"What are you doing?" the driver demanded.

My head was in agony. "Dammit, don't ask! Start the car! Go! *Get me out of here!"*

* * *

# NINE

Four days and four thousand miles to the west later, I stepped off a plane, in America.

Suitcase in hand, I hurried through the airport, taking the quickest route to the street. I'd done it. I'd found a way out of Denmark again. Whatever was happening to me, I was in for the ride, so I sold off all my belongings, negotiated a clean break from my apartment lease, and with about $15,000 in my pocket, left my home country and now found myself blinking in the sunshine of California.

I reached my destination as the sun fell. The Pacific Ocean and the palm trees presented a pleasing new geometry. Santa Barbara, California is often called the American Riviera, and my new employer suggested it as they had some contacts of their own in Los Angeles, only about two hours' drive away.

Above my new house, the seagulls rose in flocks, their shadows floating across the beach. Laying in bed, I listened to the ocean crash against the sand. Growing up in Scandinavia, I felt like one of the pioneers who'd journeyed to America before me, determined to be the creator of my own life. By now, I'd learned that the tallest fences in life are all named *fear.* Each of these fences can be climbed and conquered. What sustained me now was the knowledge that the alternative of failing in my quest was even more terrifying than my fear, so I put my chin down and kept pushing myself through unfamiliar terrain and countless obstacles, desperate to find what was waiting for me out there.

* * *

Squashing my anxieties, I jumped headlong into scheme after scheme as I set up the US division of my Danish employer. Yet the warning from the attorney never left my mind for one day.

I'd found a decent beach house overlooking the Pacific Ocean because I love the sand and the water. Standing at the surf's edge each morning warmed my soul. Only now and then did I miss home—

mostly a longing to see my mother, to sit with her before the warm woodstove, curled up at her knee in the winter chill.

Needing companionship, I bought my dream dog; an Alaskan malamute, that I named Flower. Together we strolled the beach, hugging the surfline, Flower barking to stand guard against the dive-bombing gulls. Above us the blue heavens looked huge. There I was, living The American Dream! It seemed only a brief moment ago that I was broke and out of a job, returning home in defeat. Now here I was, a blue-eyed Dane and an Alaskan malamute in sunny California, with a beautiful home and a 7-series BMW, living a life I could not even have dreamed of in my wildest fantasy as a boy.

Talk about embracing the unexpected and being out of place...yet exactly where I was meant to be!

All painful memories of my past were slowly obliterated. Rarely did I cling to the thought that at any moment all of this might be torn from my hands. Instead, I went into career-overdrive. Without any staff, I began to generate leads and contacts and business on the customer and supplier side of computer hardware.

The pressure to create a good life kept me taut with stress. I woke up every day with ideas on how to optimize and disrupt sometimes ordinary everyday things I'd seen. It was like a flame that couldn't be extinguished. Where others saw problems, I saw an opportunity for change. I always stepped outside of my comfort zone. I moved fast, without needing to take permission from anyone.

With all I had learned, I felt ready to take on the world. God bless America; this new opportunity was what I had been waiting for, ever since I was a boy, selling flowers back home.

Success or failure was in my hands. Exactly the way I liked it.

* * *

Even in this quiet American beach town, I couldn't find peace. My mind began to derail. While seated at a bar, I'd feel the room suddenly fall silent, the eye of every other patron fastened on me. Police helicopters shrieked over my bedroom at night. The beach pounded in my restless sleep, hour after hour. Sometimes I'd experience panic attacks, as everything in my apartment would reassemble itself into that Munich boxing ring, and I'd feel trapped in the corner by some faceless, unseen opponent.

The thoughts pre-occupied me day and night, in my dreams and even during my workday.

In this sleepless stress, my childhood visions returned. I saw the desert. The sun beating down. The strange woman drawing a symbol in the sand. And the millions of voices, warning me. I lay in bed, gripping the sheets, watching the blur of faces drift past. When I woke, I felt the dream had ripped me apart, into madness.

These visions of impending doom bled into my work. Each morning I found myself braced for bad news. One day, after only three months setting up and building the business in America, I received a phone call from the CFO back in Denmark, informing me that I should not expect to receive any more salary.

"What do you mean, no more salary?" I shot back.

"The company has gone bust," was the CFO's reply.

I hung up, paralyzed in shock. Suddenly the truly frightening bottom line hit me: I was penniless now and stuck in America, a foreign land.

The first thing that raced through my mind was the attorney's warning that he was going to make life hard for me and stack the deck. Even though I could never prove it, I was sure he was behind it.

I kept my eyes on the phone, expecting the CFO to call back any second, to say it was all a big joke. The instant it began to ring again, my heartbeat echoed in my throat.

The caller-ID read ANONYMOUS. *The attorney. Of course!* My stomach knotting, I answered.

"Easy come, easy go," he chuckled. Instantly my brain went into auto-pilot, dumped into the numb wreckage of my entire life imploding. I listened, feeling lightheaded, my entire body limp and groggy. His tone sounded odd. "Although frankly, you've succeeded more than I expected," he said. "I hoped you'd go home to your Mom. But now that you've learned what it takes to make money, and lose it all, I want to meet you soon and make you an offer you can't refuse."

The line went dead. Staring at the screen I sat down, collapsing into my chair, and waited. There was something unconsciously terrifying about that call. I stared at the phone, waiting, expecting it to ring any second again. Meanwhile, my mind whirred.

*Easy come easy go.*

The words had a hypnotic effect on me, sending me back to places I didn't want to go. I felt like throwing up and my head was on fire, the heat sucking the air out of me, my eyes swimming with white specks. I closed my eyes, and let my mind whirl, realizing this was the day, the exact moment when my life changed forever.

* * *

*Oh, God,* I thought, wiping my eyes with the back of my hand. My mind froze, as I continued to stare at the phone. What could I possibly do? I hardly knew anyone in America, apart from some of the contacts I'd made. I didn't know any other employers or head-hunters. Right when I got lucky and found myself in the best place of my life, the rug was being pulled out from under me!

*Here I am,* I thought, *in America. Out of a job. No money. No means to earn it. Soon I'd have no roof over my head!*

*How the hell do I get out of this one?*

Closing my eyes again, I drifted off. I was awakened by the creeping of feet in the hallway and opened my eyes to find Flower's tongue gently licking my chin. "What a bad fucking day," I groaned to my companion. She continued licking me like crazy.

The next day, as a last gesture, the company offered me a ticket back home. To me, that was like someone tempting me to accept failure. How could I return in defeat to Denmark yet again, to my friends and the neighbourhood, my dreams gone, giving up my search for my destiny?

One thing I knew for sure; the incredible thing I was supposedly going to do was not happening in Denmark. Leaving would be the end of my journey—and that was what the attorney wanted me to do.

I had no choice but to find a way to stay.

There was only one thing left for me to do.

Trust my instinct.

* * *

It turned out to be the perfect decision to make.

Not at first—because trusting my instinct meant I would be out there, alone and exposed. And to be honest, I was full of trepidation, shattered nerves and anxiety, thinking about confronting this new challenge, something I'd never done on this scale nor in a foreign country.

But one thing would be worse than failing; to have to return home.

I was willing to take my chances, and at least give it my best shot.

The plan was this: I'd set up my own company, using my last pennies and sheer utter determination. *Millions of people have done it,* I thought. *So, could I. After all, how hard could it be?*

Who was I kidding? It was super hard, and I was strapped for cash in America!

And so, my stomach doing flip-flops, and having no idea what was about to unfold, I founded my own IT distribution business from my spare bedroom.

I became a broker, a middleman, buying unsold IT hardware cheap from big computer distributors in one part of the world with excess inventory, and selling to distributors in other parts of the world looking for more goods at better prices.

I was clueless about how much work this would take. The first year I worked sixteen hours every single day, creating a network of trustworthy suppliers in every corner of the globe, learning about logistics and the challenges involved in moving parts internationally.

I generated $1 million in sales.

In the second year, my one-man show grew miraculously to $24 million. It continued to grow, and by Year Four, we turned over $47 million with only me, another salesman, and an accountant.

I was ecstatic! I was sure this was what I was born to do, and took this as proof of the universe's blessing. Yet as I trudged home from work one day, I realized it was time to make another significant change.

Being on the West Coast of America, when the majority of my customers were on the East Coast, suddenly made no sense. The three-hour time difference was becoming an issue. I decided to relocate my business to paradise…Key West, Florida.

Saying goodbye to California, I rented an incredible property from someone who had just sold his company to Microsoft. It was massive, as big as a city block, with a tropical garden, a guest house, and a swimming pool.

The move was challenging, and inspiring. I found my work wonderfully richer, and more satisfying, yet I felt more distant from Denmark and my family than ever. Here I was, with my buddy Flower, in Key West, on the edge of America, staring out into the crystal-blue Gulf of Mexico, 90 miles from Cuba. Here I could find my purpose. Here I could reach my potential. Here I could make my mark on the world.

Talk about being out of place again...yet exactly where we were meant to be at that precise moment in time.

* * *

FINANCIAL TIMES
BRUSSELS, APRIL 8, 2020

EUROPEAN DEMANDS FOR INFORMATION FROM SMART-PHONES ARE RAISING FEARS OVER THE REACH OF STATE SURVEILLANCE

With much of Europe at a standstill as a result of the coronavirus pandemic, politicians want the telecom's operators to provide similar data from smartphones. Thierry Breton, the former chief executive of France Telecom who is now the European commissioner for the internal market, has called on operators to hand over aggregated location data to track how the virus is spreading and to identify spots where help is most needed.

But the use of such data to track the virus has triggered fears of growing surveillance, including questions about how the data might be used once the crisis is over and whether such data sets are ever truly anonymous.

Still, assurances from officials and industry executives have done little to appease anxiety that privacy rights could be brushed aside as governments seek to use tools of mass surveillance in their efforts to combat the virus. The concerns about political use of data have been aggravated by the fact that the European Commission wants the telecoms companies to provide the actual aggregated data, not just access to insights from that information.

Latvia, for example, has exercised its right to be exempted from certain obligations in the European Convention of Human Rights, which grants citizens privacy and data protection rights. Slovakia passed a law last month to use telecoms data to ensure people abide by quarantine laws.

# PATH / DAY THREE

## MONEY, POWER AND TEMPTATIONS

*The only thing necessary for the triumph of evil*
*is for good men to do nothing.*

— EDMUND BURKE

# Ten

"I've got a proposition for you," the attorney said, narrowing his single blue eye at me. We sat in my office. Flower, her thick coat white and grey as a timber wolf and now grown to 120 pounds, stared the old man down like a vision of lunch. The attorney bristled.

"Just don't make any fancy moves," I warned the old man, smiling at Flower.

The attorney cleared his throat, angled his old head around the room, scanning my office, impressed. "I see you've made some money…"

"*Some* money?" I snapped irritated.

"$47 million is chicken-feed, Brian," he snarled back.

"Built on *trust,*" I snapped again. I sensed the old man was trying to antagonize me. I patted Flower gently on the back, her brown eyes boring defiantly into the attorney's blue one.

The attorney leaned back in his chair. "Like the bank in Florida who gave you a $2 million line of credit?" he inquired.

"How did you know *that*?"

The attorney scowled. "Chump change," he said. "It meant you could swim with bigger fish. But not the *huge* ones."

"I'm happy. I didn't let the fear of failure consume me. I grabbed my opportunities."

"And now you live The American Dream with your little mansion and BMW and your boat," he smirked.

*What's your problem, old man?* My mind screamed, becoming even more annoyed. Shaking with rage I glared and spat through gritted teeth, "What d'you want?"

Smiling, he leaned further forward. Now I had his attention. *What a slippery fucker.* "From now on—and consider this a modest down payment on your inheritance—for every million you've made, we'd like to match it…"

My eyes widened. "We?" I squeaked out. I sat frozen, my wild heart pounding in my throat. Dizzily I tried to take in what he was saying, then immediately wondered what he'd want in return.

"...we'll match it, *times ten,*" he interrupted.

I stared at the old man in silence, then pushed back my chair. "What's going on here? You don't look like a drug dealer."

He laughed. "No, Brian. I'm a humble attorney."

"And you don't look humble, either." I glared down at his costly Swiss watch. "Who are you?"

For a moment, the attorney stared at the wall, a strange serenity coming over him. Finally, he shifted his blue eye and peered over at me. "I'm Clark Swanson, Brian. I represent a powerful man, since deceased, who was part of...shall we say an influential corporation."

"What's his name?"

No reply.

"What's this corporation called?"

The old man shifted his blue eye to Flower, then back to me.

"The Seven," he said.

"Interesting name. Mysterious."

"It's just a name, Brian."

"Really?" I scoffed. "Seven is just a random name? I don't think so."

The old man said nothing, his hands clasped loosely together, fingers interlaced.

"Seven is considered a holy number, in most religions," I said. "Hindus believe in seven chakras. Sanskrit's Rig Vega describes seven stars. The world was created in seven days, and Noah's dove returned seven days after the flood. The book of Revelation speaks about seven seals, the Egyptians mapped seven paths to heaven, and Allah created seven-layered Islamic heaven and earth."

The attorney yawned, raised his hand, studying his gnarled fingernails. *He's toying with me,* I realized. *The slimy bastard.*

"We have seven seas," I continued, "seven planets, Gandhi mentions Seven Blunders of the World, pilgrims make seven walks during the Hajj and Umrah, there are seven doors to Hell in Islam, Buddha took seven walks after his birth, and the number is important in Cherokee cosmology, too."

"And there are Seven Princes of Hell," interrupted Mr. Swanson suddenly, "fallen angels who rebelled with Lucifer, created a war in Heaven and when defeated, twisted into hideous abominations…"

"If you believe in all that nonsense."

"Brian, *stop.*"

"There are also seven deadly sins…"

"The Founder was a movie fan."

"The *Founder?*" I watched Swanson lean back slowly. Suddenly my stomach ached, twisting in knots. Those two words had set my teeth on edge. "What's his name?"

Swanson lifted his eyes slowly, carefully. He didn't answer, just gave me that sly smile of his.

At my side, Flower growled. *I have underestimated this mealy-mouthed old bastard,* I thought. *This is worse than I'd imagined!* I concentrated on continuing my argument. "I was born on the seventh month of a seventh year…"

"At 7 am, Brian."

I stopped. Swanson chuckled. He was really annoying me with how much he knew about me. I leaned forward in my chair, Flower rising to her feet.

"Why would this Founder give me $10 million every time I make one million?"

What he said chilled me to the bone. "Because Brian, you're…special," Swanson replied. "Which is why my client, in his will, left his entire estate and business empire to one person: *you.*"

My heart pounded like a drum. I was certain he could see the naked fear on my face.

"I'm *special?* In what way? And people don't just give away fortunes."

Swanson lifted his blue eye at me, blinking. "We have great plans for you."

"Who's *we?* You keep saying *'we.'* What plans? Why would you do this?"

"It's your rightful inheritance, Brian."

"What is? I remember you told me that before, without really saying anything."

The old man sighed, staring resentfully. He seemed disappointed. "Does my proposition interest you or not?"

I paused. Sweat rolled down my cheek. "What was my benefactor's name? And why me?"

Swanson tilted his head, setting his thin lips in a grim line. "He specifically outlined in his last will that his true identity, along with his connection to you, should remain secret, until you fulfilled the conditions of his will and were ready to accept your inheritance. I'm sure you understand, Brian."

"More mystery. And, what does his estate get out of this?"

"The pleasure of helping us become…more."

"More what?"

"Don't be naive, Brian," Swanson gruffly hissed, leaning directly into my face and chuckling under his sour, old man breath.

"Do you like to be controlled like the rest of the sheep? Or do you prefer to be the one in control of your life and the lives of others?"

He raised an eyebrow, waiting. Silently I absorbed his words. Immediately Flower took notice of the tension in the room. Hair began rising on her neck as she silently crept towards Swanson.

"Control your beast," he demanded, squirming.

"Her name is Flower," I said and gripped her by the collar, pulling her back, then giving her a reassuring pat. "And I prefer to be in control, of course."

Swanson cursed, then tore his eyes away from the dog, his blank expression giving nothing away. "As to why *you*, my client believed you are the only person alive who has what it takes to run his empire, and the Trustees concur. You possess…the appropriate credentials."

"Do I?"

"Admirably. Are you interested?"

I watched his stunted, twisted, ugly mouth curl into a smile. "Maybe…send me a proposal…" I muttered.

Swanson cocked his head, gave his chin a quick stroke, and then opened a black briefcase, producing some papers which he handed to me.

I scanned them, frowning. It was the offer he'd spoken about, all right. Only a few clauses, like not giving any away to charity, the best way to pay little to no taxes. And more.

Which raised alarm bells.

To my astonishment, the last clause offered $10 million on the money I'd already made, $47 million.

That meant…*$470 million — a*lmost half a billion.

I let out a gasp, my eyes popping. I'd be rich beyond my wildest dreams. Suddenly, absurdly, I felt guilty.

The attorney squeezed the chair arms, almost in delight. His blue eye flashed at me. He opened his laptop, and with a few keystrokes turned it around for me to view the screen.

At the top it read UBS GROUP AG, then the amount $470,000,000 with my name and a recipient account number I didn't know.

"We've taken the liberty to set up a discreet, offshore, tax-free account in your name. Just say the word," he announced, his crooked old finger ready to press CONFIRM.

Shock poured through me. Watching my reaction, Flower growled. I kept scanning the screen, a muscle in my cheek twitching, close to tears, finally managing to blurt out, "I…I need to think about it."

"Are you certain?" Swanson's finger hovered over the CONFIRM button. "All you have to do is sign, then I press this button, and $470 million is yours, like that, no questions asked. And as I said, this is merely an appetizer for what's to come for you."

I hesitated, grinding my teeth in confusion. Swanson smiled, his eyes dead. Deep inside of me—or perhaps from a place outside—a small voice shrieked to get my attention. Why this pressure to make me sign right now? If I were to give away that amount of money, I surely would not be in a hurry. It was like he was unusually eager to get me to sign.

Flower showed me her teeth, looked at me with her bright eyes, then sagged back to the floor with a grunt. I was having a hard time keeping my thoughts together. Finally, I took the pen in my left hand and flipped to the last page of the papers needing my signature.

I paused, leaning forward, the pen shaking. Across the room I could sense Swanson rubbing his ancient hands together. The temptation was almost irresistible.

"If I sign here, am I selling my soul to the devil?" I asked, without even knowing where those words came from.

Swanson didn't answer. Flower sat up on her haunches. Confused, I put the pen down on the line, ready to sign while staring right at the attorney to watch for any expression on his face, any odd tone of his voice, that would either make me sign or not.

Swanson only peered down at the paper, then right back at me, with a cold stare.

"Don't be ludicrous," he said, "there is no such thing as the devil. Every man is for himself, tempted and lured by his desires and weaknesses."

The tone of his voice, as cold and dead as his gaze, instantly gave me the chills.

Without breaking our stare, I said, "Or maybe the devil's greatest deception was to convince the world that he doesn't exist, and all the shit is on us?"

"Whatever. Let's get back to your inheritance. In the event you fail to fulfil the conditions, our offer remains our private matter, and you will never hear from me again."

He gave me a tight-lipped smile that could kill. In that second, the voice in my mind screamed not to sign. *There is something wrong with this situation*, I thought. *I feel it in every cell of my body.*

The attorney was using an age-old trick to force people to sign; silence, then hand them the pen, put the papers in front of them and shut up, just stare at them until they become so uncomfortable they will do anything to break the silence.

I didn't give a damn about pleasing him. I felt like his pet rat let out of its cage, too uncertain about moving and stepping into another trap.

"I need time," I mumbled.

"Understandably, Brian. You have twenty-four hours," Swanson said and snapped his laptop shut. I

"All your clients in such a hurry?"

"He was my only client. And yes, he liked matters concluded promptly."

I stared at him sharply. "Twenty-four hours, then."

"Excellent."

Relieved, I stroked Flower's thick grey fur, smiling now. For the first time, Swanson gave me his business card, black with no name or address, just the embossed word THE SEVEN in gold and a cellphone number. Even more mystery.

Just then my desk phone rang, jarring me. Swanson leaned forward, the meeting over. "Tell me," he said, rising, gazing down at the ringing phone, "what lessons have you learned in the business, Brian?"

The phone rang and rang, the noise intolerable. Snatching the receiver, I had it halfway to my lips when there was a loud *click*. The line went dead. I placed the phone back on the hook, tempted to bolt from the office." Always diversify," I finally answered, wiping the sweat from my collar. "You're not invincible, and nothing lasts forever."

Swanson nodded, shook my hand, and said, "No, it doesn't, Brian. Not even you."

Then he left.

* * *

# ELEVEN

As soon as Swanson exited the room, I lost it completely. I unleashed an insane high-pitched laugh, the tears welling behind my eyes. Huffing and puffing, I let out a deep breath, noticing the sweat on my hands, my arms, my neck, everywhere. My mouth was dry, every muscle in my body clenched tight. *Think. I need to think.* I felt overwhelmed with excitement but stressed at the same time.

What was all this "Seven" talk about? Who is this founder? Are these the people that have been watching me all my life? Why me? What should I do? Do I take this massive amount of money? If I do, what do I have to do for them?

*I'm frightened,* my brain whispered, as tears tears ran down my cheeks. It was true, Swanson's proposition was beyond my wildest dreams. And it preyed on me.

Stress had me locked in a dance of raw fear. Stress meant one thing; taking out my boat and getting away. Now.

It was a beautiful sunny day when I reached the pier, fishing boats heading out into the harbour. Quickly I untied my boat, fired up the engines, and roared off at full speed, the wind whipping my hair.

I zoomed on the dividing line between the Atlantic Ocean and the Gulf of Mexico, the sea spray splashing my face. I leaned against the helm, watching the city recede in the distance, growing smaller and smaller, catching my breath. Beyond, there were other boats bobbing in the crosscurrent. I studied the open sea, my back to the beach and the shoreline, feeling the engine rumble beneath me. *You're alone now,* I thought. *You have time to think, in peace. Now you can—*

A voice from behind startled me.

"Quite the dilemma, Brian," whispered the voice in my ear. I spun around, one fist clenched, the other scrambling around to find a weapon. That's when I saw him. Gurung.

"What the heck are you doing here?"

Gurung smiled. "When I'm stressed," he said, "I take your boat out." He cocked his head, studying me, a big straw hat shielding him from the powerful sun.

Speechless, I almost fell to my knees. "How did you know I…never mind." What a time for Gurung to just turn up out of the blue! But of course, he's Gurung; he doesn't just arrive for no reason. "I know why you're here, "I said.

"Of course, you do. You're learning. And you have come to a fork in the road."

I sighed, nodding in agreement. The blood in my veins had turned to ice. Sensing my confusion, Gurung shifted his gaze off to the horizon; those piercing brown eyes always searching.

"This will be one of the biggest decisions you'll ever have to make." He frowned, cocking his head to one side. "Choose wrongly, then life as you know it, is over, and the course of your destiny will be changed dramatically…"

"I know, Gurung, just like with the witch, right?"

"…and not for good."

"What do you mean?"

Gurung screwed up his face. "You pursued the corporate world and money with the same determination as you did karate."

"The more money I made, the more I wanted to make."

"Yet how much did you give to help people? Did you share your good fortune with others?" he asked, disappointed.

As I watched, his face twisted into a bitter grimace. "Well …no. It's my money, and I worked like a demon to make it."

Gurung lowered his gaze. I could hear his slow intake of breath.

"Yes, like a demon, indeed," he said. "Brian, you're being led down a path of greed, wealth, and power, making that your priority."

"I'm not a bad person, Gurung, just because I want to create a better life for myself."

"Correct, Brian. However, the only way to live a life of peace and contentment is to live with fairness, integrity, and to make yourself useful to others. Remember *ikigai*?"

I nodded my head. Who could forget?

"But what's wrong with being prosperous?" I asked. "With wealth, you can do a lot of good, changing, and saving lives. If you are poor and your primary need is your survival, it is difficult also to be able to change other people's lives."

"Yes, Brian. But money coming from being bad does not create goodness."

"What do you mean?"

"How do you think The Seven generated the incredible amount of money they are offering you?"

"The Seven?" We stared silently at each other. There was that name again. "What d'you know about them?"

"First things first. Answer my question."

"I never really thought about it, Gurung."

"Well, let me tell you then. The Seven are a front for the most powerful bankers in the world—yet that is only a small fraction of their dirty business. They are the major instigators of fear and anxiety in the world today. We live in the safest time in human history, yet we have never been more anxious and fearful."

A hollow pain knotted my stomach. I gripped tighter to the boat's wheel, my only connection to sanity.

"When countries need loans," Gurung continued, "they come to these men. When wars need financing, they come to them. They have their filthy hands in everything and every business from advertising, tobacco, pharmaceuticals, water, oil and gas—you name it. They have insiders reporting to them on the board, or they secretly own the majority of the company. They run the world, Brian, and when they want to, they initiate global financial crises to set everyone back and to control new corporations suddenly in desperate need of financing."

"You mean like the financial crises that keep happening every decade?"

"Yes, Brian. It still astonishes me that people think it is a coincidence that the minute they recover from the latest crisis, a new one comes along. And that no bankers are ever put in jail."

"They probably own the corporations that run the prisons as well."

"I am sure they do, while also being in the arms trade, human trafficking, illicit drugs, and counterfeit goods, everything illegal. Imagine taking hundreds of millions of dollars of dirty money? No matter how much you want to think it is yours to keep and you can do well with it, it will rot in your hands and destroy your heart, like a festering tumour you can't get rid of. Why do you think they made the amount they offered you so tempting?"

I didn't answer but remembered how eager the attorney was for me to sign.

Gurung continued. "You're an engineer. Remember quantum entanglement, described by Albert Einstein as 'spooky action at a distance'?"

"Yes, particles that interact with each other become permanently connected and dependent on each other's states and properties, to the extent that they effectively lose their individuality…"

My mind immediately understood what Gurung was going to say. I felt a sharp pain in my belly. All around me, the wind whipped and whirled, the ocean waves crashing.

"So, imagine that you take money from a dead man's pocket, which means that the particles of the dead man are now entangled with the particles of the money and as you said, they become permanently connected and behave as a single entity. Now you take that money linked to the dead man. I think you can imagine that absolutely nothing positive or good will ever come from that money."

"I get your point, Gurung." I nodded. He was right, as he usually was, but I still had this huge decision to make.

"The Bible is full of wealthy people, Brian. And in Islam, Muhammad said, 'God does not look at your forms and possessions, but he looks at your heart and your deeds.'"

Somewhere off in the distance the seagulls were shrieking. A roaring yacht raced past us. Distracted, I exchanged greetings with the captain, admiring the vessel absently, which Gurung ignored.

"Today, most wealth is controlled and manipulated by evil people so they can dominate Earth's resources."

"You mean The Seven?" I asked, but Gurung was now in full flow.

"Money is evil when greedy people make more than they need. But in good people's hands, money *is* good because *service* is the purpose and helps people to reach enlightenment. You've been in business long enough to understand this, Brian. You've watched people spending every hour chasing money, and not giving their loved ones their time."

I winced at that, the time I hadn't given to loved ones and close friends. Time now lost forever.

"Slowly but surely, they take advantage of everyone. If you confront them, they have no problem rationalizing their greed by saying, 'it's my money, and I made it, why should I share it?'"

"So, you're saying it's the devil's work?"

"When people sell their soul to the devil, we all imagine someone standing in front of Lucifer signing a contract with a drop of their blood in exchange for fame and fortune."

I laughed at the cheesy images in my head, but Gurung was deadly serious.

"In business, people sign contracts and do things they would never do, for fame and cash. It erodes the spirit and distances us from our creator." He turned slowly and stared off at the horizon. A hissing wind filled the air. "In the film business, people sleep with directors to land roles, smoke on camera to promote cigarettes that kill, fake-date others to promote their violent movies, and take all kinds of soul-killing drugs. In the *music* business, they sing about sex, drugs, guns, and devil worship, surrounded by groupies, even when married. And they're fed drugs to cope with the punishing schedules."

"You're going to talk about the corporate world now, aren't you?"

"In *business*, bosses fire people and devastate families, employees sleep with the boss for a promotion, directors break up companies to increase profits, close factories then move overseas, firing thousands for profit and destroy anyone who goes against the corporation..."

"I remember bosses like that all too well."

"...then they dump toxic waste that pollutes the environment and make people work grueling, unhealthy hours."

Staring at the ocean, I thought about all the waste that pours into our seas, atmosphere, and lungs, causing premature death all over the world.

"Sensitive souls don't make it. Often, they kill themselves directly or indirectly, through drugs and alcohol to escape the pain and guilt."

Gurung muttered something inaudible, then fell to silence.

"Let me tell you the story of *caution*," he said, stepping forward and leaning close into my face.

"They say that in 1923, America's most powerful men met at the Edgewater Beach Hotel in Chicago. Together, they controlled more wealth than the US Treasury. Listen to what became of them. In 1936, Arthur Cutten, the top wheat speculator, was charged with evading over $400,000 in income taxes. He died of a heart attack at the same hotel before he went to trial." "Like some divine intervention, right?"

Gurung shrugged and continued. "In 1945, Leon Fraser, President of the Bank of International Settlements, shot himself in the head at his summer home in North Granville, New York. He was only 55 years old."

"Why'd he do that?"

Again, Gurung shrugged and went on. "In 1949, Howard Hopson, President of the largest American gas company, lost most of his fortune and died in a sanitarium at age 67."

"These guys haven't been so lucky, apart from their wealth."

"In 1932, Ivar Kreuger, head of the world's greatest monopoly, shot himself dead. Rumours have persisted that his death was murder and not suicide. In 1940, Jesse Livermore, the greatest bear on Wall Street, committed suicide at New York's Sherry-Netherland Hotel a week after thanksgiving. Charles Schwab, President of the largest independent steel company, lived his last years on borrowed money and left behind an insolvent estate. Richard Whitney, President of the New York Stock Exchange, was sent to Sing Sing Prison." Gurung finished, then leaned away from me again to stare at the water, now growing turbulent.

My mind fixated on all he'd said. I could feel a fluttering in my bowels, something inside me giving voice to what Gurung had left unsaid. "Wait, there's seven of them!" I gasped in surprise.

Gurung nodded.

"Were they the original Seven?"

For the third time, Gurung shrugged, "That's your world, Brian. I fear that you are about to become one of them that they have been grooming you."

"But who are they? And what do they want from me?"

Gurung stared disappointed. "Have you not been listening to what I said about where their money comes from?"

"I *have,* Gurung!"

"Yet you are still considering if you should take it or not. Your heart has grown weak and dark."

"It's not my heart, Gurung. It's the temptation."

He nodded. I could see financial temptation meant absolutely nothing to him.

"Do you know who the head of The Seven is?"

I shrugged. "No one knows. No one has seen the leader, ever. And no one knows the leader's name, or if that person is dead or ever even existed. A…ghost."

"You're scared of The Seven."

"I've seen presidents, monarchs and some of the world's most powerful leaders terrified at the mention of them. Few ever crossed them or refused their offers."

A filthy, oil-splashed fishing boat passed in front of us. As the captain screamed for my attention I slowed my engine, wheeled us back toward shore, stopping the boat at my favourite spot, the sandbank I always sat at to reflect.

Gurung crossed the deck, leaning against the railing. He bowed his head, arching his back, suddenly seeming helpless. "All religions and cultures have had interactions with them. The Bible said Mary Magdalene was possessed by seven demons and some believe in the Seven Princes of Hell…"

"…and Seven Archangels to oppose them," I interjected, and Gurung gave me the strangest look.

Too weary for much more conversation I dropped anchor, grabbed two chairs, jumped out of the boat, and placed the chairs on the sand, but neither of us sat. Fish swam between our legs in three feet of clear blue water.

Above us the gulls cawed and swooped. To my surprise and way too fast, the thought of the money again overtook my thoughts. "But Gurung, they just offered me *ten* times the money I've made so far!"

"If you accept the offer, they own you, and you will never be able to turn back."

"But, almost half a *billion,* Gurung? C'mon! Maybe some of it came from legal businesses, right?" I said but didn't believe it for a minute.

"Then choose the path to darkness," Gurung whispered. "Or enlightenment."

I sensed Gurung staring at me resentfully. I sucked in a big breath. "What do you want from me, Gurung?"

"I want you to destroy The Seven."

"What? *Me?* How the hell am I supposed to do *that?"*

The volume in Gurung's voice rose. "Do you think it is a coincidence that I am here? That you met the fortune-teller in Paris?"

"You know about her?"

"I know about *everything,* Brian."

"So...who are you, *really?"*

"Your friend, your guardian angel, your protector, guide, mentor, teacher...and the one *preparing* you."

"For what?"

"For the day, the battle against fear must be fought."

*A battle?* That hadn't figured into my plans. I slid down in my seat, placing my hands over my eyes as I shook my head. *God, why me?* "It's all too much to take in, Gurung."

"Then take in just one thing."

"What one thing?"

Gurung stretched forward in his chair, leaning in to me. "That accepting the attorney's money is the end for you. And a prolonging of fear for humanity."

* * *

# TWELVE

In virtual silence, Gurung and I rode home. When we reached the jetty, Gurung jumped out, no sign of his bad limp, shook my hand with a respectful bow, then ran off fast.

*He's in a helluva of a hurry,* I thought.

So was I.

Racing home, thoughts of The Seven sliding through my brain, I showered and changed, then sat with a bourbon watching the sunset, mulling over everything. My head was swirling with what Mr. Swanson and Gurung had said. I clamped the cold drink to my forehead, as if checking to make sure I didn't have a fever. Sad to admit, but I was torn.

An hour passed. The red sunset made my eyes ache. Eventually, I stumbled into the bathroom and stared at my reflection in the mirror, my lips trembling, searching my face for answers.

*What do I do? Is this really a trap?*

For too many years I'd lived in poverty, with my mother. I thought about the money struggles of my childhood—selling flowers, being forced to take handouts from my grandmother, then losing everything which I've worked so hard for.

Then I thought long and hard about the old attorney's offer.

What would that mean to me? Would having everything make me happy, change me into someone else?

In silence I thought about Gurung's warning, and what he was asking me to do.

*Could I refuse Swanson's offer? Then destroy The Seven, a mighty evil empire?*

Into my confused reflection I stared. This was getting crazier and crazier! Gurung was asking the impossible! It was so much easier just accepting the offer of wealth beyond my wildest dreams.

As I stared and stared my face turned white, my breath steaming the glass. A few hours and a few more drinks later, I made my decision.

I whipped out Clark Swanson's business card and sat it next to my cellphone where lit candles flickered. *Let's do this,* I told myself. Then I punched in a number and spoke.

"Mom?"

Hearing my mother's familiar voice in faraway Denmark instantly soothed me. "Brian…I was expecting your call."

"You were? Why? What's happened?"

"The American attorney called, said you'd spoken and discussed his proposal."

I sighed, then nodded, gulping air. "So, what d'you think?"

There was a long pause, then a hesitant answer. "I wish we knew more about him, Brian."

"Like who is he and who's this mystery benefactor?"

Another long pause. Sweat spread hot on my cheeks.

"It's half a *billion,* Mom!"

From the other end of the world my mother's words entered my brain. "Let me tell you a story, Brian. One morning when I was pregnant with you, I helped your Dad get ready for work, then went back to bed. Suddenly, a woman appeared at the end of my bed, wearing clothes from the middle ages with a cone-shaped hat and a long veil. My heart pounded in fear. She pointed at my belly and whispered something I couldn't understand. Then, as suddenly as she had appeared, she vanished."

"Mom, that's insane! Why didn't you tell me about this before?"

"I couldn't. I think she was trying to tell me something important or warn me. In any case, I stumbled out of bed and dressed as fast as I could, then went to tell my parents about what happened."

"Did they believe you?"

"Yes, and they thought it was an omen of something bad to come. That's why I'm telling you."

"Mom, who could this crazy offer be coming from?"

"I've got a bad feeling about this, son."

"Tell me, Mom."

She was silent for a moment. "It's probably best if we don't discuss this any more over the phone, Brian."

I shuddered. "But Mom, all that money…"

"Never forget your runestone," she said, her words making my stomach tighten. And with that, she hung up. I picked up Swanson's business card and stared at it for what seemed like an eternity. I could feel my brain and body systems all tuned to flee, to escape. My heart rate climbed, to a pace I was unable to control. Its pounding was loud, my lungs bursting, sweat glands working overtime. Suddenly my face softened. I looked up at the wall with a faint little smile. My mind was made up.

What kind of fool turns down *half a billion dollars?*

* * *

# THIRTEEN

Flipping Swanson's mysterious black business card around and around in my fingers, I breathed heavily, my mind in a spin, imagining how life could be, how much it could change so dramatically with all that money.

The candle flickered as I picked up my cellphone, my fingers poised over the numbers.

*What's stopping you?* I wondered, my shirt suddenly damp with sweat. Then I let out a huge sigh, laid the phone down, and stared at the card again. Hard.

Slowly, I reached for the candle and held the card over it.

*Burn, baby, burn.* The corner turned brown, then blacker than ever until suddenly the card burst into wild flames and I dropped it in fright. In seconds, it was a small heap of black ash in my lap.

Mesmerized, I brushed away the ashes, then crawled deeper into my thoughts. I had to admit that I was still sorely tempted by such a massive offer. Who wouldn't be?

As I tried to sleep that night, my thoughts faded into a fog. I pictured my mother and I, so poor that we sold flowers on street corners. I imagined myself as a boy, sleeping in a tiny drawer. The next morning, I rose early and made all the travel arrangements.

The rest of the morning I spent on business. During the afternoon, I checked out possible apartments where I could live. It was time for another significant change in my life, this time to get some distance between America and myself, away from the attorney, and even Gurung.

I was going to relocate the business again, this time in a part of the world where the wealthiest people enjoyed life, a place I had always wanted to live.

This would give me more time to think about what to do about The Seven, now that I'd turned down their offer.

I still had that sense of being followed and wondered if it was The Seven. Could it be? Would they track me down? Would I somehow find a way to destroy them, as Gurung asked?

Whatever I decided, or whatever fate had in store for me, I had to get away.

The very next day, I was on a plane to Monte Carlo, Monaco with my dear friend Flower. The sun was bright, filtering through the trees as we touched down in Nice Airport. An incredible eight-minute helicopter ride from Nice followed, flying by St Jean Cap Ferrat, Beaulieu and Eze, crowded with superyachts, then we touched down in Monte Carlo.

The sounds of the city swept me up in a feeling of magic. That same day, we strolled around the elegant Place Du Casino, up through the beautiful Jardins de la Petite Afrique until we found a cool apartment on Rue des Lilas on the 6th floor directly facing the casino and the Mediterranean Sea—an unbelievably expensive rent, it's true, but we paid six months in advance.

The next morning I stood in front of my apartment mirror, dreaming. I was really looking forward to an exciting new phase of my life, and to soak up some of the delights of one of the world's top destinations.

To my great surprise, Monaco was incredibly dog friendly. On many occasions, I would take Flower with me to Cafe de Paris, a fancy restaurant right next to the famous Place du Casino. The waiters would come running with a bowl of water for her, and everyone would think it was perfectly normal to have a massive, 120-pound, sled-dog in a sleek restaurant, in the middle of stylish Monte Carlo.

Not long after I arrived that things changed, and I'll never forget that night, for reasons both good and bad.

It was a Saturday, and I attended a black-tie fundraiser to rebuild Nepal's healthcare system, devastated by earthquakes and other natural disasters. A cause I was more than happy to support.

It was a glittering affair, hosted by the most powerful man on earth, the President of the United States. Standing only a few feet away, Secret

Service agents flanking him, I watched as he was presented by Prince Albert II of Monaco at the Monte-Carlo casino.

I rubbed my eyes, unable to believe I was truly here. I found myself being introduced to captains of industry, world-shakers and government policy makers, a scenario the little boy growing up in snowbound Copenhagen could never have imagined.

Suddenly, there was a loud commotion. I looked up to see an entourage of large, dark-skinned men, armed bodyguards, surrounding a dignified, important-looking man.

"It's the King of Nepal," an excited voice shrieked, and I craned my neck to see him.

*What a surprise,* I thought.

But that wasn't as surprising as who was part of his escort.

*Gurung.* I nearly choked on my drink.

He limped out of the imposing entourage and beamed at me, guiding the King's elbow, headed in my direction.

Halting right in front of me, he said, "Brian, how are you?" then shook my hand. "This is His Highness, Birendra Bir Bikram Shah, King of Nepal."

The King shook my hand. I was more than bewildered to see Gurung, never mind meeting the King, and barely managed a smile.

"And who is this young man?" the King inquired.

"This is Brian, Your Highness. Brian's on a…" He paused for a moment, then finished his sentence, "…*quest.*"

I raised my eyes to the King. The King stared me up and down, the gears in his mind grinding, then smiled. "May you find what, or who, you seek. And beware of The Seven." Then taking Gurung's arm, the two of them shuffled away.

I was dumbstruck. Raising my eyebrows, I watched Gurung and the King approach the President, Gurung introducing them, the President bowing lightly.

I didn't see Gurung again until later that night, after dinner, at Jimmy'z, an exclusive nearby nightclub; the usual noisy, dark place, packed with people talking, dancing and drinking.

Gurung stood in a corner, with a group of Nepalese. I crossed the crowded room to approach him when suddenly a hand clamped onto my shoulder.

In apprehension I whirled to see a man in the shadows. He leaned close to my ear and whispered, "I hope you decide to join the family business…Brian," and as he stepped back, I was astonished to see who it was.

The President of the United States.

Instantly my throat went dry, my face all saggy. How did he know my name? And the attorney's offer?

I stammered, frozen, wanting to say something, wanting to run. I must have looked as lost as I felt. The President waited for my reply patiently, almost affectionately. Finally, he grunted, and said, "If there's anything I can do for you…anytime…please contact me."

He shook my hand, bowed deferentially to me, smiled, and walked away.

I started to answer, but my voice was a croak. *What the hell just happened?* Again, I felt the sickening wave of self-consciousness, of being watched. My eyes scanned the casino, wondering where I fit into all this.

Just then I felt a nudge, and noticed Gurung by my side. Enormous relief rushed through, all at once. "You know, Brian," he said, "their influence goes to the very top."

"What are you doing here?"

"The King is a friend. But I really came to see you."

"The King knows about The Seven?"

"They want to recruit him, but he keeps stalling them, which means his life is at risk."

I could see Gurung's eyes were focused tight on me, which meant there was more to the story. "What d'you need to see me for?"

"You have shared your wealth, Brian. I am very proud of you."

"Thanks, Gurung, it's the least—"

"But all that is about to change."

"What d'you mean?"

"You turned them down, Brian. No one has done that before. Ever."

A sudden chill swept through me. It felt as if someone was squeezing my heart. "So," I sputtered out, "what's going to change?"

"Normally, there's a car crash, or an accidental drug overdose, an enforced heart attack, a so-called mugging, a coup, whatever."

"Gurung, please stop talking in riddles."

"You die, and it seems like a natural cause of death. Is that clear enough for you?"

Gurung stared into me, his eyes shining with sympathy and something else. I wanted to unload my thoughts. My head was spinning. I tried to drown my fears in alcohol, yet I needed to go to the restroom from drinking all that champagne.

That was the last place I should have gone.

* * *

# FOURTEEN

I felt a numbing sensation, eerie, and uncanny as I stepped through the door of the men's room. Inside, wealthy-looking gentlemen stood using the urinal and washing their hands, barely glancing at me.

"*Pardon,*" I gasped, whisking past them. I ducked into a booth and closed the door. That broke the insane reverie in my head. For a brief moment, I brought my thoughts into focus.

*The Seven. The President. The King. What did it all mean?* Suddenly, the room went quiet. Had everybody left? I looked up, a hollow knot twisting in my stomach.

Outside the cubicle, the entrance door swung open. I could hear the *click, click* of men's leather shoes. *Somebody is coming.*

*Click, click.* I leaned forward on my elbows, waiting. *Click, click.* After a moment, my eyebrows narrowed in irritation. I cursed, and reached for the cubicle door. Just then, it crashed down on top of me, and I gasped in fright.

A man in a black suit wearing a grotesque devil mask and a cute hat loomed above me. "*Wait a minute!*" I screamed, suddenly realizing it was him again, the man. "Who the hell are—" but the question was snuffed out when the man in the mask blew some kind of dust from his hand into my face.

Instantly, I gasped, coughed and choked loudly, blinded and struggling for air, face red and eyes tearful.

Grabbing me by the throat, the man lifted me out of the cubicle, then walked me across the room and smashed my face against the wall. I moaned in pain. He didn't seem to be a big guy, but he was powerful.

He grabbed my hair and slammed my head against the mirror, and I cried out in agony. My knees buckled, but I did not fall. Knowing he was right in front of me, I quickly head-butted him in the face. Unfortunately, his mask was metal, and my skull now exploded with pain. I arched my back, my brain swimming in confusion. Then he grabbed my lower lip, twisted hard and I howled, blood flowing from my mouth, as he started marching me toward the door.

I gritted my teeth, trying to stem the bleeding. Blood ran down my neck. Broken glass fell from my hair. I wiped the blood, struggling furiously, then lashed a knee strike into the man's stomach.

*Bullseye!* This time he gasped, his grip on my lip relaxing. I tried to focus, but my eyes were teary. Too late. He gripped my hand, twisted it into a lock and I groaned as he whipped out a knife.

I heard the click of the blade swishing open. I gripped the hand, slamming it back. A moment later, the assassin's blade slashed down at my head. *This is insane! Nothing on earth is making sense!*

With a loud bang, the bathroom door swung open. It was Gurung. He launched at the man.

There was confusion, blinding stabs of pain. The assassin dropped his knife, lurched back, and began crawling away. He grabbed the knife and held it high. In a flash, both Gurung and I rained kicks and punches on the man, some hitting the target but most missing.

Gurung pulled out his *kukri*. The blade flashed. He engaged in a close-combat knife fight with the man, each trying to slice the other open. Shifting position from left to right, circling each other. Suddenly the assassin launched forward, and Gurung narrowly avoided his knife, which buried itself into the bathroom stall door.

Seeing an opening, I took two steps and slammed the assassin in the back with the hardest side-kick I have ever given. He crashed into the door and fell over the toilet.

That's when two security guards raced in, guns drawn.

"Brian, run!" Gurung gasped, grabbing me by the scruff of the neck.

His powerful fist spun me around, shoving me out the door. We raced out. All I heard was the sound of a terrible but brief fight, then silence from the restroom.

Outside, in the dark alley, a gleaming black car sat. Gurung launched us at it, hauling the door open, and hurled me inside.

"What's happening?" I shrieked, as the door slammed behind me and the car sped off. Gurung blinked like crazy as we tore away and screeched through the streets, scanning the rear-view mirror for a car following us.

Nothing. Thank God.

"That son-of-a-bitch was going to kill me!" I screamed, checking my head for blood, removing shards of broken glass from my hair. Gurung veered the car to the right, gunning it down the next street. "I still don't understand why The Seven would kill me! Torture me into joining them perhaps…but if they want me to inherit then why *kill me?*"

"I don't know Brian. But that man was a professional, the kind who eventually get their kill."

Down the side streets, we roared, skidding around corners, Gurung in a sweat, constantly checking the rear-view mirror. At one wild turn I was launched across the front seat, Gurung heading uptown. Finally, we arrived at my apartment block. Gurung kicked the passenger door open. *How did he know my address?*

"Go upstairs, clean up, get some rest, and pack a bag. He won't attempt anything else tonight; there are too many police and security. In either case, I'll stay down here and watch."

I gave him a look, trying to fathom this strange but incredible man.

"How come you're always there when I need you?"

"Don't believe that just because you can't see something, it isn't there. Your eyes and your brain will deceive you."

I swallowed hard, nodded in agreement, knowing that once more, Gurung was right. Then I jumped out, looked around, and scampered into my block.

Up the apartment stairs I raced, staggering as I reached the top, ready to collapse from exhaustion. Cautiously I moved down the hallway, dazed, my shoulder aching from Gurung's wild ride. Suddenly I heard the scurrying of other feet. "Hello?" I whispered... No answer. I took a step closer, inching down the dimly-lit corridor, cracking the door to my apartment open. "Hello?" I forced my body through the door, eyes scanning. Out of nowhere Flower leapt up to me from the darkness, knocking me over and making me gasp in fright. I hugged her gratefully, then fed her a juicy steak from the fridge.

I checked all the rooms carefully, cautiously flipping on the lights. Satisfied there was no one hiding, I loosened my tie, poured a stiff drink, and stepped onto the balcony.

In the distance, I could see the casino still glittering in the night to the backdrop of the Mediterranean. People were even casually strolling out of the casino in their black ties and ball gowns. My nerves were shredded. I thought of the attack, my assassin, how my karate training instinctively kicked in, and thanked God the man didn't have guns or other weapons.

Sipping my drink, my mind searched every plausible reason for anyone to kill me. *Somebody wants me dead. Why? What was their strategy?* I thought about how I had made my millions and didn't need The Seven. I still felt good about turning down their incredible offer.

Looking down I spied Gurung sitting in the car, my babysitter, with not a care in the world.

I closed my eyes, letting this sink in. I yawned, stressed but needing sleep, and I wondered if I'd have the dream again. The vision of the desert, brush blowing and sand swirling in the wind, and from a duststorm, a figure emerging.

I felt the wind engulf me from the dream. A thin person reached out a hand to me, but the blowing sand kept swallowing me. *Who are you?* I couldn't see a face and was unsure if this was a good or a bad person.

I didn't take the offered hand. And when I woke the next morning, things took a terrible turn.

***

# FIFTEEN

YOUR CREDIT LINE HAS BEEN RECALLED… THE BANK CANNOT CONTINUE TO LEND YOU MONEY… RECALLING ALL YOUR CURRENT LOANS…

The next morning my cellphone and email inbox were crammed with nightmarish messages.

YOUR CREDIT CARDS ARE CANCELLED…PLEASE PAY IN FULL IMMEDIATELY OR FACE PROSECUTION…

I stood on the balcony, reading and re-reading each text. *What in the hell's happened?* Slipping into despair, I punched in my voicemail and desperately listened to my cellphone messages over and over again, "…call the bank urgently…" and" …pay your overdraft in full immediately or else…"

I shook my head in shock. More texts came buzzing in.

THE MORTGAGES ON YOUR U.S. PROPERTIES MUST BE PAID IN FULL WITHIN FIVE BUSINESS DAYS…ALL LOANS MUST BE REPAID WITHIN FIVE BUSINESS DAYS…DO NOT IGNORE…

I shut my phone down with a heavy heart and a tormented sigh. I had no way of repaying them. *Dear God, please let this all be a mistake!* The stakes had become much higher than I had ever imagined.

Messages continued to arrive. One stated that my customers would only buy with six-month terms, which I couldn't fund for that long, virtually putting me out of business.

"You *bastards,"* I whispered.

The messages kept coming, going from bad to worse.

I received an email from my mortgage lender in Denmark. WE HEREBY WITHDRAW OUR LOAN ON YOUR APARTMENT. PLEASE REPAY IN FULL. NOW.

Again, I shut the message down with a grim face.

Luckily, my frantic call to my Danish realtor produced quick results. By chance, he'd already found someone who either wanted to rent or buy my apartment. A meeting was set to discuss terms. I prayed that I could convince the person to buy it.

I was horrified to my core—first the bank loan, then my customers, some of them friends, now this?

Surely, The Seven was behind it all.

The conclusion was obvious. *It's no coincidence that a week after I refuse their offer, I find out that I am suddenly not only broke but homeless.*

It was clear that attorney Swanson was as good as his word; he'd do everything he could to make me fail. He was not only against me, but he was also now my enemy, an enemy I couldn't afford to have and had no chance of defeating.

Dropping the phone in my pocket, I hung my head over the balcony railing to see Gurung still down there, dozing in his car, looking calm and unbothered. Unlike me.

Seeing Gurung, my anger vanished. I hadn't heard from him since Key West, and suddenly he appears in Monte Carlo. How on earth could he possibly know I was here?

I jumped as my cellphone rang. Another bad message? Fortunately, it was Gurung. His voice was calm but insistent. "Now you can finally achieve your destiny."

I stared down to see his smiling face fixed up at me. What was he thinking? I'm near suicidal, broke, homeless and in agony, and he says that?

Flower's insistent bark alerted me to the apartment door. Next second, Gurung was inside my apartment. *Is he a part magician?*

"Brian, you must leave here now. The man will be gathering strength again and will soon make another attempt to snatch you, now that most dignitaries have left with their security details."

I nodded, whirling to look around my beautiful apartment.

"It is time," he said, "Time for you to meet the Bruja." All at once I wanted to find a deep hole and crawl in. *Meet the Bruja? Just like that? Dear God, this crazy fool!* I felt myself sinking deeper and deeper into depression.

"I would wish we had more time to train and prepare you, but we're running out of time. Now that you have declined their offer, they are hunting for you."

My mind spun. Inside, I knew he was right, but I felt sick.

"But before that, you must meet someone else. A man who can help."

He looked at me for a long time without saying anything. My mood was so bad, I almost laughed. I was exhausted and bruised after our fight with the man. Flower sat looking up at me as if she could read my thoughts. I knelt and hugged my beautiful dog to my face.

"Time to go, Flower," I sighed, and went to pack a bag.

Five minutes later we were in the car. With Flower in the back seat, Gurung drove me to my realtor's office. I slipped my keys through the letterbox, together with a note that told him to take or give away everything in my apartment. I wasn't coming back anytime soon.

Out of the city our car plunged, Gurung driving faster and faster, my hands gripping tight to Flower's fur. Before I knew it, we'd crossed into France, racing through Beausoleil heading up the narrow winding roads towards the A8.

Gurung sped along one of the world's most stunning coastal drives, along the D53, Route de la Moyenne Corniche D6007 and then the D51. The journey was breathtaking, especially on such a sunny day, and I kept my eyes fixed on the calming waters of the Tyrrhenian Sea, thoughts racing in my brain.

"The drive takes about eight hours, Brian," Gurung explained with a grim look. Suddenly, I felt weary and closed my heavy eyes.

I dozed a little and woke up to see signs for Savona, still on the epic coastal drive. From deep inside my subconscious, I felt a strange twinge of relief.

Struggling to stay awake, I heard Gurung's voice. "You have special powers, Brian," he said. "Everyone does."

I looked at Gurung. He stared straight ahead. Calm. Unreasonably calm.

"Like what?" I groggily asked.

"Sixth sense. Intuition. Foreboding, the appreciation of the world and nature and most incredible, miraculous really; *love.*"

I was feeling dizzy again, losing focus. "When you put it like that…"

"These things and more are unique to humans. Truly amazing gifts that most people have forgotten, and never awake to how special they are."

Leaning back in my seat, I pressed my eyes shut, expelling a breath. In my temples, I felt a headache raging. We swerved into the countryside, passing signs for La Spezia. I knew that once we saw road-signs for Pisa, we'd turn inland; the road hilly but a joy to watch.

"And joy. Don't forget joy," I said to Gurung, and he smiled.

"You're going somewhere very few people go to meet a very special person."

The signs said Livorno, and I slumped back in my seat, weary, thirsty, hungry.

Another sign flashed past, the E76 past Florence then the E35 at Arezzo by-pass, and we stopped at a roadside tavern to let Flower do her business. Then we snacked on amazing gnocchi, a personal favourite.

I was barely able to stagger out of the car, I was so exhausted. My fingers pressed into my temples with such immense pressure that I worried my flesh might break apart. We sat in a booth by the corner, Gurung opposite me. "You're going to the Vatican, Brian. The Congregation for the Causes of Saints, responsible for investigating miracles and paranormal matters."

"Paranormal?" I said, trying to clear my mind while Flower slurped from a deep bowl of water, splashing it at my feet.

"You'll meet a man who is sent all over the world to investigate everything from statues of Jesus or Virgin Mary shedding tears of blood, to exorcisms and miraculous healings and apparitions."

"Phenomenal," I said with a smirk at Flower.

"He was also the last person to meet the Bruja and knew of her last location."

"Sounds exciting, but…dangerous."

"The clock is ticking, and you have no choice." Gurung pressed his hand over mine, the message unmistakable. "You have to find her before The Seven find you."

* * *

# SIXTEEN

A massive room, plunged in total darkness. The only light seeps from six hidden spotlights in the ceiling.

At a vast picture window, a black-haired man stands in silhouette, solemnly staring out at a stunning panorama of Lake Davos with breathtaking views of the lush, green, snow-covered Sertig Valley lying between the snow-capped Fluela Wisshorn and Blackhorn mountains. Helicopters zoom past from a sizable heliport, fenced off, armed security guards ringing the fence.

The man turns to face the lavish Intercontinental Hotel, the venue for the World Economic Forum in Switzerland. The hotel is massive, ultra-modern and egg-shaped; yellow brick and concrete with a thousand windows glinting in the hot morning sun.

Guests and tourists mingle with delegates and speakers, many escorted by security details, weapons bulging obviousy under their thick winter coats.

At the entrance to the hotel, giant banners on either side proclaim: *World Economic Forum. Where Leaders Meet.*

Outside, the world looks cold. Down in the street, eddies of wind swirl snow into spirals. Gleaming black limos pull up and security details swarm, VIPs emerging to be escorted by a ring of guards toward the bustling entrance.

"The news, sir," a young woman announces, then grabs a TV remote.

The black-haired man turns. A giant plasma TV screen comes to life, and the young woman zaps its broadcast to the news channel, flipping through different reporters speaking German, French and Italian, the black-haired man nodding in understanding until the woman eventually finds an English-speaking channel.

A reporter is outside the impressive venue, snow swirling, and talking earnestly to the camera:

*"...non-profit World Economic Forum is headquartered in Cologny, Switzerland, where the average price for homes is around 10 million Swiss francs, roughly 10.2 million USD ..."*

With a blank expression the black-haired man stares. The footage changes to reveal a sprawling range of buildings, the Alps in the distance, then reverts to the reporter:

*"...with the motto 'Committed to Improving the State of the World.' This year, 2,000 global-shaping delegates from academia, journalism, politics, and business..."*

The man at the window smiles. Sniggers.

*"...with Heads of State, Prime Ministers and Presidents will attend, the theme 'Creating a Shared Future in a Fractured World'..."*

The man at the window grunts, shakes his head in disbelief. "People believe anything," he snorts, then struts to the head of a long teak table.

There, spotlights pick out six other people: five men, and a woman, all very expensively power-dressed, impassive, self-important, and almost regal.

The Seven.

"Update me," the man snaps from the darkness as he sits in a deep, black leather chair, checking his Patek Philippe.

One of the men leans forward. Max, a hefty man in his 60s, wearing a grey suit with swept-back salt and pepper hair, looks at the black-haired man. "Project Fear kept us in control for centuries, sir. And it remains highly effective. Our global PR, advertising, and political programme keep people everywhere running scared."

Max zaps a remote. Images appear on the white wall displaying a map of the world, many countries with red blocks. Newspaper headlines: FINANCIAL MELTDOWN. TV ads are showing slimy politicians, and sweatshops are making cheap clothes and food. And more.

Max sits back smugly. The black-haired man nods, satisfied.

Max smiles and continues. "We've persuaded humans to buy our powerful lie; life is limited, they need a job they hate, to save up and buy things they don't need from us, and they should welcome retirement to get a pension that we control, then die without ever having lived. We've saddled them with debt, locked those who could afford it into a mortgage, and threatened them that they'll lose their homes if they default on payments to *our* banks. Project Fear ensures that no one wants to get arrested for protesting or falling back on payments. Also, our relentless PR machine, and our ability to manufacture cheap, quickly disposable trends, create panic about keeping up with what people think they need to be happy."

Sniggers around the room. The lone woman at the table, her voice slicing through the darkness like a knife, says, "Kerching."

Max chuckles and continues. "What they don't understand is, *we* control their happiness. However, some people have become too powerful and influential since the last financial crisis ten years ago..."

The black-haired man grunts loudly, a grunt of cold disgust, gestures for Max to get on with it. Max clears his throat, talks faster.

"It's time we create another one. We take over their assets and resources and put the sheep back on the treadmill again to rebuild, sir."

Max smiles, smugly. Without missing a beat, he adds, "Using advertising and subliminal tools; we give humans a quick fix. They are dumb but dangerous animals driven by factors outside their consciousness, and need to be protected from themselves. We have successfully manipulated their life choices and engineered their consent, so they think they decide what they really need."

Everyone in the room laughs, even the black-haired man.

"We have turned them into herds of consuming, pleasure machines," Max says, "so that we can control them. They are trapped in an endless cycle of short-lived pleasure and long-term dissatisfaction, and..."

Suddenly the young woman leans in close to the black-haired man and says, "Your keynote speech is in three minutes, sir."

The black-haired man looks at the woman, narrowing his eyes. The woman is utterly beautiful with major plastic surgery and looks ageless, with dyed-blonde hair, big blue eyes, scarlet lips, a lot of diamond jewellery, and a smile like a shark.

The man shoots her a patronizing stare, frowns and mutters, "Finally, somebody who speaks shorthand." Then he turns to a tiny, lizard-like man of about 80; body bent double, thick glasses on, toying with worry beads.

"Project Social Control update," the man demands.

The lizard-man licks his lips. "Our DNA project is highly effective, sir. We've hijacked 57% of DNA from the world's industrialized countries, 79% of that from shell companies offering ancestry information and disease prevention. And 20% was submitted... anonymously."

The Seven snigger together. Max shakes his salt-and-pepper head. "People are fools. There is no such thing as anonymous DNA."

The lizard-man nods and continues. "We just keep stealing health data on earth's population."

The man in charge smiles, liking what he hears.

The lizard-man laughs casually. "We've launched the most complex cyberespionage attacks on public and private health insurers, biobanks and genome sequencing companies, stealing patients' personal and sensitive genetics data. Just last week, sir, we hacked the UK Biobank, the single largest public genetic repository in the world, with samples of the genetic blueprints of half a million Brits."

Impressed, the black-haired man nods. "So, all in all, sir, the project is highly effective, and we now hold the most precious thing a human can ever own; their genome."

The black-haired man looks perplexed. The woman at the table interjects, trying to make him understand.

"They're also using the gene-editing algorithm CRISPR. It removes disease genes and enhances desirable human traits like strength, sight, or speed..."

"Which improves your overall DNA...for a price," the lizard-man snorts.

The woman doesn't like being interrupted and tries to hide it, snapping, "*And*...we're developing the ultimate delivery method, a gel which delivers CRISPR gene-editing which contains DNA coding and activates targeted genes while leaving healthy cells intact."

"*If* you can afford the upgrade," the man in deep shadow finishes, then adds, "Bill Gates warns of inequality, favouring only wealthy people."

The woman nervously sits back. Everybody is quiet, waiting. The black-haired man bends into the spotlight, thinking.

"I...*like* it," he says, and the woman smiles.

"Our AI Project..." the fifth man—a short, bald and round man in his 30s with a ruddy, alcoholic face—begins, but the black-haired man raises a finger, and he stops dead.

The man lets him sweat, then raises a finger.

"...is highly effective, sir..."

The man pauses him with a single gesture, licks his lips at the young woman, and then waves his hand for the fifth man to continue.

"Our predictive crime analytics decide if someone is likely to commit a crime. If they are, using our DNA phenotyping, our scientists can create a simulated face from a drop of their blood using their genetic markers. Then, by activating the cameras in cellphones and laptops of unsuspecting users, and using global surveillance, we can locate them anywhere in the world."

The fifth man sits back in his chair, comfortable, sturdy, and smug.

"So...people have lost hope, their connection with others, communities, and nature. They are asleep, politically ignorant, spiritually bankrupt, and their worth is money, not self. And, they abuse substances. All of this adds to the global mental health epidemic, and people feel...empty."

The others gape at him, waiting for what's next with trepidation.

The black-hairedman drums his fingers. Pausing. "Good job," he finally says.

The others in the room fall silent. The man smiles then suddenly slams the table with his fist. The room rumbles.

"Then why is Brian causing us so many problems?" he shrieks.

All in the room are taken aback by his sudden fury.

"He's...*determined*..." the lone woman at the table bravely states.

The man doesn't look happy, and his eyes bore into hers. She gulps and continues.

"...to follow what he believes is his path. We will make him truly see, sir."

She stares across at the man, eyes blinking crazily. The man smiles and gives the woman an approving nod, and she exhales with relief. The man's female assistant leans in close to his ear and whispers, "Your keynote speech is *now,* sir."

"They can wait. I have other plans," he says and gazes at his assistant lustfully. His pulse suddenly rises. Looking around the table at anxious faces, he asks, "Where is Brian now?"

* * *

# SEVENTEEN

In the car I awakened in a sweat, as if from a dark dream. Breathing heavily, I looked out the window to see it was approaching nighttime as we raced past a sign that read Terni. A scream was still echoing through my head, brought on by my dreams.

*Stop, please make it stop,* I pleaded with my brain. Seeing my agony, Gurung rammed his foot down on the gas, and picked up the pace of his driving. Next thing I knew, I saw a road sign that read, Citta Del Vaticano.

The Vatican.

A city-state, the smallest on earth, surrounded by Rome, and headquarters of the Roman Catholic Church. Home to Pope Francis, the first Jesuit Pope, a good man from Buenos Aires and humble, living modestly in the Vatican guesthouse.

As we drove closer, I wiped my lips with a trembling hand, settling back in my seat. I turned my face to the sun seeping through the car window and closed my eyes. We managed to find a parking space because we'd need to walk.

Our starting point was on the side of the Tiber that's home to the famous Colosseum, Pantheon, and Termini Station, then we headed west toward a bridge to cross the River Tiber.

We chose the prettiest bridge to walk across, partly because it's pedestrian-only, and the one leading directly to the Castel Sant'Angelo. Cleverly it's called the Ponte Sant'Angelo, or Sant'Angelo Bridge.

I gaped at everything; my brow tightened in wonder. I thought about the Vatican's treasure trove of iconic art and architecture. Its Museums houses ancient Roman sculptures such as the famed "Laocoön and His Sons" as well as Renaissance frescoes in the Raphael Rooms and the Sistine Chapel, famous for Michelangelo's ceiling.

"The spiritual home to over one billion Catholics," Gurung stated sharply, "the Vatican is also a tourist trap. And the Vatican Bank has assets of $8 billion, plus."

Gurung sighed. This wealth conflicted with his belief system. It certainly affected me as I thought about all the poverty in the world.

In no time, we were heading towards an office Gurung called The Congregation for the Causes of Saints.

"How d'you know where it is?" I asked. But he just flashed his customary enigmatic smile.

As we crossed a big, open yard, I could see a man in black with a white dog collar standing there, clearly waiting for us — a *priest.* I shoved my hands into my pockets and kept walking.

At either side of an archway stood a Swiss guard in their uniform; blue, red, orange and yellow with a distinctly renaissance appearance.

Gurung noticed me watching them.

"The Swiss guards are the Pope's bodyguards. They're equipped with traditional weapons, like the halberd, and firearms. Since the assassination attempt on Pope John Paul II in 1981, the emphasis has been placed on non-ceremonial roles, with training in unarmed combat and small arms."

I nodded, fascinated at the extent of Gurung's knowledge.

"Recruits to the guards must be unmarried Swiss Catholic males between 19 and 30 years of age who have completed basic training with the Swiss Armed Forces," he finished as we reached the priest.

The priest eyed Gurung, then turned around without acknowledging us. This made me nervous for some unexplained reason. I drew in a deep breath, Gurung taking my arm to steady me.

"Stay calm," he whispered, his eyes as solid as two stones set in his skull.

As we walked off, I felt the urge to turn back. Glancing over my shoulder, I spied one of the guards pull out his cell phone.

* * *

The priest was short and roly-poly, with no hair and perfectly smooth, alabaster-like skin, wearing round steel spectacles and an air of mystique.

"Ronaldo Del Duca," he said, introducing himself, then smiled.

Together we headed across the yard, past beautiful, ancient, dirty-blonde sandstone buildings, then into a modest office, heaped with papers, filing cabinets, scientific, medical and religious books, high-back leather chairs, and in complete contrast to the messy room, white, state-of-the-art, touch-screen Apple computers.

There was a huge map of the world on the wall, and I stared at literally thousands of different coloured pins on it.

"How many cases d'you investigate in a year?" I asked Ronaldo as he poured coffee from a steaming pot into three mugs.

"Too many," he said, handing Gurung and me a mug each.

"Interesting job," I said, as we all sat back in comfortable chairs and exchanged smiles.

"How do you investigate miracles or paranormal events, Ronaldo?" Gurung asked.

"Everyone asks that," Ronaldo answered. "I'll try and keep it simple."

He composed himself. "The Catholic Church has done some odd things. But paranormal activity is investigated with sincerity and urgency, whether we're deciding on putting our gold-plated seal of approval on Vatican-certified miracles to canonize a saint, or carefully dispelling a wayward demon who set up shop in someone's body."

"Not like *The Exorcist* or *The Conjuring* then?"

"Perhaps," Ronaldo answered. "Brian…what if some of those stories were real?"

That stopped me in my tracks. Sweat suddenly beaded on my forehead. I creased my brow at the ridiculousness of Ronaldo's claim, deciding to keep silent, to listen.

"I deal with thousands of cases a year, like legitimizing miracles in the Catholic Church or performing exorcisms. My paranormal investigations usually involve working with a team of doctors and scientists to determine whether paranormal phenomena has occurred."

Gurung and I exchanged impressed glances.

"My office investigates, and if proof of a miracle exists, the person who performed the miracle may get beatified."

I nodded absently. Gurung's face remained impassive, his words slow and deliberate.

"The Curandera—the Bruja—healed a lot of people, Brian. Ronaldo was sent to investigate," he said, and I nodded.

"Beatification is one of the first steps to becoming a saint and is necessary for a miracle to be officially recognized by the church."

"And did she perform a miracle?"

"Let me continue. Each case investigated by me is opened by the bishop in the diocese where the individual under investigation lived or died. Bishops wait five years before opening a case, though I make allowances in exceptional cases, like with Mother Teresa."

I gave him another impressed look, and the priest smiled, sipped his coffee, and then continued.

"The path to the verification of a miracle isn't easy. I evaluate whether the person who allegedly performed the miracle is *virtuous* enough to have performed it, before deciding whether it happened."

"And the Curandera was virtuous?"

"She was. But I also need significant evidence that the individual in question was exceedingly *holy,* and people have been drawn to *prayer* through her example, must be present..."

"Was she? And were they?"

"You're an impatient young man, Brian."

"He's on a quest, Ronaldo," Gurung interrupted.

"I know, Gurung."

I shivered. All at once my impulse was to run from the room. *How did he know?*

"So, if the congregation rules that a person was a servant of God, the case is passed to the Pope, who can beatify candidates for sainthood."

"It sounds complicated," I said.

"It's very difficult to prove someone performed a miracle. For it to be considered by me, it must meet certain requirements. Miracles, like curing disease, must be instantaneous or sudden, complete and permanent, and without scientific explanation."

"And the Curandera did that?" Gurung asked, beating me to it.

Ronaldo hesitated. "*Possibly*. We're still investigating."

"And how d'you do that?" I pressed.

"All of her qualifications must be *proven,* and the burden of proof with medical miracles, after I rule a person is virtuous enough to have performed a miracle, lies with Consulta Medica, a board established by the Vatican in the mid-1900s and made up of a hundred renowned Italian, Catholic physicians."

"How does anyone ever get through all of them?"

"Only five Consulta Medica doctors review the miracle, examining things like CT scans, X-rays, and medical reports.

"Most modern miracles are medical," Gurung added.

"Yes, more than 95% of the cases cited in support of canonization involve healing from disease."

"So, your doctors have to say, 'We don't have any natural explanation for what happened.'"

"Quite, Brian. Consulta Medica is involved in nearly all of my investigations. For miracles that happened because someone prayed to a saint after his or her death, the prayers are investigated. If Consulta Medica can't produce a scientific explanation for the miracle, doctors pass the case to a panel of cardinals and priests who look for evidence of healing prayer. If healing prayer occurred, the panel issues a declaration."

"It's not only complex but very convoluted."

"The Church must always be careful, Brian. Miraculous healing in response to prayer is a proof that the potential saint is in heaven with God. The Pope can beatify the applicant if he chooses. This is the final step, before being officially declared a saint."

"The Curandera is going to be a saint?" I asked incredulously.

"Possibly. Sainthood applicants would need two verified miracles to be canonized unless the individual in question was a martyr. In the case of martyrdom, the Pope may simply declare sainthood."

I nodded to myself, and once again, my head was in a spin trying to absorb so much information.

"So, where did you investigate all this?"

"In Chimayo, New Mexico. The local bishop contacted me, told me the Curandera healed countless serious illnesses with nothing more than herbs and words."

"And you believed him?"

"Bishop Cruzeria is an honourable man. Of course, I believed him."

"But what did *you* think?"

"The locals swore blind she cured them and helped countless others. As to her, she was…captivating. I have high hopes and nothing but respect for her."

"Is she still there, in Chimayo?" Gurung asked, looking deadly serious.

Ronaldo shrugged.

"Will she become a saint?" I pressed.

"Perhaps in time."

I smiled, still puzzled, while my brain struggled to piece together the jagged connections these men were prophesying. Looking pleased, Gurung thanked Ronaldo for his time, stood, reached to shake Ronaldo's hand and prepared to leave.

"How will I know her, even if I get to Las Chimayo?" I asked.

The priest fished around in his coat, then produced a creased photo from his wallet. Handing it over to me, he said, "Keep it."

I lowered my gaze to the photo. It showed a stick-thin, interesting-looking woman with long, jet-black hair, high wrinkled cheekbones and brightly coloured clothes, adorned with about 10 pounds of glittering Native American jewellery and holding a beer, of all things. Again, I felt the malevolent insanity of everything, and found myself exerting every ounce of my will just to keep from fleeing.

"She also said someone would come. A man on a quest to open the eyes of humanity, and usher in a new era with no fear."

I nodded, realizing that's how he knew of my mission. I stared down at the photograph, my brain feverish, my mind exhausted. Suddenly, Ronaldo gripped my hand in both of his and stared deep into my eyes.

"Miracles come in many guises, Brian. Each child is a miracle, and sometimes they're even more special."

He stared intently into my eyes with a warmth and a certain strangeness that made me wonder what he was thinking.

"Sometimes, a miracle isn't what someone *does,* Brian, but remembering what someone truly *is.*" He continued gripping my hands, with much force. The silence between us spoke volumes. Only a few years ago, I'd awakened each morning without a single purpose in life, other than making it through each day to the next.

Now all that had changed.

* * *

# EIGHTEEN

It seemed a thousand years since we'd entered this room. My brain was full of whispers. *I can't believe this. I can't believe any of this! Who do these people think I am, a savior? Why me?* I found myself wanting desperately to confess my anxiety, my fears. Yet after a few mumbled niceties, Gurung, Flower and I left, saying a warm farewell to Ronaldo. As we strolled back over the bridge towards our car, Gurung kept looking over his shoulder.

"What is it?" I asked.

"We're being followed. Don't look." Of course, the first thing I did was look.

I couldn't see anyone suspicious. Gurung said nothing. We kept walking. Suddenly I felt the whole world was going crazy.

"He's good, a professional; suggesting you're in danger," Gurung announced.

I stared at him, perplexed. "Is it The Seven?"

Gurung raised a hand, silencing me. "I don't know. But let's get out of here."

We hurried to the car and jumped in. I gave Flower a nervous stroke, mumbling a few anxious platitudes.

Gurung observed the rear-view mirror, then gunned the car to screech away.

"Where will we go?"

Gurung disengaged the turn signal, snapped the headlights on, eyes fixed on the road, blocking out my words.

"Take me to the airport, please," I said, my mind still in a state of shock.

"Where do you intend going?"

"Copenhagen first, I guess. To see if I can sell my apartment. And then Santa Barbara, to see if I can save my business and home."

"You can't, Brian. They're lost."

I scanned Gurung's eyes in the rear-view mirror. In them I saw something like pity. Then I noticed his fists tighten their grip around the steering wheel. "How can you be so sure?"

"Who do you think is behind it?"

I weighed his words, said nothing, and just slumped in my chair.

*The Seven.*

Their tentacles are everywhere, and I wondered what chance I stood against them. Flower squirmed against me as if she understood.

"Can we ever defeat them?"

"Have faith."

"Like Ronaldo? I wish."

"Fiumicino airport is under an hour away. We'll head there," Gurung said as he deftly switched lanes, veering and weaving like a madman, car horns blaring.

In spite of Gurung's warning that my homes were lost, I produced my cell phone, googled flights from the airport and saw that the cheapest flight to Copenhagen required a change in Charles de Gaulle airport in Paris.

"Are you coming with me?" I asked Gurung as he once again checked the rear-view mirror.

"No, Brian. I have things I must do," he said, grimly glancing into the mirror again, face tense.

I nodded, sad to see this part of our journey end. "How far is it now?"

"35 minutes."

He held up his hand, signalling no more talking. *Great! No more questions meant no more answers!* Flower gritted her teeth and gaped up at me with that wide-eyed child's expression of befuddlement. We drove along the busy A91 via Cristoforo Colombo, past Ponte Galleria, then we saw signs for Fiumicino airport.

My mind felt stiff and numb, from all the driving. Shortly, Gurung pulled onto the off-ramp, and within minutes, we parked outside the entrance at the bustling airport, and my nerves ramped up a notch.

Gurung kept a close eye on traffic, spinning his eyes left and right, particularly watching a man in black leathers wearing a black helmet on a shiny new gunmetal-grey Moto Guzzi motorbike, which pulled in alongside us.

As he jumped off, Flower eyed the man carefully. She growled, from deep in the back of her throat, and I sensed her fear.

"Wait, is that him again, the assassin?"

Gurung didn't answer. I leaned against the door a moment, for support. *Careful now.* Settting my jaw I climbed out, cautiously glancing at the man, then I snuck Flower out and silently put a lead on her. Gurung and I looked at each other awkwardly, my eyebrows knitted in confusion. His eyes shone.

"Farewell, Brian. Be safe, healthy, and happy, my friend," he said, as he leaned out through the open driver's window and hugged me, for the very first time.

I had tears in my eyes as I hugged him back, hard. As we parted, Gurung's old eyes looked faded but still sharp.

"And beware of The Seven. They reek of evil."

I nodded grimly. "What did Ronaldo mean? About a miracle?"

"Whatever you think he means."

Gurung gave his usual enigmatic look, and I smiled, shaking my head.

I saw Flower's head cocked to one side, her face wearing that look of entrancement. I heard Gurung release a long breath that seemed full of apprehension. As I glanced over my shoulder, the man on the motorcycle had disappeared.

* * *

Check-in took quite some time, the busy airport packed with tourists. Fortunately, clearing security took no time at all, as the Italian guards were busy watching a football game.

I left Flower at the check-in counter, to be loaded with the other passengers' pets into the plane, then headed toward my gate. At the desk, I watched the other travelers, most of them stylish Italians, for any sign of surveillance, but didn't notice anyone. Which didn't mean the man wasn't still following me.

With Flower safely in the hold, and the plane full, we took off on-time for short flight to Paris.

I settled in, a magazine on my lap, and silently mulled over everything that had happened.

From meeting enigmatic Gurung, a weird fortune-teller, a King, a U.S. President, government heads, a mysterious attorney for a client connected to my family, then a charismatic Vatican miracle hunter; it was an intoxicating cocktail.

It was all I could do to control my thoughts from exploding into madness. My brain on fire, I fell asleep.

The stop-over at Charles de Gaulle, a sprawling, scruffy airport I never liked, was a total nightmare. As I sat in my seat, buckled up and ready to depart for Copenhagen, a swarthy flight attendant spoke quietly to me, explaining that somehow a man had broken into the hold and seemed to be searching for a particular animal…and somehow Flower had escaped.

*Oh shit! Flower!*

The inside of my body filled with blinding panic. I knew exactly who that man was.

The flight attendant then told me the worst possible news. "The airport is so massive and surrounded by woods," she explained, "that when this happens, they rarely ever find the escaped animals."

I gasped in horror. *Flower! Dear God, no!* Tensing to scream, I leapt from my seat, the attendant shouting at me to stop. The other attendants tried to cut me off, but I shoved past like an insane man, bolted down the narrow metal steps, reached the bottom and whirled around in a panic, eyes scanning everywhere for Flower.

"Flower! Where are you, girl?" I raced to a heap of bags on a baggage trailer, the handler looking at me crazily, then sprinted to a small hut, yanked the lock ceaselessly, then searched all over the runways for what seemed like an eternity.

*"Flower!"* I shrieked. *Madness. This is madness!* I ran and ran. My lungs were burning. There was no sign of my precious dog, and I felt sick.

I glanced up to see the pilots in the cockpit staring at me. I kept running, weaving in and out of planes. Eventually, the flight attendant found me and insisted that I go back to my seat. I told her a flat no, and she threatened me with the police, so with a heavy heart, I returned on board.

Staggering back down the aisle, I reached my seat. I slumped into it, turning my face to the window. And there, staring back at me, was Flower, sitting in the seat next to mine!

I couldn't believe it! "Flower!" Ecstatically I hugged her tight, many of the other passengers applauding enthusiastically, as tear after tear rolled down my cheek.

Soon the flight attendant arrived, and Flower was removed from my bear-hugs, and taken back down into the hold. As the engines roared for take-off, my suspicions were aroused. This was the work of The Seven; they sent this man. He tried to kidnap Flower to use her against me, or to separate her from me. But why? It was clear that attorney Swanson was hell-bent on destroying everything I held dear and bring me to my knees.

As we got underway, I asked for some bread, cheese, and a glass of wine, but didn't touch it as I had that strange feeling again. A tightness in my gut.

*I am being watched.*

Hesitantly I sat forward. Looking up and down the aisle, I pondered. I stood, stretched, looked around at the passengers who all seemed harmless enough, then after asking about Flower, I got myself comfortable and tried to doze off, that nagging feeling still there.

That nagging worry continued through the rest of the flight. Arriving in Copenhagen, I took a taxi straight to the apartment in Nyhavn. It was an incredible place, overlooking the old harbour and sailing ships, 170 square metres in the best location in the city. Even better, two floors beneath me, was the best ice-cream shop in Copenhagen, baking warm waffles every day.

I knocked on the door. No one answered. *That's odd.* I pushed the door, and it slowly swung open. "Hello?" I called out, but the realtor didn't answer. It felt great to be back, feeling I had at least one home left. As I crept down the long and narrow hallway, I looked back, hearing breathing. The next second, someone came from behind me and slammed my head violently against the wall.

* * *

# Nineteen

I opened my eyes. Instantly I closed them again to block out the pain. Explosive images raced furiously around in my head. My legs buckled, as my body lurched forward.

My assailant was propelling me powerfully towards the dining-room. Dizzily I turned to face my attacker—he was wearing a balaclava robbery hood concealing his face, immediately recognizable by his eyes, it was *him,* the assassin who tried to kill me—same medium height, slim athletic body, elegant and expensively-dressed in a dark suit, eyes burning with intensity.

He twisted me to my left. In a split second, I saw the face of my realtor, tied up in the corner, duct tape covering his mouth. His eyes were wide open and filled with terror.

My assailant tossed me easily to the floor. I landed painfully, the throbbing in my skull enveloping my senses. When I turned to him, he held a stun-gun, the electric flame flickering back and forth.

*Well, shit! I am dealing with a totally insane man!* In an instant, I jumped back, getting just out of reach of the stun-gun. As soon as my heels hit the ground, I wheeled and smashed the side of the man's face with a swift left hook, as hard and brutally as I could.

He barely flinched. *Holy fuck*. I knew I was in grave danger.

The man stood there for a second, just staring at me, his intense eyes gleaming like a predator ready to pounce.

His hesitation gave me the millisecond I needed. I tore past him and ran down the hall towards the front door. *Oh God!* I stupidly locked the door behind me when I entered!

Luckily, the keys were still in the door. With my heart pounding, I gaped back over my shoulder as I fumbled with the keys trying to open the door. The man aimed the stun-gun at me as he hustled down the hallway, swiftly approaching.

"*What the hell are you doing, man? Shit!*" Grimacing, I bent over, my hands still fumbling with the key in the lock. The masked man leapt at me, with a guttural cry of death. I leaned against the door and gave him the hardest karate sidekick I could muster with my heavy Timberland winter boots, slamming him right in the chest, sending him staggering backwards and the stun-gun flying.

*This is madness!* "Who the hell *are* you?" I screamed. I tore open the door and stumbled out into the street, crouched and whirled in case there was another assailant outside, but only saw the boulevard crowded with local citizens enjoying the day.

Blood running down my face, I tore into a restaurant, causing a commotion with all the diners, and called my friend who was a cop. I drew my first breath for what seemed like forever and slumped into a chair; panic, fear, and shock consuming me.

All around me the diners sat watching, their eyes closing in from every side. I nodded, tried to speak, then dropped my head to my chest, helpless. Within minutes, a SWAT team arrived. Rousing me, we bolted upstairs to my apartment, kicked down the door. There was no sign of the attacker.

The SWAT officers left. Dismayed, I stared at each empty room. Later at the police station, I sat like a bewildered child. While giving my testimony, the Sergeant told me that based on what they had found at the scene, had I not been able to defend myself, most likely, I would not have gotten out alive.

The realtor had been found with his throat slit. No fingerprints in the apartment. No clues.

My eyebrows raised as the Sergeant told me this. Feeling like a fool, I hobbled pathetically out of the station. My mind analyzed and discarded the facts as quickly as they came to me. *Dear God, what is happening?* I'd almost lost my life, my realtor had been murdered, all my belongings from the apartment were gone, and I'd lost my last chance to save my home.

Two weeks later, the apartment went into foreclosure.

As I prepared to leave it for the last time, I stared around at the walls, my thoughts spiralling into one another in confused contortions. I knew that sooner or later the killer would come after me again. Sooner or later he would get me. I couldn't continue to be so lucky to barely escape.

What I didn't know was how quickly we'd meet again.

* * *

I needed time to think. I needed answers. I needed to disappear.

In the middle of the night, after leaving the police station and picking up Flower from my Mom's, I ordered a taxi. Hanging up the phone, I gazed out my mother's window, and to my surprise, there a taxicab sat, motor chugging at the curb. Without hesitating Flower and I raced downstairs and jumped into the car.

The driver wasn't friendly or talkative, and I told him to head north, then began browsing on my phone. At the next stoplight, my phone pinged with a text message. *'It's your driver. I'm outside waiting for you.'* Instantly, my eyes darted to the driver who stared back from the rear-view mirror, his piercing eyes narrowing at me.

Flower snarled. Immediately, cold fear raced through my veins. Filled with a terrible sense of dread, I recognised those eyes—the same man who'd attacked me in the apartment!

The traffic light turned green, and the man accelerated fast. I knew I only had a split second to get out alive. As we exchanged glances from the mirror, I suddenly rose from my seat and with all my strength, smashed his face off the steering wheel, making him veer to the left sharply. He put his hand around my throat, strangling me. I lowered my head, gripped the seatbelt tight, and held onto Flower just as the car crashed into a parked van, smashing the windshield.

Everything was pandemonium. I kicked the door open, and Flower and I jumped out, then scrambled along the street with a furtive glance behind, and then turned another corner until I was sure he hadn't followed us. This was my neighbourhood, and I knew everywhere like the back of my hand.

We crept down the center of a dark alley, peeking our heads out into the street. Satisfied, I backed away, hailed a cab and had the driver drop me at a remote cabin in the middle of the woods, an hour outside of Copenhagen. The cabin was miles off the beaten path, across a primitive wooden bridge, just a large kitchen with a cast-iron stove and two small rooms. It was not in my name, and I was confident that the assailant would not find me here.

When I arrived, the thermometer on the outside wall read -20 degree Celsius. *Great,* I realized, *one of the coldest winters in memory, and I'm hiding out here!* The cabin had no telephone or TV service. It had snowed heavily the night before, and the building was surrounded by one metre of thick heavy snow. Instantly I build a fire in the old wood-burning fireplace. Flower loved it, although she'd also sleep outside sometimes, burying herself deep in the snow covering her nose with the bushy tail. Crazy damn dog.

For me, it was too bloody cold and pitch dark most of the time to sleep in these cold Nordic conditions, but somehow, I felt we were safe; it gave me time to think and re-evaluate my life, its purpose and the mistakes I'd made. And my quest.

I was thankful for the solitude and the peace. I wasn't afraid to die, and I wasn't scared to live, I was just lost as to what my role and purpose were.

In the bitter cold I had a hard time keeping my thoughts together. In spite of understanding I was on a quest, I didn't understand what my creator wanted from me. *If I'm going to follow your true purpose,* I pleaded, raising my eyes to the heavens, *perhaps you could clue me in, God.*

There was no reply. Instead, images of the assassin with his fists tightening around my throat replayed, over and over. At night, I would stand outside, knee-deep in the snow with Flower sitting by my side, both of us looking at the starry sky. Sometimes I would kneel to pray to the sound of the tall birch trees swaying in the cold and howling wind.

My eyes scanned the snow-covered countryside, filled with an impulse to pack everything up and run. I prayed for answers, for guidance, and a second chance, promising to do better and be less selfish. I knew deep inside that I could not escape my fate and would have to face my worst fears.

But what I didn't know was that my trials were only beginning, and salvation would be far off.

After what seemed like an eternity of praying and listening one day, without finding answers, I packed my bags, and we walked out of the forest towards the nearest town, two miles away. From there we got in a cab and went straight to Copenhagen Airport.

* * *

# TWENTY

Drained and distressed, I flew back to Santa Barbara in a last attempt to save my home.

On the plane, I rubbed my aching head, trying to sort out my impressions. *Why is everyone so intent upon seeking me, hounding me, trying to murder me?* The Seven seemed to know with certainty my every step; how I couldn't even begin to surmise. *Why, God, why?* The aftershock the police warned me of never came. I lay back in my seat and thanked God that my years of boxing and fighting had prepared me for a battle, yet I never imagined I would be in this kind of a battle.

A fight to the death or not, I was ready for it. I was now absolutely convinced The Seven were behind everything—how else could so many malicious events happen right after I turned down their offer?

By the time I arrived at the sprawling Los Angeles airport, it was early in the morning, and I looked and felt like crap, uncomfortable in the same sweat-stained suit and shirt I'd worn for days.

Anxiously, I collected Flower, sighing with relief that she was safe.

I took her outside the terminal for a walk, went to a store, and bought a cheap cell phone as I'd given my other phone to Gurung in case they were tracking me. I grabbed some breakfast, fed Flower some steak, and then flopped on an airport seat for a short nap until our connecting flight to Santa Barbara airport.

I had no idea what to expect when I got there.

* * *

The trip was uneventful. After landing and disembarking at lovely little Santa Barbara airport with its Hispanic red-roof tiles and swaying palm trees, I raced to collect Flower.

She wasn't too impressed with me after all these flights and wailed right in my face as I hugged her.

Short on cash, but exhausted, I decided to take a cab home. I used my new cell phone and called a cab company, and we waited outside in the blazing sun.

Twenty minutes later, after driving through the city, we arrived outside my home, Hacienda-style, in the foothills, right behind the old mission church and the beautiful, blooming rose garden, with a view over the city and the ocean.

I loved this house. *God, how I wish my mother could see this! Lord, I hope I can save it.*

Hopping out of the car, I instantly saw a foreclosure sign posted in the front yard, and my heart sank.

I stood before the sign, Flower bellowing her disapproval, my mind screaming. *The Seven. Of course! What next?* I nodded dully, feeling a dreadful mix of shame, shock, and disappointment all at the same time, my eyes welling up with tears.

Fumbling in my pocket for my keys, I dropped them, picked them up, and then ambled disgustedly to the front door. Stabbing the key in the door, to my horror, I discovered the locks had been changed.

*Are you kidding me? I can't get into my own home. Now what?*

In a rage, I stalked past Flower, who picked up on my anger and took a piss at the foreclosure sign as I marched around the back.

Looking around furtively, I smashed a window with my elbow and climbed inside my own house. Dusting myself off, I looked around sadly, knowing it was time to say goodbye to the home I'd worked so hard for.

When I'd bought it, this home was a small shack. While it was being renovated, I'd slept on the floor on a mattress among the sawdust, my clothes in plastic bags, dusting myself down each day to head to work.

Nothing had come easy for me. I'd accomplished things most people wouldn't do in order to seek a better life for myself.

As we walked the perimeter, the neighborhood dogs howling and baying at Flower, my throat tightened, and I shed a few tears. A minute later, I cleared my mind of mourning. That's when matters got even worse.

Opening my phone to check emails, I discovered more terrible news.

ALL OF YOUR ASSETS WITH THE BANK HAVE BEEN FROZEN, read the first message.

I sank my fingers into my hair. Instantly I felt crushed. I read on, my shock growing, a gnawing in my churning stomach growling as I read …AND YOUR CREDIT CARDS ARE ALL DULY CANCELLED.

By now my confusion was rapidly turning to anger. *These motherfuckers.* My eyes stung. Tears came rushing out as I read the bottom of the email to see all the money I had in the world after all my hard work.

The balance was $10,000.

That was it. Just $10,000 to show for all my blood, sweat and tears over many long, punishing years.

"Bastards!" I spat, then stomped over to the sink and filled a kettle, slumping over it.

I closed my eyes, helpless to pull away from my anger. *Calm down, calm yourself,* my brain commanded. I ignored it. I felt grim, and by 9 am, I had called my mortgage-lender to arrange a meeting, which he was extremely reluctant to have, for some reason.

*The long reach of The Seven,* I thought. Was it them behind my bank cancelling my credit card and freezing my assets?

Checking my wallet, I noticed I was low on cash. My eyes bulged, then I closed them to keep from drowning in my negative thoughts. Short on funds or not, I took a taxi downtown. Outside a bank, I had the driver pull over, using an ATM to draw out as much money as I could, in case the banks took over. Then we drove to the meeting.

*Don't do anything stupid,* I told myself. Mr. Dilbert, my mortgage broker, was a friendly man—at least he used to be. Now, he couldn't get me out of his office fast enough.

"Listen," I pleaded, "all my money is tied up. My banks aren't allowing me to liquidate any assets to allow me to pay off my mortgage."

Dilbert seemed pre-occupied and anxious. "I have no other option but to put your house into foreclosure," he said. He stood, motioned to the door, meeting over.

I was devastated, hoping he would be a little flexible.

"I have assets," I continued, trying to remain calm, "just not ones I can realise right now."

Dilbert, however, didn't want to listen to that. Again, he showed me the door. I had lost my house once and for all.

Outside, I stood alone in the street, trash swirling in the Southern California wind around me, feeling like my world had collapsed, wondering what I should do.

I glanced over at Dilbert's office. He was on the phone, typing something into a computer, looking furtive. Noticing me, he strolled over and closed the blinds.

The burning taste of sweat dripped down my throat. *What the hell? Was he speaking to The Seven?*

Gripping my cell phone, I scrolled down to see who I thought might help me in my distress. Names flashed through, many of them business connections, others overseas, most of no help whatsoever.

I called some friends in LA, but they'd experienced some bad luck in the stock market and couldn't help, knee-deep in their own problems.

Grumbling, I shoved my phone in my pocket. *Great! What else can I do?*

My thoughts flashed back to Ronaldo, the Vatican miracle hunter, mentioning that the Curandera was somewhere in Chimayo, New Mexico.

Having nothing to lose, and intrigued about what Ronaldo said about the Curandera, I figured why not?

I checked my wallet again, flipping through what little cash I had. Not much, I quickly realized. I sighed.

I couldn't afford to fly, so I anxiously called another cab. Fifteen minutes passed. *Come on, come on!* Finally, a taxi arrived, dust flying, exhaust fumes sputtering, and Flower and I chugged back to Santa Barbara airport along with my three suitcases, the last of my worldly possessions.

My plan? Rent a car to drive to New Mexico. Simple.

It was boiling hot and growing dark now, as I lugged the heavy cases in a wonky trolley, sweating hard, breathing heavy.

Not one of the car rental agencies would rent me a car.

"You don't have any credit cards," said one after another.

"How about a debit card?" I asked. Still, their replies were the same.

"Can't help you."

"Why not? I have cash and a debit card?!"

"Policy," they echoed.

Storming out of the last rental office, I let my fear and anger jell. I'd never heard the word *No* so many times in my life! I sat on the sidewalk on Fowler Road, steaming mad and sweating in the same suit I had worn for weeks. Flower panted to keep cool, eyeballing thousands of expensive cars speeding past us.

I only needed one car and cursed my luck.

Filled with frustration, I gazed up into the clear, midnight blue sky and begged, "God, I need some help, *please!* I can't do all this on my own!"

Overhead, the skies rumbled. I groaned, feeling Flower groan at my side. Suddenly her head lifted, eyes narrowed and squinting off. I followed her gaze, looking to my left to see one small car rental agency I hadn't noticed before. With a tremendous sigh, I strolled over, desperate to convince the clerk to accept my debit card, even for the tiniest, shittiest car that would accommodate me, my dog, and three suitcases.

*Ding!* rang a bell, as the door swept open. Across the room, a man sat at a computer, looking bored. Hearing a growl, he peered down at Flower, who peered back. The man approached, bent down, stroked her, letting her lick his gloved hand.

I quickly explained my predicament.

The man listened, squinting at me. He turned and spoke directly to Flower. "Hey, girl. Why did the other agencies not rent your owner a car?"

I shook my head. *That's weird,* I thought. I explained why I needed to get to New Mexico to find a friend. Again, the man listened patiently, squinting his eyes, nodding with sympathy—then turned to Flower, ignoring me.

"I might have just the perfect solution," he told her. Flower wagged her curly tail, then started howling the way only Alaskan Malamutes do.

The man's gloved fingers typed a few keystrokes into his computer. *Please, God,* I thought. *Please help me.* The man sighed, massaged his head, then typed in a few more keystrokes and turned to Flower. "I've got a car that needs delivery to Miami. Would your owner be prepared to drive it, do his business in New Mexico, then deliver it there?"

I blurted out, "Of course I would!"

The man smiled. His smile wasn't as big as mine when I spied the car that needed to be delivered.

He walked me out to a beautiful, shiny, and brand new, top-of-the-range black Cadillac SUV, with chrome gleaming, black leather seats, and tons of space for me, Flower and my cases. He also gave us a GPS for the road, free of charge.

For the longest moment, I stared at the car, teary-eyed. *A miracle!* And this miracle had given me an olive branch—from out of his pocket the man produced a number to call in the event of an accident, returning to the office for a warm blanket for Flower.

*Angels do exist,* I thought. *Unbelievable.*

I laughed at myself, thinking I wouldn't be surprised if I came back to find another clerk at the front desk five minutes from now, one who's never heard of the one who just saved us, as if our rental-car angel never worked there.

I rubbed away tears, shook the man's hand until it nearly broke. Soon I was on my way out the door.

Sixty seconds later, I plunged the key into the ignition and started the car. The engine purred. As it roared I nearly jumped a foot out of my seat. *Thank God something's going right!* Relief swept over me. My crisis had been averted. Good things were beginning to happen.

I thought of the journey ahead. Nine hundred & sixty-three long miles, just over 14 hours of driving, along the famous 1-40E road toward Chimayo. A long trip, and I wondered what lay in store for me.

As I drove off, I noticed the door to the rental agency shut with a curious *ding!* With a laugh, I imagined a strange scenario: a young Hispanic rental agent, tied up with an extension cord in the back room, mouth plastered-over with duct tape, blood draining from his bruised face as he tried to free himself, his inaudible screams muffled.

*Yeah, right,* I chuckled. Then the gloved agent went over, locked the door, and turned out the light.

* * *

# TWENTY-ONE

I drove. And drove. Mile after mile raced under my wheels. I drove until whenever the gas tank was pegged at EMPTY, or Flower needed to stop, or I became bleary-eyed and exhausted from staring at the zooming asphalt.

Eventually, my stomach gnawed at me. Bleary eyes I could handle; hunger pangs I could not. We stopped at a little diner a hundred miles outside Flagstaff for food, letting Flower relieve herself.

I decided to call my Mom. *She must be worried sick about me.* I dialed, waiting patiently. The phone rang and rang. Eventually, she picked up, and I told her what happened, leaving out all the gory violence, then explaining that I was heading to New Mexico.

Like the amazing Mom she was, she immediately asked me if she could send me some money. *Oh, Mom!* She never stopped reminding me that when I'd made my money, I had called to tell her I was going to pay off all her loans on her home so she could retire.

No big thing—to me, anyway. One day, I just called her bank and asked how much she owed on her home. The banker sounded shocked. I guessed it wasn't every day a small-town banker received a call from someone's son in America. The next day, all her loans were paid off.

I had waited a long time to be able to do that for my Mom, who so deserved it.

"I want to tell you something, but you might think I'm crazy," she suddenly whispered.

*I can't believe this,* I thought. *What next?* "Well Mom," I sighed, "you worked in a psychiatric ward for 32 years and saw a ghost with a coned-shaped hat in your bedroom. Why would I think you're crazy?" I laughed, as if I could already hear her answer.

"The cone-shaped lady gave me a warning of bad tidings, Brian," she said.

"And look how that turned out, Mom."

"Just this morning, I rode my bike to the Brugsen supermarket, like always. Suddenly, out of nowhere, a crow swooped down and gently landed...*on my head!* I was shocked, people turning their heads at me on my bike with a crow sitting on my head! The weird thing is, the crow didn't hurt me; it just sat there. Then as suddenly as it appeared, it flew away. I immediately thought it was one of my ancestors warning me. Maybe my Dad or his Mom, perhaps? But about what?"

"I don't know, Mom, but crows are considered omens of evil."

From the other end of the line there was a long silence. "Be careful and call me when you get there," my mother said and hung up.

Mind racing, I sat in the corner of the diner, leaning forward, watching the road outside. After a huge cheeseburger and French fries, and a chunky T-bone steak for Flower, paying with what little cash I still had, we finished and exited.

*So much for Mom calming me down,* I thought. The call with my Mom pounded in my brain. I didn't believe in coincidences, and neither did she.

Still, I was glad she'd told me about the crow, though the omen it spoke of made me feel woozy. I stretched my muscles and Flower hopped happily into the car and sat with eyes beaming, looking out the windshield as we drove off.

We passed road-signs that read Mojave National Preserve, then eventually, Williams, Flagstaff, Coconino National Forest, Winslow, Hopi Reserve, Holbrook then a few tiring hours later, a cool, bright road sign that read, Welcome to New Mexico. Land of Enchantment.

Further on, another sign read Albuquerque, and I got excited, knowing I was close.

Just before we reached Albuquerque, I turned off at a road sign to Chimayo, now only 90 miles. *A 90-minute drive.* My heart shuddered.

I was excited but extremely tired. I yawned, blinked my eyes over and over, took a swig of water and kept driving, foot pressed hard on the accelerator, wind whipping over the Cadillac hood, the engine growling.

Finally, I smiled at a sign that read Chimayo. 10 miles.

*Chimayo! We're getting close to where the Curandera lived and worked,* I realized, with a rush of adrenaline. Only 10 miles away. I hoped I'd find her.

For the next few minutes I watched the road whip under our wheels. Ten miles later I stopped the car, the weather starting to turn bad, light snow falling, and I googled *Chimayo.*

"The Lourdes of America," it read, "A Roman Catholic church in Chimayó, New Mexico, United States. This shrine, a National Historic Landmark, is famous for the story of its founding and as a contemporary pilgrimage site. It receives almost 300,000 visitors per year and has been called 'the most important Catholic pilgrimage Centre in the United States.'"

I shut down the phone. *No turning back now.* Impressed and apprehensive, I drove east and headed into Chimayo.

We circled through town, following the GPS. The old church looked magnificent, with a walled courtyard, a bell-tower on each side, pointed caps on the towers, a metal pitched roof and elegant doors. I understood its lure immediately and could imagine the Curandera healing people within its stunning, sacred grounds.

*I need to find the priest who met her,* I thought. *Bishop Cruzeria.* And as exhausted as I was, I needed to search now.

But now, the snow was blowing heavy. The windshield wipers struggled to clear the glass, making it nearly impossible to see. The wheels of other vehicles kicked up snow. Soon the car was sliding, skidding and fishtailing crazily.

*Get a grip, Brian!* I slowed down, as it was just too dangerous to continue. Gripping the wheel tight to regain control, I scanned desperately for a place to park.

Spotting one through the piling snow, I slid carefully into a parking spot and looked around. There were very few people. *Where is everybody?* I cut the engine, apprehensively climbed out, my breath immediately steaming, and asked if anyone knew the Bishop. Every one of them gave me funny looks, then hurried on.

Something about the unease I felt in their eyes alerted me. I didn't blame them for hurrying off; it was blowing snow like crazy. Yet I whipped my head around, staring into the snowstorm, my eyes stinging with pain. *Did I come all the way here, for this?* Massaging my aching chest, I told Flower to stay in the car, hearing the strain in my voice. Then I started walking off, into darkness.

To the right, two hundred yards in the distance, I spied a squat building. I squinted into the snow, trying to see more clearly. I walked towards the obscure square shape, each step treacherous, and my shoes crunching on the ice.

Suddenly I heard racing footsteps. A spit of light exploded in my face, blinding me. Hot, searing pain exploded in my skull. I squeezed my eyes shut until I could see no more, then raised my hands over my head.

* * *

# TWENTY-TWO

My vision blurred, I put an arm over my eyes. Through the mists of pain, I heard a man's voice.

"Who are you? Answer me!"

I shielded my eyes, blinking through the pain. "I'm Brian!" I hollered. "Who are you?"

"No one."

*Great, more mysteries!* I swayed on my feet, the light blinding me.

"Can you turn that flashlight off?"

"Why are you here?"

"To see Bishop Cruzeria! I came a long way."

"Why?"

"To ask for his help. Who are you?"

"Help for what?"

"I need to find someone."

"Who?"

"Can you stop with the damn flashlight?!"

*Click!* The light died. As my eyes adjusted to the darkness, I noticed a small, skinny-legged man with kind eyes, a white dog collar fastened around his throat, and thinning grey hair. In his trembling hand, he held a Maglite.

Squinting, I craned my head to get a better look at the man who'd shoved a light in my face. At once I recognized him. "Bishop Cruzeria?"

He examined me very closely, eyes narrowed.

"Who is it you seek?"

"The Curandera."

"Who's that?"

*More games! When will all this insanity stop?* "I think you know, Bishop. Father Del Duca said you'd know where she is. Wait…"

I rummaged through my pockets, producing the photograph Ronaldo gave me from my wallet and showed it to him. He nodded but didn't look convinced.

"Anyone could have that photograph."

"They could. But with Ronaldo's signature on the back?"

He snatched the photo, flipped it over to see the scribble. He kept his eyes steady, his gaze calm. *Dammit, hurry up, old man, I'm freezing out here!* Finally, he smiled.

"We have to be extra vigilant. Many seek her, some for evil reasons."

"Many..." I replied, my eyes stinging. "You mean...The Seven?"

The Bishop stared at me, nodded slowly, and held out his hand. For a moment, I stood paralyzed with shock.

"Bishop Cruzeria, Brian. Apologies for the interrogation."

We shook hands, and he gestured for me to follow.

Snow blew heavily, almost knocking me down. The Bishop didn't seem to mind as we trudged through it in silence, finally reaching his little house; a tiny bungalow on a beautiful street, the rooftops, cars, trees, bushes, and plants all covered in a thick blanket of snow.

He opened the door, gesturing for me to follow. My shock eased. I entered his home, papers, and cartons piled high everywhere.

The Bishop disappeared into a room. I could hear his hushed voice on the phone. Relief flooded through me. *Finally, somebody who can help.*

After a minute, he reappeared, a smile on his face. "Ronaldo says hello," he explained.

I sighed, the Bishop shrugged, and we shook hands. I sat, dusting the snow off my neck. So far, my first minutes in Chimayo had been a bit frightening. We shared some bread and cheese, the conversation turning to the Curandera, and a warning that a stylish man had recently been asking about her.

*A stylish man?* A silent scream shrieked in my ears. It was him again. The man who tried to kill me. But how did he know I was here?

Eventually, Ronaldo mentioned the last time he saw the Curandera was in the town of Angel Fire. Instantly I leapt to my feet, ready to race off.

The Bishop held up a hand. "The weather is treacherous, Brian," he said calmly. "Why don't you stay the night here?"

"Thanks," I replied, "but a witch in a town called Angel Fire? Sounds just like the place I wanna be." I smiled ironically.

The Bishop smiled, though I could see he didn't buy my same conviction about meeting witches. However, I was desperate to meet the Curandera, so there was no discussion. No debate. With a flask of hot tea as a gift, and warnings about the road conditions, I headed off into the night, snow stinging my eyes, breathing heavily, the first rays of moonlight stabbing down through the clouds. If a trap was being set, I was walking right into it. There would be no rest for the weary, and there would be no escape.

* * *

# Twenty-Three

An hour's passed. Bishop Cruzeria is preparing his bed when he hears the sound of car tires crunching outside. His first thought is that Brian has gotten lost and returned for further instructions.

He sighs, grabs his flashlight, stepping outside. The headlights from the car suddenly flash up, blinding him. He holds up his hand to shield his eyes from the light.

"Brian?" he calls out. "Is that you?"

He listens for a reply. There is none. The Bishop squints his eyes, fixing them on the vehicle. Suddenly the hum of a car window rolling down can be heard.

"Brian?"

No reply. For the briefest moment, the Bishop almost bursts out laughing. He clicks on his flashlight, aiming it at the vehicle, eyes poised to acknowledge his new friend.

Suddenly he is hit by the massive force of a bullet striking him in the chest. There is no muzzle sound; searchers tomorrow will agree no cartridge could be found. The Bishop drops to the ground, in complete shock. His back pressed against the ice. Suddenly he begins convulsing. In thirty-nine seconds, he will pass away from a massive heart attack.

* * *

# Twenty-Four

Chimayo to Angel Fire was 74 miles away. I knew it was a crazy decision on such a bad night, but I had come so far and was determined to see this Curandera, this witch, now. Tonight.

I drove cautiously, following the road-signs for Angel Fire, climbing higher and higher. There was very little traffic, although one car seemed to be following me. I tried not to be paranoid, and kept my eyes on the road.

*Follow your instincts. No one's trying to kill you—at least not here. And if they are, you're not helpless.* Thirty minutes later, the snow eased a little though the icy wind continued to howl. I passed ice-covered road signs with fantastic Native American Indian names—names like Owingeh and Ohkay, then Velarde, Embudo, Dixon, the mountain Picurus Peak, then Ranchos De Taos.

A mile further, the weather turned treacherous again. I suddenly found myself in thick snow, the tires slipping, wipers struggling to keep flakes and slush off the windshield.

I opened my eyes wider, straining to see. Tires scraped up the icy road. I gripped the wheel tighter, my breath steaming through parted lips, my face chalk-white in the windshield's reflection, staying calm as possible, under control.

Then it happened.

Out of nowhere, an animal—the shape of a magnificent stag deer—skittered across my headlights. *Dear God!* In a panic, I swerved hard to avoid it, losing control of the Cadillac.

Headlight beams stabbed into the darkness. Snow swirled everywhere. I was blinded, the car fishtailing, the wheel lurching wildly out of my control. I arched backwards, expecting an impact, Flower howling, my mind screaming. I collided with a road sign, the car rolling violently, then it plunged over the side into a steep ravine and the darkness below.

I braced myself, the auto interior rising and falling. The last thing I heard was Flower moaning, then an unceasing howl of icy wind. The freezing wind swallowed me. I blacked out.

* * *

# TWENTY-FIVE

A heavily stained yellow leather workboot crunches through the snow. Kicks a fat, badly worn tire. A curse growls, in a strange, guttural accent. A man's cracked and lined hand yanks at the twisted driver's door, which won't budge.

The snow is heavy, falling on a beat-up old red vehicle by the roadside; a '62 Chevy pick-up truck. It looks ready for the scrap heap—paint flaked, bodywork bent and rusted cracked windows, lights damaged. Inside, it is filled with garbage.

The curse growls again. The man's hand yanks even harder at the door, pulling, tugging, until at last it creaks open slightly.

The man, a skeletal, Native American Indian with deeply etched brown skin, spits on the ground and looks around. Behind him rises Taos Pueblo; the only living Native American community designated both a World Heritage Site by UNESCO and a National Historic Landmark.

The man doesn't care about that. He pulls and heaves and wrenches at the reluctant door, and it creaks open, an inch at a time. At last it yawns wide, and he hurls his skinny body inside, jumping into the driver's seat, trying the ignition.

Nothing. Just clicking. The battery dead.

The man curses then climbs out with difficulty. As the drifting snow pours down harder, he lays both brown hands on the hood of the car, his lips moving in disgust.

Feverishly he works on the engine. Minutes later, he nods happily, climbs back into the Chevy, tries the ignition, and the car coughs a little.

The Indian sighs, tries again, and the vehicle explodes into life, the engine spluttering loud from a ruined exhaust.

The Indian smiles, showing just a few yellow stained teeth and reverses the truck from in front of a long row of beautiful, low, brown adobe buildings, snow-capped mountains in the distance, scrubland for miles and miles.

"Firewood," he mutters. His breath steams in the cold night air. He shoves the truck in first gear and then speeds away.

* * *

THE NEW YORK TIMES
JULY 13, 2019

FACIAL RECOGNITION TECH IS GROWING STRONGER, THANKS TO YOUR FACE.

SAN FRANCISCO — Dozens of databases of people's faces are being compiled without their knowledge by companies and researchers, with many of the images then being shared around the world, in what has become a vast ecosystem fueling the spread of facial recognition technology.

The databases are pulled together with images from social networks, photo websites, dating services like OkCupid and cameras placed in restaurants and on college quads. While there is no precise count of the data sets, privacy activists have pinpointed repositories that were built by Microsoft, Stanford University and others, with one holding over 10 million images while another had more than two million. Kim Zetter, a cybersecurity journalist in San Francisco who has written for Wired and The Intercept, was one of the people who unknowingly became part of the Microsoft data set.

"We're all just fodder for the development of these surveillance systems," she said, "The idea that this would be shared with foreign governments and military is just egregious."

Matt Zeiler, founder, and chief executive of Clarifai, the A.I. start-up, said his company had built a face database with images from OkCupid, a dating site. He said Clarifai had access to OkCupid's photos because some of the dating site's founders invested in his company…

NEW YORK TIMES
AUG. 1, 2019

CHILDREN AS YOUNG AS 11 ADDED TO N.Y.P.D. FACIAL RECOGNITION DATABASE

With little oversight, the police have been using powerful surveillance technology on photos of children and teenagers.

Still, facial recognition has not been widely tested on children. Most algorithms are taught to 'think' based on adult faces, and there is growing evidence that they do not work as well on children.

The National Institute of Standards and Technology, which is part of the Commerce Department and evaluates facial recognition algorithms for accuracy, recently found the vast majority of more than 100 facial recognition algorithms had a higher rate of mistaken matches among children. The error rate was most pronounced in young children but was also seen in those aged 10 to 16.

"I would use extreme caution in using those algorithms," said Karl Ricanek Jr., a computer science professor and co-founder of the Face Aging Group at the University of North Carolina-Wilmington.

Recent studies indicate that people of colour, as well as children and women, have a greater risk of misidentification than their counterparts, said Joy Buolamwini, the founder of the Algorithmic Justice League and graduate researcher at the M.I.T. Media Lab, who has examined how human biases are built into artificial intelligence.

"If the facial recognition algorithm has a negative bias toward a black population, that will get magnified more toward children," Dr. Ricanek said, adding that in terms of diminished accuracy, "you're now putting yourself in unknown territory."

# Path / Day Four

## Searching for a Balance – A Spiritual Path

*The battle-line between good and evil*
*runs through the heart of every man.*

— *ALEKSANDR SOLZHENITSYN*

# Twenty-Six

Inside my mind, a violent eruption shrieked, clashing with the incessant screeching of metal. A shattering crash slammed through my brain. Rushing cold darkness enveloped me, pierced by the screams of pain. From out of the roaring chaos, a man spoke something in a strange accented voice, which sounded like Native American Indian. Spiralling into madness, I struggled to understand these incoherent words invading my brain.

"Dead?" whispered a woman's soft voice, also accented, but sounding Hispanic.

*Dead?* A wave of panic ripped through me. *Who are they talking about?* Occasional sounds of twisting metal clashed with the shrieking in my head. I was in a daze, having that dream again, the sun beating down on me in a desert, walking, wandering, holding a white pebble in my hand with strange carvings, searching for something, or someone, and seeing the blurry outline of a woman's figure again.

Only this time, there was more.

I blinked. In a swirl of wind and sand, the woman approached, her dark eyes throwing shafts of light. She stooped, wrote in the sand a capital D with her finger, and then looked me right in the eye.

A scream filled my mind. I panicked and ran. As I turned back to see if she was giving chase, the desert sands beneath me split open, and I was falling, into an abyss of total darkness. I clawed the air, reaching out for anything I could grab onto. As I plunged downward through the air, the darkness swallowed me. I could feel the impact coming, closer and closer, and I kicked and clawed again, closing my eyes, grabbing at anything. Finding nothing.

Suddenly I opened my eyes. In agony I rolled over. I was in a dark cave. A roaring bonfire was blazing in front of me. Lit up like a fiery demon, on the other side stood a gnarled old woman. A witch…

The witch leaned forward, staring at me. *My chest. My chest is in torture!* I realized. I closed my eyes to block the witch from my sight, then squinted between my curled eyelashes to observe she was no longer there, no longer standing across the bonfire. Instead, she was leaning right over me, her fiery breath whispering into my ear.

*Brian…*

*Let me alone!* My mind shrieked.

Pushing up my aching frame, I staggered backwards, eyes desperately scanning. Angling myself, I spied daylight spilling in from the cave's opening. *The way out!* I stumbled, lunging toward it, my hands clawing the air, expecting any moment for the witch to grab my shoulders and pull me back.

*Let me alone! Let me—*

I fled toward the opening. The light outside was blinding. I felt trapped in a stone tomb. Gasping for air, I raced toward the crack of sunlight, terrified that the witch was right behind me, slapping my boots against the red clay floor and crossing the cave until I broke through—

And stopped. Suddenly, another bolt of panic surged through me. I screamed, lashing out at anything that could hold me, anything I could grasp, my legs buckling as I realized—

*I'm at the edge of a cliff! High up on a steep mountainside!*

I twisted to my left, feet plunging halfway over the edge, trying not to fall. I lurched backwards. *Back, get back, get back!!* I clawed to find the heavy rock wall, unable to rip my eyes away from the edge. For a crazy moment, I saw myself; a tiny figure standing outside a cave atop a high and mountainous cliff, a black abyss yawning beneath me.

I whipped my hands up to my head.

*LET ME ALONE!!! PLEASE!!! LET ME ALONE!!!!!*

Suddenly, I sat bolt upright. A thin, shadowy woman was looming over me, and I was half awake, lying in a comfortable little bed.

*This is insane!* I thought. *How did I get here?* Shock waves bolting through me, I tried to focus, but it was no use, and my next thought was shot through with terror.

*Flower! Is Flower alright? My God, Flower!!*

I whipped my head back, thrashing my hands into the air. The next thing I knew, a rough tongue was licking my fingers. *Flower! Thank God!* I breathed a sigh of immense relief.

From somewhere in the room, a man's voice cursed something unintelligible, almost in anguish. The woman looming over me crossed herself. Grimacing, I sat forward, exposing the bandages on my chest and stomach.

A sharp bolt of agony exploded in my temples. Memories flashed. Haunting me. Paining me.

Jarring words blasted out of my mouth. "Where am I? What happened?"

The woman bent down to examine me. An ancient Native American man also crept forward. Both gaped at me, eyes roving over my body, open-mouthed.

"Was I…in an accident?" I asked, their four questioning eyes leveled at me. My mind struggled to remember. "There was a cave with a witch, high up on the mountain and…" Suddenly the pain inside my head exploded again, and I flopped back on the bed, weak, moaning.

Memories flooded my mind; the car crash, the pain, waking up in a cave with a witch, struggling to overcome my worst fears, the pain and suffering in my past, and the dream I had in the cave, the same recurring dream from my childhood.

"Was any of it real?" I blurted out.

The woman shook her head and glared at the ancient Indian.

"How do you know *this* is real? Maybe you're *still* dreaming?" she replied.

She paused. The old Indian man shook his head in exasperation. The pain in my temples accelerated. There was something familiar about this woman's voice...some stab of recognition…something frightening...

I closed my eyes, letting my mind wander. I was too confused and weak to think clearly and didn't know if the dream was reality and reality was a dream. Crazy. It all felt crazy.

"Your dog attacked my timber wolf," the woman said suddenly.

*Timber wolf?* I opened my eyes, trying to focus them. "Sorry…she's usually very placid," I managed in a feeble voice I didn't recognise as my own.

The pair stared at me in astonishment. I managed to crane my aching neck to see Flower sitting at my bedside, staring up at me, wagging her bushy tail and cocking her head. For the first time, I noticed that she had bandages wrapped around her chest and her right leg.

"Hey, Flower," I groaned. Flower nodded back, sliding forward to greet me on silent feet. "Thank you so much for saving her," I replied to the pair.

"Wasn't us," the man grumbled. "Found her like that after the crash. I don't know who stitched her up. Whoever it was, they knew what they were doing and saved her life."

The man squinted at me, baring broken, yellowed teeth. Then the woman dropped a fat slice of red meat on the floor and Flower instantly scrambled over to wolf it up hungrily— strangely keeping a close eye on the woman.

While Flower licked at the meat I squirmed atop my bed. I arched backwards, checked my body for signs of injury, but other than the bandages couldn't see any blood or apparent injuries, thankfully.

Slowly my eyes scanned the room; everything was finally coming into focus. I could now see this woman was about 60 years old, 1.6 metres tall, attractive with high cheekbones and lined brown-skin setting off brilliant white teeth, long raven-black hair, wearing faded blue Levi jeans, a cosy fleece, and fur winter boots.

Suddenly it hit me like a bolt of lightning.

"You…you're…*her,* the witch from the cave!"

My voice trembled, and my heart pounded in my chest like a drum.

"Are you calling me a witch?" she snorted in anger. "I'm a *Curandera,* a healer who just saved your life."

"Sorry, and thank you so much," I said as she glared at me indignantly. My mind raced. I weighed the two of them carefully with my eyes. "How did I get here, from the cave?"

Apparently the Curandera thought this curious. "What cave? You had a car accident, and my good friend Ahote brought you here," she said. I looked across the room to see her companion, a skeletal brown-skilled man about 70, an American Indian, now standing at the stove. He turned and gave me an almost toothless grin. I waved weakly.

"You got lucky. Ahote's '62 Chevy pick-up hardly ever starts. He thought you were dead," she grumbled and gave him a hard stare.

I peered over at Ahote, my temples pounding. "Is this…an American Indian reservation?"

Ahote smiled back, then mumbled something in a language that I couldn't understand. The old woman approached him, stroking a hand on his stooped back.

"Ahote said, 'A man, well-dressed in a sleek car, seemed to be looking for you,'" interpreted the Curandera.

A loud buzz went through my brain. "Was he wearing a Borsalino hat?"

"Yes, he wore a hat."

*I knew it!* I inclined my head toward the Curandera. "He's an assassin," I said, and the pair gaped at me once more.

Feeling a stabbing jolt of pain in my shoulder blade I stared at the ceiling, my brain whirring furiously. *I should have known!* It was him, the guy from the fundraiser in Monte Carlo. He followed Gurung and I to the Vatican and attacked me in Copenhagen at my apartment. *It had to be him.*

"Ahote saw your headlights in the creek and pulled you out of your crashed car."

I smiled, groaned, pressed my back against my pillow and looked around at my surroundings. The place was a tiny log cabin. Every spare inch was cluttered: religious crosses decorating every free space on the walls, a giant statue of the Virgin Mary, hand-woven Indian carpets on the floorboards, an old fridge, and a sink heaped with dirty dishes, a bright red altar with statues. There are also photos and mementoes, a pile of handwritten notes strewn on a table, beautiful Native Indian paintings, some finished, some works-in-progress, bookshelves with tarot cards and packed with books on medicine, traditional healing and herbs, traditional Chinese medicine and on the wall, diagrams of human anatomy.

On many wooden shelves stood glass jars full of different coloured plants and herbs, all labelled in a scrawled handwriting. Incense burned, giving the place a pleasant, healing aroma.

I angled my head back to the two of them. "Where is this place? Was the cave I saw just a dream? I'm bewildered."

There was no reply, only a hush in the room. Then it all came back to me; the fiery cave full of red clay. I gazed across the room and in one corner, I spotted my boots; smeared in dried, red clay.

*It was no dream. The cave really happened!*

There was the clatter of approaching feet. The woman scurried across the room as fast as her old legs could carry her, carrying something tight in her fist. "Why is there a picture of me in your pocket?" she shouted in a fury, suddenly right in my face, her cheeks blood red.

I gulped. "Picture…of *you?"*

She tilted her head, wise eyes probing mine.

"Answer my question!" she insisted and jabbed a bony finger into my chest, her eyes turning black and menacing.

If I had any doubt before, it was gone. Her face transformed at that moment, from a wise old woman into the menacing witch. At that moment, I cursed my luck, and my heart skipped a beat, realizing I could be in terrible danger.

*I'm in her den, the Bruja! The one Gurung warned could welcome me, or kill me.*

"Aldo…Ronaldo Del Duca gave it to me," I stuttered, fighting terror.

"Why?"

"Because…I'm…"

"Spit it out!"

"I'm…" I glanced at Ahote, then back to the woman, "I'm on a *quest."*

She studied me closely, like a raven ready to peck out my eyes. "What quest, Brian?"

I shuddered. "How come everybody knows my damn name?! And I'm on a quest to find out who is behind The Seven, stop them and all the fear in the world," I shouted back at her.

There was no reply. My thoughts suddenly filled me to the brink of tears. Sweat rolled down my neck. "What's *your* name?" I blurted out, trying to distract her from killing me.

The Bruja grunted, just stepped away, and then hustled to the tiny stove where a pot boiled. She made fresh tea, poured some leaves into mine, then came back and handed me a steaming hot mug.

"*How long have I been here?*" I pleaded again. In terror, I stroked my chin, feeling four to five days of growth.

"This will help your aches," the Bruja said and sipped hers as I took the mug in my shaking hands, gratefully drinking.

"This place, as you asked, is my hospital. And my home, and my mountain. She is…sacred."

I sipped my drink and looked out of the small window to see a small, rickety gate, brush blowing in the wind, rocky hills behind, just a few bushes growing in a very remote, inhospitable, brown dirt terrain.

All at once, I found myself struggling to breathe and wondered if I had chest or lung injuries.

The Bruja noticed. "Don't worry, Brian. We're 3,500 metres above sea-level. That's why it's hard to take the air."

I wheezed, gasping. Slowly my wheezing subsided. But she was eyeing me warily, her gaze full of poison, and I felt something wasn't right. *Why had I been brought here?*

"Because of your…search," she answered. "Quests are precious."

*Wait, did she just read my thoughts*? I glanced at Flower, always a great judge of character, but Flower just sat, staring at the Curandera curiously.

I yawned, feeling my chest tighten.

"It's Tiponi," the Bruja interrupted, hands outstretched to me, while she and Flower had a staring contest—which the old woman won, and my dog looked away, suddenly uninterested.

*Tiponi. Is that her name? It rings a bell.* "Why here, Tiponi?"

"It's *Miss* Tiponi," she snapped, her words sending a whistling noise through her pursed lips. She studied my face. "In winter, no one takes this dangerous road, especially in a snowstorm. Apart from you…and the stranger with that hat."

*Hmmm.* "I guess I really am lucky."

She gave me the strangest look. "You'll need more than luck."

"What d'you mean?"

"The evil ones won't find me, or you, here."

Her eyes gleamed. Straight away, I knew she meant The Seven.

I nodded grimly, scanned the room again, my eyes clearing, and noticed a lot of American Indian items. The Bruja's sharp eyes took in my interest.

"The Rockies were home to Paleo-Indians, then indigenous natives, like Apache, Arapaho, Bannock, Blackfoot, Cheyenne, Crow, Dunne-za, Flathead, Kutenai, Sekani, Shoshoni, Sioux, Ute, and others."

"Is that why you came here, Ti—*Miss* Tiponi?" I asked.

She took a sip from her mug, didn't answer. "Taos Mountain, part of this chain, is called Pueblo Peak locally, or Mó-ha-Loh or Má-ha-lu by the inhabitants of Taos Pueblo. It is 12,305 feet high."

"Um…why are you telling me all this?"

"It fails to interest you?"

I wiped the tea from my chin, sighed. "Please, tell me more."

She stared into my eyes, grunted, and then continued.

"Locals call her 'La Sierra de Los Indios' and tourists call her 'Skull Mountain' because of the strange skull shape seen on her southeastern slope after heavy snow. And you are here, because the mountain, she allowed it."

Captivated by that thought, I watched her closely as she moved gracefully toward the kitchen. *Strange woman. But is she Curandera or Bruja?* I asked myself.

"I have a question for you," she asked, and again I wondered if she could read my thoughts.

She smiled, then glanced at the mug of tea in my hand.

"Why shouldn't I kill you?"

* * *

# TWENTY-SEVEN

In that second, the steaming mug in my shaking fist, it all came flooding back: Gurung's dire voice, warning me not to accept any of the Bruja's offers of food or drink. *My God! What have I…!*

"And what have you lost?"

For a moment, I didn't acknowledge her. Flower's growling snapped me back to reality. "Lost? My business," I shakily answered, "my homes, most of my money and belongings…"

"Are these things important to you?"

"I thought so, but now…"

"Now, you're not so sure."

Startled, I dug my fingernails into the bed. Flower sat up, and with her eyes bored into the Bruja, took two steps toward her, then backed off and sat down again with a low growl.

The Bruja just smiled and went on. "The sacred mountain slopes leading to Blue Lake are home to the ancestral dead. That makes the mountain holy. 'Faceless Ones' appear wrapped in blankets and stand against trees there."

"Why do they do that?"

"They stand sentinel over the paths to Blue Lake. This is a magical place."

I nodded, waiting for her response, full of trepidation.

"What did the attorney say?" she asked.

My heart stopped. I couldn't believe she knew about the attorney and wondered how she could but covered up my anxiety.

"He offered me an inheritance from some dead guy."

"How much?"

"Half a billion dollars."

The Bruja didn't even blink. "Your response?"

"I turned him down."

"There's regret in your eyes."

"Hardly surprising. I'm totally broke."

The Bruja didn't reply right away. "This man, no one has ever seen him, or knows if he even existed."

"From what the attorney said, he existed alright."

"That was a significant sum. Why refuse it?"

"No one will ever own me."

"Then you leave me with only one choice."

"I don't know what you mean."

Quick as a flash, she raced over to me and dangled a small glass of potion in my face.

"I've poisoned you. This is the antidote."

* * *

# TWENTY-EIGHT

Fear rumbled through my guts. Desperately, my brain went back over every second of my conversation with Gurung. *This is the edge of madness,* I thought. "So, you *are* the Bruja, the witch, not the Curandera, the healer!"

"That depends on you."

"How come?"

The Bruja didn't answer. She stared at me, dangling the bottle of strange potion. My chest tightened, and I gasped, clutching it in fear. Drenched in sweat I tried to stand, my legs weak and buckling, my knees wobbling. I flopped back on the bed, groaning for air. Reaching inside my pocket, I clutched the runestone my mother gave me for comfort so long ago, feeling its strength.

"What's *that?*" she asked, glancing at the white pebble.

"A runestone," I wheezed. "My mother gave it to me to protect me."

She looked at me with surprise.

"Maybe, just maybe…"

"Maybe what?"

The Bruja looked unsure. Genuine doubt flashed across her face. Finally, she opened the antidote, bright sunlight glinting off the bottle, and let me drink a little.

I swallowed greedily, spluttered and coughed, my lungs on fire. My breathing eased and I pitched back on the bed, drenched with sweat. Suddenly I felt all the air in the room being sucked away from me. My arms and legs felt as numb as sticks.

The Bruja chuckled. Her voice ringing in my ears, I blacked out again.

* * *

I had another dream. This one was completely different, in complete contrast to the blinding sun of the parched desert of New Mexico.

I was soaring. My body propelled upward into the sky, then twisted downward. I swooped down a snow-capped mountain range like I could fly, then past a heavily wooded forest, down into a deep valley, over tall, elegant skyscrapers whose lights twinkled in the black, starry night, then toward an imposing building; a glossy hotel.

Next thing I knew, I was in a gigantic room—a meeting room—in virtual darkness, massive picture windows throwing a spotlight onto six people, five men and one woman. They sat in high-backed chairs around a long wooden table, all attentive and nervous, looking at a seventh man, deep in shadow, who sat at the head of the table.

All were wearing faceless white masks.

"Where is Brian now?" the seventh man asked, and stared hard at the others, who all looked even more anxious.

No one answered. I hovered, at the picture window, my gaze fixed on the man.

All at once, his face transformed, the muscles tensing, and he looked instantly alert, staring around the room. *He's looking for me!* I shut my eyes, feeling an urge to vomit. And at that moment, I somehow knew these were The Seven.

"Mr. Norburg, sir?" a young woman called, but he ignored her.

When I opened my eyes again, I was there, inside the room. Alarmed and confused, I slipped back into the shadows and remained silent.

The man's expression hardened. He growled, heaved himself to his feet, and then crept along the length of the cavernous room. The woman began to speak, but the man stopped her, a bony finger at his thin lips.

My breath was as shallow as possible. Through his masked face, which showed neither sympathy nor sorrow, I could sense he was pure evil.

Recognizing my presence, he prowled the room like a pro-boxer looking to land a blow, peered left, then peered right, then swiveled his eyes my way and scurried in my direction.

He came closer. And closer. A slow, sinister smile spread across his face. He could smell me, like a predator feeling its prey.

Creeping towards me, he stared into my eyes with laser-like intensity.

Fear and terror kicked in. I bit my lip, my legs trembling and my teeth chattering.

The man blinked. Cocked his head. Suddenly with lightning speed, he clamped his hand around my throat, strangling me, snatching me up off the floor and lifting me high in the air. His long fingernails dug into the back of my skull.

Higher and higher, I was lifted. My gaze whipped around the room desperately. I clawed and kicked and tried to squirm free, but he pulled me close, closer, and closer to the edge of his mask. From inside the mask, his eyes gave me a condescending look. Whatever he was, he was not of this world. He smelled of something ancient. Of something sinister. Of something…

He lifted me higher, rocking back and forth on his heels. I could hear his laughter echoing in the big room. Abruptly he licked his teeth, then cackled again.

My breathing was ragged now. His grip around my throat was so tight that I was losing consciousness. *Oh, God! I knew it, this time I'm going to die!*

* * *

# Twenty-Nine

I woke in a sweat, the laughter in my head vanishing, my heart pounding, my neck throbbing with excruciating pain, the dream of me in the huge meeting room instantly fading. And the man. The man who knew I was there.

*How could he know that?*

"Good dream?" a soft voice said, and I looked over to see the Bruja cooking something on the stove, steam surrounding her in a cloud, a twinkle in her knowing eyes.

My face felt weird. Frozen. I didn't trust her yet to tell her what I had just dreamt, but somehow from her grin, I sensed she already knew.

"Well?" she asked again.

"I don't think so," I replied flippantly, then touched my face and suddenly jumped. My flesh was covered in needles. Razor-sharp steel needles! In horror, I gasped.

"Chinese acupuncture. I'm healing you."

I touched my face gingerly all over, got up slowly, went over to the wall, and looked at a mirror.

My face was covered in needles from the top of my head to my chin and above my eyes. *I look like Pinhead from the damn Hellraiser movies!* I stared in disbelief, almost falling over backwards in shock when upon spying the red finger marks formed from the powerful compression around my throat. I felt the frightening sensation of gasping for air frantically.

I realized that everything was happening to me. Whether I'd dreamed it or was now living it. Whether I was awake or asleep. Whether I was truly dead or alive.

I glanced out the window to see if it was dark.

"What time is it?"

"Does that matter?"

I thought about that and nodded. *She's right.*

"What did you put in the tea?" I asked, rubbing my throbbing neck, delicately touching each of the razor-sharp needles. I tried to walk toward her but found it impossible to stand, and instead, I swayed, swooned and flopped back on the bed, massaging my neck.

"Got any Tylenol?"

"Chemicals? Inside your body?"

She snorted, turned from the cooker, glided to the shelves packed with glass jars and bottles of herbs and potions, grabbed one, and walked over to me.

"Rub that on your neck."

I read the label, FEVERFEW, and cracked the bottle open, then poured some strange glop onto the palm of my hand, rubbing it on my throbbing neck.

"You know a lot about natural remedies."

She drifted back to the cooker. "No, I know *everything* about natural remedies."

"Smells good. What is it?"

"The mule deer you killed."

My jaw dropped. I sniffed the glop, in disgust.

"But…I thought…I…"

Miss Tiponi looked at me, then suddenly let out an uproarious laugh that floated over my head like beautiful music, forcing me to smile. *She might be a witch, but she's one fascinating lady.*

"You're right about that," she said and continued cooking.

I turned to say something to Flower, but she was watching this strange woman cook, her eyes glittering toward the flame. At last, my neck was feeling better, and I stood, reeled a little, took a step forward and caught myself, then walked to the shelf of herbs, reading handwritten labels.

"All plants are our brothers and sisters. They talk to us, and if we listen, we can hear them."

"How…interesting."

"It's an Arapaho Indian proverb. And you don't find it interesting."

Opening my lips to speak, I changed my mind. *How the heck does she know these things?*

"That's why it's your first lesson."

I looked at the labels again. ALFALFA, INDIAN HEMP, ANTELOPE SAGE, ARNICA, ASHWAGANDHA, and countless more. Flower and I gaped at each other.

"Go into the garden and get me some black cohosh."

"What, black...*cohosh?* I don't know what that is."

"You will."

I shrugged, refusing to argue with her. "But why do I need to know about herbs and plants?"

"You ask too many questions," she snapped, and ladled some steaming broth into two bowls and stepped to the table, set for two.

She gestured for me to sit. I didn't say anything. I walked shakily over and sat on a rickety wooden chair, eyeing the broth gratefully.

Gripping a wooden spoon, I held it over the hot liquid. I was about to eat when I looked up to see her eyes closed, her hands planted on the table, her lips moving slightly. Then she opened her eyes and started eating.

"Um...what were you doing there?"

"Thanking the mighty creator for putting food on our plates..."

I smiled. She glared and added "...you ignorant peasant."

I nearly choked on my food and looked at Flower on the floor, happily gnawing at a meaty bone by the blazing fire.

Pretending nothing had happened, I started eating the food, trying to forget my troublesome thoughts. It was delicious.

"You need to learn about herbal remedies, so you don't poison your bloated body with chemicals."

By now, I was eating greedily, broth dripping off my chin. As the soup slid down my throat, I realized that Miss Tiponi might be rude and offensive, but she talked a whole lot of sense.

"Um...what happened to my car?" I asked.

"Ahote called some Indian friends to remove the ugly blight on my sacred mountain."

My heart beat wildly. "Oh God! I was given that car almost for free! How am I going to tell the guy at the rental agency?" In a panic, I looked around. "Where is my jacket?"

"What for?"

"To call the guy and apologize. There's a piece of paper in my pocket with a number."

In desperation I looked to Ahote. "No phone here, son."

My shoulders tightened. I took a deep breath. *No use in insulting my hostess,* I sighed. "Good soup," I answered, beaten down again, but ravenous.

Without a word, Miss Tiponi refilled my bowl, then sat, eyeballing me.

"Um…why are you staring at me?"

"I'm deciding if you're worth it."

"Worth what?"

"My time, you idiot!"

I ignored her and continued eating. From across the room I heard Miss Tiponi chuckle.

"What did you dream about?"

I put my spoon down and frowned. *Should I tell her?* "I was flying, through a mountain range, into a swanky hotel…"

"Not that one, the other one. The one in the desert."

I gaped at her in amazement, wondering how the hell she could possibly know that.

"I'm a *Dreamwalker*, Brian."

*A Dreamwalker?* "What's that?"

"A *Dreamwalker* is one who works with, and within, dreams to understand, to create, to heal, to meet with *elderhearts*, to journey this realm and to work with other worlds and realms, to teach…to be one with the creator."

She just stared at me until I looked away.

"What did the person in your dream write in the sand?"

I scoured my memory, fumbling to recall. *Of all the questions!* Then it hit me. "It was one letter. Capital D."

Her lips moved as though she might even smile, then resumed eating her broth.

"I have to unpick all the nonsense in that stupid head and rebuild you."

I rubbed my head, realizing I was still a bit sleepy. "And am I…" I gulped. "…*worth* it, I mean?"

"Probably not. But you are the man who's supposed to free the world of fear," she said and chuckled, sarcastic, peering again at my runestone. "Your mother was a wise woman. A characteristic you don't share." She chuckled, sipping her soup and shaking her head. "Where are you from?"

"Denmark," I answered. She gave me a blank stare.

"It's in Europe," I added, but she just kept staring.

I moaned, feeling my stomach churn. The penetrating eyes never strayed once.

*"Vikings?"* I said.

Her face instantly changed, her eyes dancing, and she leaned closer, studying me as if seeing me for the first time.

"I see it now. I can work with that…maybe."

She seemed preoccupied, then leapt to her feet, snatched up the bowls and tossed them in the sink on top of the others.

"Time to go," she said.

"Where are we going?"

"*We* are not going anywhere. *You* are."

I frowned, closed my eyes, thought for a moment, my lips moving in silence, trying to find the right words. At last, I stood, following her to the front door, which she yanked open.

"Out you go."

"What for?"

"You're going to learn about herbs, Brian."

"But…it's pitch black."

"You must embrace the darkness that you've always been afraid of, for what's in store for you."

I clenched my fists, my fingernails digging into my palms. *How did she know?* I'd never told anyone I was scared of the dark.

"With all the needles in my face?"

She shook her head like I was a moron.

Poking my head outside, I looked up at the sky, now completely clear, no sign of the snowstorm, the mountain covered in a peaceful, thick white blanket.

"What do you see?"

"Stars," I replied.

"You really are stupid," she snapped.

I shrugged my shoulders, thinking she just might be right.

"That's where we come from, Brian. The stars."

"You sound like Gurung."

"We sound like each other."

I nodded in agreement.

"Maybe, one day…"

"One day, what?"

She sighed long and hard, muttered something, then almost whispered, "If I accept you—*if*—I will teach you to be pure and strong and prepared to find The Seven and free the world from the shackles of fear."

I glanced at her sidelong. "You've met The Seven?"

She sighed, lowered her head, gently placed a hand on my back, and kept it anchored there. I moved closer to her, relieved, content even with such growing acceptance. Finally, she lifted her eyes to the sky, shook her head dismissively, and muttered.

"Takes longer when people are pig-headed." Then with her hand behind me shoved me outside, into the dark.

* * *

# THIRTY

I woke with a jolt the next morning to find Miss Tiponi, the Bruja, leaning over me, pulling out needles from my face. I could smell coffee and tobacco on her breath. Yanking two needles from my cheek she studied them with hollow eyes.

"I usually use 32-36-gauge needles, which are thinner than the needles you see at the doctor's," she said as I winced in agony.

*"Ow!!!"*

"However, to treat your pain, I've selected much thicker needles," she continued rolling needles between her brown fingers and pulling them out one by one.

Each needle removed sent pain shooting through my skull. In some parts of my face, it hurt so bad that my entire body jerked and jolted. In other places, it was like an electric buzz travelling from one location of my body to another.

*"Ow!!!"*

"Don't be such a crybaby! You're experiencing a stronger Qi sensation because of your internal injuries, but it will greatly reduce your pain."

I clenched my teeth to get it over with. *Hurry up, will you please!* Finally, one by one, all the needles were removed, and my entire body slumped over in blessed relief.

"Stay here for a moment before you get up," she said and left the room.

I lay back, my head spinning in circles, and finally dozed off again. In my dreams I heard unearthly howling, and was running through a forest unimaginably dense and dark.

When I woke, the forest had disappeared, though the bizarre howling still burned in my head. The Bruja was nowhere to be seen. I leapt from my cosy bed, petted Flower, and went looking for her.

I groped through the semi-darkness of early dawn, sweat breaking across my forehead. Through the window I could see her, sitting on an old, worn-out brown leather couch, wrapped in a warm, brightly coloured and patterned Indian blanket, smoking a black cheroot and drinking her disgustingly strong, steaming hot coffee from an old tin mug.

"Good morning, Miss Tiponi," I said with a smile.

She grunted, "Feeling better?"

"Yes, much better, thank you."

"Hungry?"

"Famished."

"Pity. You have work to do first."

"Of course," I blurted out, my shoulders drooping. "What are we doing?"

"You're a bit slow, aren't you? *I* don't do the work, *you* do."

"Sorry. So, what am *I* doing?"

"Gathering herbs to identify them and learn about their healing properties."

"But I don't know anything about herbs."

"Did I not say that was your first lesson?"

"Yes, you did, but…"

"Let's go then," she snapped and pointed up at Skull Mountain, looming high and gargantuan over us. Sizing the mountain up, she moaned, shaking her head. "My legs hurt today."

She wanted me to carry her up to the peak.

I closed my eyes, took a deep breath, and drawing on what strength I possessed started hiking.

It was a steep and loose track, slippery with rocks, definitely not suited for anyone with balance issues like me, and here I was carrying old Miss Tiponi on my aching back. My muscles felt as stiff as a statue. After an exhausting fifteen-minute climb, a section of the track had eroded, leaving a significant drop-off. I rolled violently forward and quickly stopped.

"Be careful," she said, sniggering at me.

We continued up some steep sections, followed by a short climb. My lungs were bursting. *How much farther?* My mind pleaded. My legs were burning inside and freezing outside, so I had to stop and lean up against a tree for a small rest.

"We don't have time for this shit," she hissed at me. "Get your act together. Your life will get a lot harder than this, so if you can't help a little old lady up a small hill, you're dead meat."

*Little old lady? Small hill? This is a fucking mountainside!* I thought to myself, my anger growing with the shooting and stabbing pain in my back, legs, and feet. But I didn't dare tell her how I felt. Better to just keep moving.

One excruciating step after the other, we staggered forward. The daylight was quickly passing. It was physical and mental torment since I couldn't see the top of the mountain. There was no way of knowing if I was putting too much effort in too early, so I had to keep a calculated pace if I was going to last.

"Did you bring any coffee?" she said.

"No," I hissed, annoyed.

"Don't you get testy with me, young man, or I'm gonna send your ass right back to where you came from," she warned.

I kept my walking, staggering, plodding forward, and kept my mouth shut.

The climb was strenuous, and the uphill gradient unrelenting. With each treacherous step I struggled in my muscles and my gut to hold my fears together. I felt so tired that I began weaving a bit.

"Steady, we're almost there," she said.

*Wonderful!* But she was lying. The steady slog up the mountain continued through rock scrambles and slippery pathways. We mounted higher. And higher.

Then suddenly, an impenetrable pall of fog enveloped us. My eyes flew open. I squinted but couldn't see one metre ahead of me.

"We need to stop," I shouted back to her.

"Keep going, use your senses, feel the terrain."

I gasped for air. I advanced. I almost lost my balance and slipped.

"Don't you dare drop me, boy!" she shouted. "Stop using your damn eyes and instead sense what's in front of you!"

What was in front of me was a steep thousand-foot drop. I closed my eyes, took a deep breath. Under my breath, I cursed. The sense of walking through a dense soaking wet fog, carrying her on my shoulders, was a complete nightmare. The pain in my legs was agonising, and she kept kicking me in the side like I was some damn mule.

Onward we plunged. My feet trudged forward, beginning to drag. I slipped, and twisted to my left, but kept walking. The deeper we went, the denser the fog became, increasing my panic. Suddenly, the fog cleared, and the landscape that unfolded as we climbed higher was incredible.

Out of the corner of my eye, I saw the Bruja grin. I plodded forward, my strength stretched to the breaking point. My arms and leg muscles throbbed painfully, and the pain in my back was becoming severe. I panted hard, then finally we reached the peak, my breath whooshing and moaning out in one last gasp. I collapsed on the ground.

"Get up and look at the view."

I crawled to my feet, a hollow pain knotting my stomach. I looked at the spectacular view, the snow blanketing everything, and felt the mountain's power just as Miss Tiponi waved at two of the Faceless Ones, thin people wrapped in heavy Indian blankets, their eyes barely seen, who bowed with deference.

We stood taking in the incredible landscape and the magic. The Bruja lit a cheroot, puffing peacefully. After about 10 minutes, she turned and headed back down the path.

"Wait, I thought I was gathering herbs?"

"Idiot. We're 12,000 feet in the sky. How can they grow here?"

My mouth flapped as I tried to work out what was happening.

"I just wanted to see the view from the peak and smoke a cigarette. It's been a while."

Then she galloped down the path like a sprinter and shouted, "Moron, I *have* an herb garden!"

* * *

Down to earth, in more ways than one now, I rooted around her herb garden, gathered leaves, stored them in different jars. Then Miss Tiponi started my first lesson, sitting on her couch sipping tea to relax us.

"People have used plants for remedies forever. Evidence dates back 60,000 years in a Neanderthal graveyard. They studied animals and discovered what herbs and plants helped various health conditions."

I was astonished. How could people in ancient times possibly discover that?

"Now, modern man needs to *rediscover* them," she said like she was reading my mind again.

"How can they?"

"With your help…maybe," she said and cocked her head at me.

"Written records of herbs date back over 5,000 years to the Sumerians, who described medicinal uses for laurel, caraway, and thyme. Ancient Egyptians from 1000 B.C. used garlic, opium, castor oil, coriander, mint, indigo, and other herbs for medicine. And the Old Testament of the Bible mentioned herb use and cultivation of plants like mandrake, vetch, caraway, wheat, barley, and rye."

She looked at me, long and thoughtfully. The fierce intelligence I saw in her eyes made my bowels quiver. I was amazed to make these incredible discoveries about just how intelligent the ancients were.

"Herbalism—sometimes referred to as folk medicine, botanical medicine, herbal medicine, and herbology—utilizes plants, plant extracts, fungal and animal products, minerals, and even shells."

As she spoke, her mouth flattened into a line of bitter determination. I hung on her every word, just like I had with Gurung, soaking up her incredible knowledge.

"Today, herbs are available in tablets, capsules, powders, teas, extracts, and fresh or dried plants. Many are beneficial; however, be wary when taking these powerful supplements. Some can cause health problems, especially if they interact with other drugs. Consult a doctor before using herbal supplements, always follow label directions, and women in particular need to be cautious when pregnant or nursing."

Her knowledge was incredible. "Show me," I asked, and she got to her feet, scampered inside her cabin, then appeared with a massive book titled *Herbs and Plants Used by Native Americans.*

"This reveals many of the herbs and plants used in history, as well as today, in Native American remedies and across the world. Read and learn, Brian."

I took the heavy book and sat cross-legged by the herb garden. Flipping through pages, I whispered to myself, amazed.

There were thousands of different kinds of herbs and plants, all listed alphabetically, and I started to read, intrigued.

The first one alone was an eye-opener.

Alfalfa, I read, to treat digestive problems, blood clotting, and jaundice. It is also used for arthritis, muscle problems, high blood sugar, energy, bone strength, bladder and kidney problems, and easing menopause symptoms.

I flicked pages and read studiously.

*Ginseng to heal a variety of ailments and for spiritual and ceremonial purposes. Also for flu, colds, fever, sinus problems, swelling, and as a laxative. The Iroquois smoked it like tobacco, the Seminole used it in sweat baths, and the Cherokee, Creek, Houma, Mimac, Mohegan, and Potawatomi used it for a variety of medicinal purposes.*

I kept reading, my gaze fixed on each word, eyes widening larger and larger until they turned glassy. At one point, I laughed aloud and said to Miss Tiponi, "Ginseng was used by Meskwaki women to get a husband and Pawnee men as a love charm…"

"That's why you Europeans in the 1700s quickly saw its benefits," she said, scowling at me.

I read and read for the whole day, hunched over this magnificent book in her garden. As the sun went down, I took the book inside, eyes glued to its remarkable knowledge, and sat at the table, poring over it.

Watching me, I could feel the Bruja's lips twisted in a lopsided grin. I jotted the main discoveries in a notebook, flicking backwards and forward through the alphabet.

*Hemp used for syphilis, fever, worms and asthma; allspice for menstrual cramps, upset stomach, flatulence, and toothaches; licorice for coughs, diarrhea, stomach aches, and after childbirth; mistletoe for blood pressure, lung problems, epilepsy, and as a contraceptive.* Bleary-eyed, I kept reading. *Cherokees concocted a tea for headache; the Creek made a concoction for lung troubles; Mendocino Indians used the root to induce abortions.* Fascinating! *Navajo Indians used antelope sage as a contraception; arnica to heal wounds; ashwagandha, they believed, restores the body, rejuvenates the mind, improves zest and vitality, and is an antibiotic, aphrodisiac, diuretic, narcotic, a sedative and…*

"Ashwagandha is *incredible!*" I said aloud, and Miss Tiponi looked over from her cooking.

"You're taking a lot of notes."

"I don't want to forget how amazing these natural remedies are. Listen to this: *Aspen trees treat fever, scurvy, cough, pain and inflammation, similar to aspirin.*"

"I know, Brian. I wrote the book."

Surprised, I flipped to the cover, and there she was, looking earnestly at her readers and dressed in traditional Native American garb.

"Aspirin has existed since 1899, Brian. But it's still a chemical in your body. One of the single biggest issues in the modern world is health, and drug companies make billions when natural remedies exist. It's one of the worst scams in history."

"I see your point, Miss Tiponi," I said, then I went back to my notetaking.

The Bruja grunted, stirred her pot on the stove. "You've *almost* impressed me. Keep the book."

"Thank you, Miss Tiponi. It's a real revelation."

"It's more than that. It's a bible for health."

I hefted the weighty book in my hand, marveling at its genius, and hers. The Bruja stopped stirring, then turned to me, with gleaming eyes.

"So, Brian. What have you learned today?"

"That herbs and plants can feed or heal us. That nature is the ultimate provider. That we don't need chemicals. That the drug companies convinced us that we do…"

She grunted an interruption. "…and tomorrow morning, I'll tell you all about manipulation."

An uncomfortable silence floated between us. I nodded excitedly, already looking forward to the following morning.

"And what else did you learn?"

"Um…I'm not sure…"

"That you need to work on your fitness and strength like as Gurung and I said, and the fortune-teller, for the day of the battle."

I struck the palm of my hand against my head. "So *that's* why I had to carry you up to the mountain!" and she almost smiled, slurping her broth with a wooden spoon and nodding in satisfaction.

"Tell you what I didn't learn."

She looked up at me and waited.

"What you gave me that could've killed me, and what the antidote was."

She smiled this time, bent over the stove with her spoon, sucking up more broth between her teeth, then resumed her cooking, adding more mysterious ingredients. I shuddered to think what those ingredients might be.

* * *

# THIRTY-ONE

"*Brian, wake up!*" a voice bellowed in my ear. I bolted upright in alarm, to see Miss Tiponi peering into my eyes, within inches of my sweating face.

"I'm awake!" I shot back, pulse throbbing.

The Bruja threw back her head and cackled. "I don't mean *now*, dummy. I mean, all the time, every single day."

I sighed, sat up, yawned, swung my legs to the floor, scratched my head, and climbed out of bed.

"It's a bit early for school to start, isn't it?"

She shook her head and meandered to the stove, where coffee sat in a pot and eggs sat on two plates next to some toast.

I stretched, groaned in pain, stooped to stroke Flower who was chewing a big bone and headed to the bathroom, where I did my business and stumbled back, bleary-eyed, to sit at the table.

The Bruja carried the plates and coffee over. She now had me drinking coffee, which I never really enjoyed before, and as she sat, we gave thanks to the creator, then started eating.

"Today, you're going to discover how they manipulated us," she said, dipping toast into her egg. I nodded puzzled.

"Who? The Seven?"

"It's them today, but before that, there was master manipulator, Edward Bernays."

"Who's he?"

"An Austrian-American from the 1920s who was the nephew of a famous psychologist, Sigmund Freud."

"Him I've heard of."

"The founding father of psychology, a renowned expert on human behaviour."

I nodded but wondered where this was heading.

"In World War I, Bernays worked for U.S. President Woodrow Wilson, using propaganda to gain support for the war by persuading

Americans to intervene in World War I and bring democracy to all of Europe."

"And he succeeded."

"He shaped public perception, and amazed that it was so easy to get the sheep to buy a slogan, he figured he could do the same in peace-time. However, propaganda was a German war weapon and a dirty word, so he invented...*public relations.*"

"That's smart."

"What was even smarter was that he took ideas from the best, Uncle Freud. His psychoanalytical techniques infiltrated the subconscious and unconscious minds of the public. Bernays also used ideas from two of the best in crowd mentality, Gustave LeBon and Wilfred Trotter."

"How d'you know this stuff?"

Unflustered, she went on. "Soon, big corporations hired him to sell more products. One was American Tobacco, who were after female smokers. Smoking was unladylike, meaning they missed out on 50% of potential consumers. Bernays changed all that."

"That's kind of disgusting," I said, just as Miss Tiponi lit up another cheroot, filling the room with dense clouds of choking smoke.

"How he did it was masterly. Women had just won voting rights, and because they usually smoked in private, he launched a fake protest at the New York Easter Day parade in 1929. He hired pretty women and called their cigarettes 'torches of freedom.' That word tapped into the female psyche, and there was a media feeding frenzy. That stunt set American females alight."

She refused to meet my stern gaze at her cigarette packet, and I smirked.

"Wow, it makes you think about all the advertisements that are so persuasive."

"Precisely. Women thought, 'Hey, we can vote like men, so we can smoke too. It's not manly; it's women's rights.'"

She blew a big puff of smoke at me and winked.

"Smoking mushroomed among women as a result, and persuasive lies became a staple in marketing."

"Not just in marketing, politics, and the corporate world, too, everywhere."

"Indeed. What Bernays realized was that selling people an *idea* or a *feeling* was more powerful than simply listing a product's benefits, or comparing it to competitors. Obvious today, but it was so successful then, every advertiser in the world copied him."

"Smart guy. Pity he didn't apply that huge brain differently."

"Pity indeed, because a certain man used those self-same persuasive techniques during the war. You might know his name, Nazi propaganda Minister…Josef Goebbels."

"So that's where the Nazis got it! Some legacy."

"Not just him, Brian. U.S. corporations and politicians worshipped Bernays. President Herbert Hoover praised him for transforming Americans into 'constantly moving happiness machines.'"

"Buying stuff they don't need or want."

"Bernays was also one of the first in celebrity endorsement. He was hired by Calvin Coolidge to improve his public image, so the PR genius invited stars like Al Jolson to breakfasts at the White House. Once again, the media and public lapped it up. Coolidge stormed to election victory in 1924."

I shook my head in astonishment at the power of PR and the mighty who employed it, and still do.

"Bernays' daughter, Anne, said he didn't trust people who could 'vote for the wrong man or want the wrong thing.' And he said in his pioneering 1928 text, *Propaganda*: 'The conscious and intelligent manipulation of the organized habits and opinions of the masses is an important element in a democratic society. Those who manipulate this unseen mechanism of society constitute an *invisible* government…the true ruling power of our country, and many others.'"

"You mean…The Seven."

"They've used Bernays' methods brilliantly. They govern people, mould their minds, form their tastes, and suggest their ideas. Yet nobody's heard of them."

"D'you know who they are?"

She disregarded my question. There was a pause as we both looked up and saw the morning stars floating in the sky. "I was healing a woman in The Enchanted Circle..."

"What's that?"

"The area around Taos. Anyway, a man tried to recruit me..."

"Why?"

"They wanted the wisdom but didn't have good hearts to learn. So, he invited me to join them."

"Which you turned down."

She shrugged. "What do I need money for?"

She exhaled an enormous puff. For a long moment, the silence in the room lingered. Putting my hands over my eyes to make an eyeshade I finally asked, "Did you learn anything else about The Seven?"

She shook her head, blowing out smoke rings. "I wish. They created our democratic society, Brian."

"Every aspect of our lives has been orchestrated by them?"

"Deep inside, men's hearts beat with darkness. So, why not distract us by tempting us into wanting things, then getting them? A society of mindless consumers. We do jobs we hate, to earn money to buy things we've been conditioned into lusting for. Ever shopped like that, Brian?"

I nodded, immediately feeling guilty that I'd been manipulated.

"We sweat at work; we need rewards. So, with the money we sweated for, we buy stuff and feel good, like our drug of choice."

"It all sounds so…ludicrous."

"It is, but it keeps us in line. Anyone with cash can get that high by buying the latest must-have toys."

"No more gadgets for me, then."

"There are industries of persuasion employing millions all over the world to distract us from our humdrum lives or killing each other. But they also take our eyes off the ball with big things, like politics."

I stared at her thoughtfully. My mind was bursting with this new information, at once both wild with thought and densely quiet, until it was absolutely overloaded. "Want me to carry you again?" I joked, looking for a break from all this heavy stuff, but Miss Tiponi just shook her head.

"Instead of protesting against the establishment, corrupt politicians, police, financers and greedy businesses, we buy happiness in a bottle, or a holiday, a new house or car, whatever."

"So, people don't make a fuss about all the corruption because they're buying shit, even though they're shackled with debt?"

"Precisely, Brian. But not only that, the never-ending hype machine and the manufacturing of cheap, disposable trends destabilize us, giving a sense of panic. They exaggerate the evolving nature of the world by creating *artificial* change, persuading us to keep up with trends, which ultimately makes us anxious."

"It's just so cynical, like a plot from a disaster movie!"

She nodded. "Naomi Klein said in *The Shock Doctrine: The Rise of Disaster Capitalism*, 'In moments of crisis, people are willing to hand over a great deal of power to anyone who claims to have a magic cure...'"

Suddenly it was all too much. My mind screamed for a break. Pushing my plate aside, I went outside and sat on a big boulder and looked at the beautiful view, as my view of the world was beginning to change significantly.

Miss Tiponi followed, sitting on a rock nearby. My eyes went to hers, like steel drawn to a magnet. Setting her jaw tight she spoke, a new tone of anguish in her voice.

"The Seven have doped us into feeling that the world is frightening, making us likely to submit to their politicians with easy solutions to complicated problems, so that we can reclaim some sense of calm."

I sighed. "What happened to the master manipulator?"

"His influence is still exerted today, by admen, marketers, PR agents, corporate psychologists, and politicians. Speaking of Presidents, Bernays helped four more after Coolidge. And, he practically invented consumerism."

For a moment we sat, saying nothing. To my right, I saw the shadows across the mountain growing long. I stood and looked at our world, all the wonderful nature and beauty, and the darkness that is encroaching it, while Miss Tiponi talked about a world I didn't know existed.

"Bernays was convinced that he stabilized a savage world and protected democracy from the worst tendencies of human nature through consumerism."

"And what d'you think?"

"The prominent philosopher Herbert Marcuse said the opposite, that the sense of achievement we get by spending and consuming is hollow and makes us unsatisfied, leading to a kind of schizophrenic existence."

"A disconnect between spending and satisfaction."

The Bruja nodded.

"So, it's like some not-so-merry-go-round of eating, sleeping, working, spending, screwing, searching for joy but failing, then you rinse and repeat?"

"Yes, Brian. It doesn't work, so people feel sad, disappointed, and angry, depressed, and betrayed total failures. So, they turn to substance abuse or mindless TV. Even the young generation of the super-rich celebrities have begun to notice—see here, the other day I read, eh, I mean *someone told me* that Kylie Jenner—you know, the Kardashian family—said, 'What I think is so amazing about having everything, and feeling like I have everything, is that I don't really find happiness within materialistic things. Like, it's cool if I can buy myself a new car, and I think it's amazing for a week, but then the thrill is over, and I'm like, 'Oh, so I guess that wasn't really happiness.'"

I gave her a huge smile. "Miss Tiponi, am I going to find gossip-magazines hidden around the cabin?"

"Absolutely not! That's preposterous, how could you even think that…but if you find one do let me know," she said and winked at me.

Trying to look serious again, she narrowed her eyes and looked at me closely before continuing. "Looking back at his life, aged 100, Bernays said, 'Sometimes it seems sort of like having discovered a medicine to cure a disease, and then finding out that so much of it is being administered that people are getting sick from the overdoses.'"

Before I could reply, she stood, patted me on the shoulder, then turned and started walking back down the path. I trailed after her, in her shadow, brooding on my thoughts.

"Miss Tiponi?" I shouted. She stopped and turned. "The Seven... they seem invincible to me. How can we ever defeat them?"

She shrugged, pursed her wrinkled lips together. Dark thoughts seemed to cross her mind. She looked at Skull Mountain in the snow, then back at me and whispered, "You can't...not alone at least," and I grimaced.

"First, you have to believe that it is possible. The Seven will be destroyed by a lion leading an army of sheep that need guidance to face their worst fears and transform their lives, not by a sheep leading an army of lions as Alexander the Great said..."

The wind gusted. Far away, I heard the howl of a wolf. I sat on a rock, and the Bruja frowned at me.

"Getting stronger is only one of the tools you need. Love is the other and most important thing you need to carry with you. Martin Luther King said, 'Darkness cannot drive out darkness; only light can do that. Hate cannot drive out hate; only love can do that.'"

I thought about that as I rubbed and stretched my throbbing legs.

"They will tempt you at every turn to become like them. As greed and envy grow within you, your chances of defeating them diminish. After greed, vanity enters - believing yourself to be important and powerful, and then, in the end, pride comes. And all the other vices come from that."

I stopped what I was doing and stared at her.

"We know that The Seven have an interest in you, though we don't yet understand why. But when the time comes, you can use that to your advantage and get close enough to discover if they have any weaknesses."

My eyes left hers and swept across the mountains. I tried to visualize the things she was saying as really happening; it was difficult to believe it was taking place in the actual world. Standing, I strolled to her, feeling the weight of my task ahead. Miss Tiponi seemed to sense that.

"There is no guarantee you will succeed, but it is your quest, and you have no choice. Either they will destroy you, or you destroy them. Life, as you knew it so far, is over; the quest is your life now."

On the last sentence, her voice dropped into a deeper, more desperate register. Her eyes were not just gleaming now, but blazing. My head was spinning, and my heart was pounding in my chest.

"When will I be ready to leave?"

"Soon. But before that, you need to know the other way, the terrible way we're manipulated."

I gazed deep into her eyes and held my breath. Then my heart sank. Any hopes I had of finding a way out of this quest had now disappeared.

* * *

# THIRTY-TWO

"It's…fear," Miss Tiponi continued, and I cocked my head, listening intently. "And it's all about money and power."

We were back in her cabin. She poured me some more tea and continued, looking grave.

"You see, Brian, people, and corporations that perpetuate fear generate vast sums of money and power."

I sipped some tea, its taste bitter, like a warning of what I was about to hear.

"Fear is worth billions, probably the biggest market in the world. Think about it. Politicians, Big Pharma, lawyers, mass media, insurance companies, and more all sell fear. And, you've heard from Mr. Bernays how manipulation works. Fear is no different."

The word *fear* registered a twitch in the corner of my left eye. I leaned in closer, listening intently so I didn't miss a single thing.

"Since cave-men times, humans were tuned to respond to fear." She stared over as if smelling the fear in me. Immediately I thought back to the attack in my place in Copenhagen and knew exactly what she meant.

"Our brains are highly complex organisms, and one thing experts say is that we're not wired to be happy all the time."

"I know that feeling all too well," I muttered.

"Brains react to stressful situations, so its main job is to keep us alive and safe…"

"…and that's why it's easy to make us fearful all the time."

"Exactly. The corporations and politicians that corrupt and exploit our weakness are human. *We* are human, so we're susceptible to corruption, just like them. And when we try to assess danger, emotional overload fails us."

She stared into my pupils, assessing my reaction. Her words were hitting home as I remembered all the times in my life I was anxious and afraid.

"What I'm saying might not seem like much, but it's *everything*. If fear is about certain danger, anxiety is 'an experience of uncertainty.'"

"And *uncertainty* is what fear-mongers play on."

Miss Tiponi smiled like a proud schoolteacher. "Exactly. That's how politicians and corporations influence you."

"So, if people are persuaded to feel anxious about their families, finance or homes, and the other side wants to influence our thinking, and our actions, they offer *certainty* or the illusion of it."

Miss Tiponi's eyes softened, looking pleased with me. "They combine *uncertainty* with the concept of a growing threat to your day-to-day routines or your entire existence. Researchers say this leads to a heightened desire for authoritarianism."

"Like…a conspiracy theory. The problems aren't random but engineered by a group like The Seven, so the other side offers certainty in an uncertain world."

"Correct. Choose your enemy. However, I guarantee you that it won't make you anymore peaceful."

I paused to think about that and realized that it was because our fears were manipulated. Miss Tiponi narrowed her eyes, then lit another cigarette.

"So, media, advertising, and political campaigns could be described as neurological warfare," I added. Miss Tiponi grimly nodded, so I continued.

"There's a lot of real problems facing humanity today, but we must face them together without feeling anxious and scared, with clear heads and compassion for everyone, not just the people who look like us, or agree with us."

"Well said."

I kept my eyes on Miss Tiponi. Everything we'd said made me more confident in the reason I'd been brought here. For a long moment I pondered. "That's why I need to get out there, find them, and destroy them. How long before I can leave?" I said, with a questioning look.

She gave me an exasperated gaze, pointing her cigarette at me. "It took you five years to get your black belt."

I was amazed she knew that. *But, of course she did, you moron. Haven't you learned anything yet?* I studied her creased brown face, streaked with shadow bars cast by the sunlight. For a moment, I was speechless.

"Timing is everything Brian, yet in our world, we're more concerned with how events occur in space than in time. Our society is focused on what things are made of and how they work, but little attention is paid to the timing of things. As an example, if you do two things exactly the same way at different times in your life, would you expect the outcome to be the same?"

"Probably not," I answered.

"Exactly," she continued, "Carl Jung called this synchronicity. He believed life was not a series of random events but rather a manifestation of a deeper order, where everything is connected, with each of us embedded in a universal completeness, where synchronicity serves a role similar to that of dreams, with the purpose of changing a person's egocentric behaviour and thinking to greater unity. However, right now time will have no meaning for you, Brian," she said, then stared hard into my eyes which got heavier…and heavier…and suddenly I was falling again, being whirled back into the abyss, the darkness of my dreams enveloping me.

* * *

# THIRTY-THREE

"Wake up, Brian, wake up!" a voice said in my dream.

But I didn't want to wake up. I was having a lovely, warm and fuzzy dream, racing with Flower and the pack of wolves to the peak of sacred Skull Mountain, then showering under the waterfall, naked.

"*Wake up!*" the voice yelled louder, and now I recognized it as Miss Tiponi.

*Later,* my mind said, *wake me later. This is too nice a dream.* Suddenly the voice screamed like the wind: "*WAKE UP!*" Rough hands shook me awake, and I moaned softly, "Okay, okay, Miss Tiponi. I'm awake," and squinted my eyes at her.

But Miss Tiponi wasn't by my side—she was making coffee at the stove.

*Weird.* Outside, it was dark, and on the porch, I could see Ahote, leaning against a post and smoking, his eyes glaring at me.

He kept his gaze riveted on me, looking grim. *What's* he *doing here?* I wondered.

I tossed my bedclothes aside and swung my legs out, then rose out of bed. I bent and stroked Flower's head. Flower jutted her chin out, begging me to rub it.

"What time is it?" I blearily asked. As soon as I did, felt foolish because Miss Tiponi looked at a wristwatch that wasn't there and snorted.

I gazed around as if hypnotized. "Why are we up so early?" I asked as she handed me a mug of coffee, which smelt delicious.

"Always asking the time and impatient," she said.

I rubbed my unshaven face, irritated. We drank our coffee in silence. Ahote kept staring at me, seeming perplexed. *Is he trying to intimidate me?* I thought, trying not to be perturbed. Minutes later, we were all packed into Ahote's vehicle, bumping along as it coughed and spluttered along the dirt road.

I sat between them, Ahote steering, jerking the wheel back and forth as if he is at a ship's helm. *What a strange couple,* I thought. *Is Ahote her only friend?*

"Have you ever been married?" I asked the Bruja. Ahote sniggered, and they both started talking in Native Indian, sprinkled with some Spanish which I recognized as 'idiot, stupid white man' and 'foreign fool.'

I waited for their sniggering to pass. Then I laughed at myself and sat back, gazing at my hollow eyes in the rear-view mirror.

Eventually, a road sign read TAOS PUEBLO INDIAN RESERVATION. UNESCO WORLD HERITAGE SITE and I rolled my eyes at Miss Tiponi's little joke.

*A reservation.*

Again, Miss Tiponi seemed to read my mind and even cracked a smile.

"You're very privileged, Brian. Few people will ever see, or experience, what you are about to see."

*What the hell does that mean?* I wondered. Then gazing around at the breath-taking sights, Ahote ramming his foot down on the gas, we roared off, and I instantly forgot my question.

"This is one of the most photographed and painted places in America," Miss Tiponi pointed out.

It was easy to see why. The view was truly magnificent the adobe buildings glowing red in the rising sun.

"It's incredible to think that up to 1900 these adobe homes had ladders outside to the roof which were pulled up in an attack. The walls are very thick for defence, too. It's the biggest pueblo structure of its kind in the world."

"Smart thinking," I said, and Ahote grunted at me.

"Electricity, running water and plumbing is banned, and Taos Indians only started using furniture recently in their two rooms, one a living and sleeping area, the other for cooking, eating and storage."

"It makes cooking and heating a little difficult," I answered. Miss Tiponi nodded.

"This is one of the oldest continuously inhabited communities in the United States, Brian," she continued.

Ahote veered the truck left, then right, and the brake when a stray dog ran across the road, pulling up outside a large adobe house.

"They're one of the world's most secretive people. Their language has never been chronicled, and their culture is a mystery to outsiders, as well as their beliefs."

"Incredible," I said, smiling between Miss Tiponi and Ahote.

A gale of wind from the northwest swirled around the house. The sun was beginning to rise. For some reason, it gave me the ominous feeling I was running out of time. The next thing I knew, I was grabbed roughly. I tried to shout for them to wait but managed only a rasping sound. And then it was too late.

* * *

My arms were so numb I couldn't move them. The world spun dizzily until suddenly I noticed I was surrounded by a herd of bustling animals in the rising sun, all crowding around me.

I'd been dragged into a snowy clearing. From somewhere, intense heat was making me sweat.

*Miss Tiponi?* My mind whispered. I tried to speak but only managed a hoarse cough.

Out of the corner of my eye, I saw flames. The flames swelled and grew, obscured in rising white steam, like a lunatic's vision. Suddenly, primaeval drumbeats boomed, a haunting Native Indian chant began, and the animals around me started to sway, then dance, all in perfect rhythm, chanting in unison.

*What the hell?! Miss Tiponi!!* I tried to lift my arms clumsily. White steam drifted all around, billowing in my eyes, then abruptly lifted. That's when it hit me; the animals were men, dressed in whole deerskins and buffalo-skins, complete with huge head-dresses.

*I'm flipping out,* I thought. I watched them in a state of shock, trying to gain my bearings. Huge deer, antelope and buffalo horns were draped with sprigs of fir trees, swaying above these bare-chested men in the bitter cold.

My mind reeled. The hissing of steam and the roaring flames drowned out my thoughts. I almost nodded off, as if I'd fainted. Suddenly, to my surprise, I found myself capable of moving. I waited patiently until my sense of touch returned. Then with a scream that I was certain would rip my throat out, I began dancing with them.

Moving. Swaying. Undulating. Shaking.

My face relaxed; a sense of almost indescribable bliss flowed across it. At that very moment, the sun rose above Skull Mountain, bathing the beautiful buildings and all the dancers red, in what looked like blood.

Dancing on shaky legs, I looked down at my body, amazed to see I was naked above the waist, like the other men.

I had no real idea how that happened, but the dance was so incredibly tribal, primordial, captivating and hypnotic, I just kept going.

Moving. Swaying. Undulating. Shaking.

I tried to understand. *Is this another dream?* I caught the occasional glimpse of Miss Tiponi, and she seemed to be in a deep trance, surrounded by Native women who were bowed down, heads lowered, as if they were worshiping her.

The dancers threw another log on the fire. The sun rose higher and higher. The drums beat faster and faster. The dance became more and more frantic, my body rolling and wobbling, rising and falling, my feet slapping the ground at lightning speed. *How is this even possible?* Around me, the other dancers seemed mesmerized, caught up in an ecstatic trance.

Moving. Swaying. Undulating. Shaking.

Faster. Faster. Faster. Faster.

My brain pounded at the insane speed of the drums. I felt as if I were about to have a cerebral hemorrhage. Suddenly, a man was right in my face, and I jolted back, in fear.

*Who the hell...!* I thrust open my jaws to cry out. But it was just Ahote, bathed in the glow of the rising sun, his body covered in red paint, sweat pouring from him, his eyes glazed.

The drums beat faster and faster. The dance became more and more frenzied, the chanting louder and more insistent, and I joined in, my eyes shut, not wanting to be awakened if it was a dream, fully immersed in this phenomenal experience.

*What an unbelievable sensation,* my mind groaned. Then suddenly, the dancing and chanting stopped.

I opened my eyes. The Native Indians had formed a circle around me, everyone silent, every pair of eyes glued to mine.

I felt frightened. Intimidated. Behind me, the flames from their bonfire sizzled higher and higher. Ahote appeared in the middle of the ring and started talking to me in his language.

I couldn't understand a single word. I stared panic-stricken.

Back and forth my eyes moved among the dancers, struggling to comprehend. Then a mighty deer appeared in the circle, its antlers massive and impressive. It snorted at me, then seemed to nod at me, then turned and clomped away.

There was a hush from the Indians. The bonfire sizzled.

Now I was certain I was going to have a heart attack. My mind lurched for me to run, yet I stood frozen. Next thing, Miss Tiponi joined us and embraced me, rocking me back and forth.

As she did, Ahote backed away from me, and the other Indians backed off, gazing at me with respect I didn't understand.

I gave the Bruja a searching look. There was a stubborn gaze in her eyes. Any second now I expected to wake up. Next thing I knew, the blazing fire roared higher, and a mob crowded around me again, a bunch of Indian women, and I was dragged away.

The women giggled, laughed, and stared at me as they stripped me and put me in a tin bath full of cold water, and I yelped in surprise.

*"Owww!!! What…?"*

They scrubbed me clean, dragged me out, dried me at the blazing fire, and then left me to dress.

Bemused, I dressed and stumbled away from the clearing to see Miss Tiponi waiting for me by Ahote's old vehicle. Through the windshield, I could see Ahote inside, a cigarette perched on his lips, weathered old hands gripping the wheel.

A wrinkle of irritation passed over his face. We jumped inside, and the car shuddered away. I gave the Bruja a strange look.

"What was that all about?" I asked.

She smiled. "It was the day the buffalo came out to dance, Brian."

I didn't reply. I didn't know what to say.

"It's called the Buffalo Dance," she added. "A celebration of winter, a re-enactment of life and death among beautiful animals, the birth of tragedy from the spirit of the hunt."

I stared at her in astonishment. "It's…incredible."

"The men emerge from the kiva, the underground chamber at the heart of the pueblo's traditional religious life, chant in Tiwa, the native dialect of Taos Pueblos, then dance before hunting."

Ahote grunted, snorted out a cloud of smoke, and then nodded his agreement.

"But why did they include me in it?"

"They know you're on a quest. They hope that you succeed in your hunt to find The Seven. And make the right decision about your future. When you do, you save all of them and all of humanity."

Her eyes blazed with certainty. "I hope so too, Miss Tiponi," I said.

"No white man has ever done that dance with them. They believe in you, Brian. And you have gained something remarkable; their deep respect." Miss Tiponi stared deep into my eyes for a long time, then looked away. Happening to catch her reflection in the window glass, I could've sworn those old eyes had tears in them.

* * *

# Thirty-Four

"This morning's lesson is magic," the Bruja told me the following sunrise, as she sat on her couch on the porch while I tended the herb garden.

My heart skipped a beat. My brain was still buzzing from the night before. Calmly I met her gaze.

"Only, it's *not* magic," she said and held up a set of bright, oversized cards. "People just think it is," she said, puffing on her cheroot.

I stared. I gulped. Tarot cards. *What craziness was next?*

"They assume it's nonsense, mumbo-jumbo, parlour tricks. It's *not.* It's real, very real."

Rising, I wiped the dirt from my hands, then strolled over to examine them. They looked ancient, worn, garish, and ornately illustrated. I stared at her doubtfully.

"You should know how they work."

"Really?" I said, sitting beside her as she stubbed out her cheroot.

"The choice of a card is exactly what your higher self already knows, Brian. This is what Tarot occultists call 'the conversation with your higher self.' The cards always work. It's not magic—tarot cards are a soul map, a sacred mirror."

*A soul map?* My interest grew. I'd always thought tarot cards *were* superstitious nonsense, supernatural mumbo-jumbo. Suddenly I thought of the German woman in Paris, the fortune-teller.

"Precisely, Brian," Miss Tiponi stated, doing her mind-reading thing again.

I drew in an irritated breath. She smiled, then shuffled the deck, held the cards out to me, and I hesitated, finally plucking one out of her hand.

Shakily I held it aloft. It was the death card, a horrible, armoured ghostly skeleton wielding a scythe on a skeletal horse, body parts scattered on the ground.

*Holy fucking shit!* I gulped, but Miss Tiponi said, "The death card is good. It symbolizes the ego, death, rebirth, and transformation."

She chuckled. Her eyes glowed as she stared at me.

I believed her. I leaned forward so that our faces were only inches apart. "Exactly where I am right now on my quest," I said.

The Bruja nodded her agreement, reshuffled the deck, and then picked a card for herself. She gave me a thoughtful look.

"Not forgetting your inheritance."

She gazed at the card, cocking her head to one side. All at once, the whole pack of cards tumbled to the couch as if in slow-motion.

As they fell, I regarded each with a critical eye. The magician card, the high priestess, the hermit, the card of fortune, the card of death, the card of the devil, the world, and judgement card.

Suddenly I didn't like the look on the Bruja's face. She gasped and looked stricken, watching each card land. The look in her eyes filled me with immense terror.

"What do the cards mean?"

She shook her head. I was beginning to feel very ill. The look in her eyes was the most frightening thing I'd ever seen. Then leaping to her feet, the Bruja grabbed my arm hard and dragged me inside.

Once inside the door, she bent forward, her voice struggling to remain calm. "Terrible danger is coming, Brian! You must prepare for the final battle to eliminate fear!"

*Final battle? What?? My quest hadn't even started!*

"When is it, and where?"

She hurried to my bed, produced my bag and started tossing my clothes inside, one after the other, her throat making soft whimpering sounds, whispering, "I need you to listen carefully."

"I'm listening."

"Remember, your survival will not depend on your physical strength but instead, the size of your heart."

I nodded, understanding what she meant.

"Forgiveness is important, Brian. People usually emerge from difficulties like yours either more compassionate and forgiving or blaming everyone and feeling like a victim…"

"I never did. I accepted responsibility for my life." I watched, as faster and faster she piled clothes in my bag.

"I know, Brian. And most importantly, you must forgive. That doesn't mean forget, but shed the anger and the disappointments and understand that people that hurt others, only hurt themselves. They are young souls with much to learn, and they will learn."

"I understand."

"People will seek to hurt you with words, trying to downplay your wisdom. They will call you a phoney and a liar."

"I've heard those accusations before."

She kept piling clothes in my bag, at desperate speed.

"Remember, it is hard for people to accept they might have wasted their lives, been scared to be with the one they love, or followed their true passion, or having their sinful lives exposed. It takes strength to accept those things. So, what comes out of their mouths is not about you—it's *their* pain, fears, and disappointment. Disconnect yourself from their words."

Suddenly I felt the old woman's fear race through me. "Like when someone says you're ugly, they feel ugly themselves?" I said. "Or they call you stupid, but feel dumb themselves? Or you're not good enough when they feel incapable, or you're wasting your time, they mean they wasted their time, or you're sick and need help, they're crying out for help themselves?"

The Bruja fell silent a moment. As she did, alternating waves of fear and horror raced through me.

"Good, Brian. Some will recognise that you have things to teach them and have the strength to admit it. They will join you eagerly to change their lives. Others with weak hearts will hate you for exposing them, and in their anger, they will try to hurt you with words and more. But stand firm in your wisdom and beliefs. The more opposition you face, the more it means that you are on the right path."

She finished packing my bag, tossed it into my hands, then eyeballed me calmly.

"The most important lesson to carry with you throughout your life, in everything you do and with everyone that you meet is..."

"...all about *love?*" I blurted out.

She shook her head. "The game of destiny is won by loving, rather than in being loved. Do you understand?"

I nodded. "I do, Miss Tiponi."

She grasped my hand, entwining her fingers in mine, emotion building. "It is always, only and ever about *love!* Love is your true North Star, Brian. But remember that you cannot control the course of love, for love, if she finds you deserving, will direct your journey and teach and comfort you in ways you can't imagine. Love is the most powerful force in the Universe, transcending time and space, and the closer you get to her warmth, the closer you are to the source of everything."

"My creator," I said.

Gently the Bruja nodded, tears streaming down her cheeks. She pulled me close, threw her arms around me, hugged me tight, wiping the tears from her eyes as she cleared her throat. I waited. Finally, I asked so quietly that my lips barely moved.

"What did the cards say?"

We looked at each other for a second. Her eyes grew worried.

"They are reaching out to you."

"Who? The Seven."

"They will make you an offer. You must accept it."

*Accept it?* Hearing those words put me in the grip of such fury that I almost couldn't speak. "No, *no!* Not all that money," I pleaded, only half meaning it because I was still reeling to be truthful about turning down half a billion dollars.

"I know how much that hurt," she said, her mind-reading antenna on. "Sorry, Brian. It's not money, it's…opportunity." She paused, and I could see the truth in her face. "An opportunity to get closer to them. It will help you find out what evil plan they have for humanity and how to defeat it, and them. And with that, your destiny."

"They'll contact me?"

The Bruja didn't reply. In her silence, the world seemed to revolve sickly before my eyes. "I wish there was more time, Brian…"

"Me too. It all seems so…overwhelming." Tears pooled in my eyes. "Thank you for all my gifts, and for saving me."

"Maybe one day, you'll save me."

"It would be my privilege."

"Speaking of gifts, Ahote has something for you."

She stepped back, eyes glowing. Hearing a grunt, I turned. Clearing tears from his eyes was old Ahote, his beat-up, and banged-to-hell Chevy looking surprisingly shiny and clean outside.

My own tears came rushing now. *We all understand what's at stake,* I realized. I strode up to him, shaking Ahote's gnarled hand. When we finished, I found the Chevy's keys clenched in my fist.

"What's going on?" I asked puzzled.

Ahote grunted, started jabbering away in his native tongue, leaving me even more confused. Finally, Miss Tiponi said, "It's his gift to you," and she nodded toward the Chevy.

I was stunned. My arms rashed out in goosebumps. "I can't take this! Please tell him I'm humbled, but he needs it more than me."

Ahote grunted something to the Bruja. She turned to me.

"He says it's a gas-guzzler and needs a fortune spent on repairs and won't last the journey anyway."

Laughing, I hugged Ahote close, then embraced Miss Tiponi again. She hoisted my hastily-packed bag in the air.

"But why? And why now?"

"You'll know," she said, forcing the bag into my hands. "And don't forget your money."

"You *knew* about that?" I said, stepping over to my bed, where I knelt, pried open a floorboard and grabbed a tin can packed with crumpled dollar bills.

But there was something wrong. There was a lot more money here than I had left.

"The Indians on the reservation collected it for you."

"But," I stammered, "They have so little…"

"They have *this,*" she said, tapping her temple, then added, "and you have a quest."

I juggled the tin can in my hands, for a moment also juggling the moral dilemma. At last, I sighed. "Please tell them I'm honoured to have met them and give them my deepest gratitude."

"They already know, Brian."

Reluctantly, I gripped the bag, thrust the can of money inside, as the Bruja shooed me hurriedly outside to the truck.

Climbing inside, I switched on the engine, listening to it purr. Out of the corner of my eye I noticed Ahote look away, in a surge of emotion. "Take care of my damn truck," he muttered, his hand waving. I nodded. At the last moment, I looked around at the cabin, Skull Mountain, the herb garden, her timber wolf, then took a glance at Miss Tiponi herself, realizing that perhaps I'd never see her or them again.

She smiled. All at once, a thought seemed to enter her mind. She ran ahead, skidded to a halt, stooped over the ground looking frantically, then hastily snatched up a rock, hurrying back to me.

She handed me the stone and clasped my hand around it tightly.

"Scientists call them meteorites. I call them…star-stones."

Clutching the stone, I nodded. "Where we came from," I answered, gripping her hand, nodding my appreciation for everything she'd done.

"It can protect you, like the runestone your Mother gave you."

I smiled, pleased she'd remembered that. She raised an eyebrow, waiting for me to say something. Sadly, I did. "Goodbye, Miss Tiponi…"

"…call me Tiponi…"

I sniffed back a tear. "…and thank you for everything. You're a saint…Tiponi."

She laughed. As we hugged, Flower raced up alongside the Curandera's timber wolf, who licked my hand.

I gazed back into the cabin. For the first time, I noticed a raggedy school tie hanging on the wall—on it, a cluster of seven shooting stars crossing the night sky. Next to it, a faded, dog-eared old photo of kids in school uniforms, all wearing the same shooting-stars tie.

My mind fumbled to understand. Seeing this, Tiponi handed me a scrap of paper. On it, she had scribbled an address in Florida.

"What's this?"

"That's the Grays' place."

"The Grays?"

"Go and see them, things will become clearer," she said, her bony fingers caressing my cheek, and with that, she headed back into the cabin.

I stood where I was for a moment, irresolute. With the wolves and deer watching, Flower and I jumped into the now cleaner, more pleasant-smelling old pick-up, which coughed and spluttered when it started. For the longest time, I paused, before putting the gear into drive.

Five minutes later, the truck was clattering its way down the sacred mountainside. As we bumped and thumped along, my eyes met Flower's. It occurred to me that I'd probably aged appreciably since the day our car plunged off the cliff. Now I felt powerful; physically, emotionally, and spiritually. A new man completely, so much wiser and stronger.

Flower read the newfound wisdom in my eyes. And with one last sad farewell wave at Ahote and Tiponi, I raced towards my future, knowing exactly where I was heading next.

* * *

WORLD ECONOMIC FORUM
NOVEMBER 7, 2018

MIND CONTROL USING SOUND WAVES?

Well, to get straight to the science, the principle of non-invasive neuromodulation is to focus ultrasound waves into a region in the brain so that they all gather in a small spot. Then hopefully, given the right set of parameters, this can change the activity of the neurons.

How dystopian could it get?

I can see the day coming where a scientist will be able to control what a person sees in their mind's eye by sending the right waves to the right place in their brain. I guess that most objections will be similar to those we hear today about subliminal messages in advertisements, only much more vehement.

THE SCIENTIST
JANUARY 19, 2009

SOUNDWAVES THAT TURN ON GENE EXPRESSION.

The team focused high-intensity ultrasound--sound waves above the audible range. Because the waves are focused on such a small area, researchers can target high levels of energy at precise locations in the body, said Moonen. The intense pulse heated a tiny patch of tissue in the body to between 42 and 44 degrees Celsius...

# PATH / DAY FIVE

## CORPORATE AND BETRAYALS

*When your time comes to die,*
*be not like those whose hearts are filled with fear of death,*
*so that when their time comes, they weep and pray for a little more time*
*to live their lives over again in a different way.*
*Sing your death song, and die like a hero going home.*

— *CHIEF TECUMSEH*

# THIRTY-FIVE

Tension wormed under my skin. I steered the clattering old pick-up truck down the bumpy, dusty, pothole-filled road, gripping the wheel tight between my trembling fists, then onto the main road, headed for the open highway, knowing I had a long journey ahead, 29 hours and almost 2,000 miles.

Most of the Chevy's dashboard instruments were cracked or broken, the gas tank registering FULL no matter how far I drove, the speedometer inoperative, frozen in time at 39 miles-per-hour. *Instinct. Follow your instinct.* Behind me, Skull Mountain grew smaller and smaller in the distance. I hoped the Chevy would make such a punishing journey and smiled at the thought of Ahote shining it up for me pumping it full of gas, and once again, was amazed. Amazed and grateful.

As we drove, Flower dug around under the seat, and discovered a big bag of her favourite dog-biscuits, a juicy bone and a big raw steak, all in a plastic bag on the floor. She gnawed the steak bone, closing her eyes to moan in ecstasy.

A warm feeling soaked through my gut. I felt so humbled and privileged to have met Tiponi, Ahote, and the Indians, who were all so benevolent and kind to me. I would never forget the wisdom and teachings of Tiponi, as long as I lived.

Which might not be as long as I'd hoped.

I flipped the visor down to ward off the blazing sun. I was heading along the I-20E to Florida to see the Grays, as instructed by the Curandera.

I closed my eyes briefly in relief, letting the balmy breeze race through my hair. I looked up to see a black flock of crows rising suddenly from pasture as we thundered by. The wind and sun on my face felt good. I resisted the temptation to speed faster, though we were passed again and again by motorcycles and cars doing 80, knowing a blowout on this stretch of empty road in this old truck would be the end of us.

After driving for a few hours, it was getting dark. I felt weary, and Flower would need walking, so I pulled into a deserted gas station.

Flower jumped out gratefully, shaking herself off and stretching. Together we wandered around the filling station, no signs of life, just a few flickering lights on the inside, tumbleweeds drifting lazily in the breeze.

I looked up at the magnificent, clear night sky and remembered Tiponi whispering to me, as if in a dream. "Brian, 99% of your body is comprised of atoms like the hydrogen in your deep blue Danish eyes. This came from the big bang when the universe was created. Other atoms in us like oxygen, carbon, and calcium in our bones and iron in our blood, came from the heart of exploding stars, billions of years ago. So, when native cultures claim that they come from the stars, don't laugh."

In the past, I had laughed. Here I was again, looking up at those stars, my eyes unexpectedly welling with tears. I wiped the tears away with the back of my hand and exhaled a deep breath, then looked around in the darkness for Flower.

"Flower? Where are you, girl?"

No reply. I closed my eyes for a moment, listening. Opening them, I stared off across the dirt road overgrown with dry grass. Concern giving way to suspicion, I spun around and ran light-footed back toward the truck. "Flower?" Something forced me to run faster. Breathing heavily, dust scudding into the air, I skidded to a stop before the truck—no Flower. *Shit!* Fortunately, there she was, rushing out of the back of the rickety building, where she'd done her business.

Overcome with relief, I knelt and hugged her, shaking her by the shoulders with a gentle scolding. Then we jumped back into the Chevy, too exhausted to keep driving, and in no time at all, I was dozing, snoring, fast asleep.

And straight into what felt like an out-of-body experience.

In the dream, I was floating outside Tiponi's cabin. As usual, the old woman sat on her beat-up couch smoking a cheroot—only this time, there was a strange smile on the Bruja's face. *That's odd,* I thought. *What does that smile mean?*

Crows begin gathering in the tall trees around the cabin. As I floated above, they ceased their babbling.

I lowered my gaze and looked back at the Bruja. Tiponi calmly stood and sauntered inside the cabin, with that odd smile still covering her face.

Seconds later, I saw why.

Out of the dense brush surrounding the cabin strode a well-dressed man wearing a long black coat and a hat, a massive Rottweiler by his side. In his left hand, the man carried a strange-looking composite gun.

*What are you all about? AND WHY THE HELL ARE YOU IN MY DREAMS NOW?* I wondered. Suddenly the door to the cabin was flung open, and Ahote stepped onto the porch, looking squarely at the man. In his hand, Ahote held a long axe with a gleaming spike end. Miss Tiponi's timber wolf sat growling by his side.

The wolf eyed the man, then let out an unsettling, low rumble from its throat, slowly baring its teeth while staring intensely with amber-coloured eyes from the strange man to his dog.

Meanwhile, Ahote fixed his eyes on the man, then nodded.

"I've been waiting for you, Azazel," he said calmly.

The man's eyes gleamed. "Ahote, my brother, the gatekeeper of the all-seeing Bruja! Finally, we meet again!" he said with a cold smile and a sarcastic tone in crisp, educated, accented English.

The dog and the man strode forward. The timber wolf growled, flashing bare teeth. Twenty metres from the cabin, the man stopped and the Rottweiler began growling at the timber wolf, sensing the imminent fight.

An uneasy sensation ripped through me. *What's going on here?*

"You've been busy, Azazel," I heard Ahote mutter.

*Azazel. So that's his name.*

The man named Azazel seemed to be expecting Ahote's reply. "All the killings ascribed to me over the years are just," he said softly. "Others, not."

Ahote narrowed his eyes. "What happened to you? You were once a glorious clever being, full of light."

"Still am, brother, just not when it comes to humans," the man said, leaning down to stroke the dog which gazed up at him adoringly.

"It was you who patched up the Malamute at the scene of the car accident."

The man just smiled. "Very good Ahote, very good."

I shuddered. *The car accident? Please tell me what's going on,* my brain thundered. *Why do I see this?*

A startled look crossed Ahote's face. "Why are you here?"

The man switched the strange-looking gun to his other hand. "For the boy."

"What do you want with him?"

"He is in the way."

"In the way of what?"

"I can't tell you."

Ahote laughed. "So, you're taking orders now, Azazel? Like an errand boy? I thought you refused to bow to any man."

The man leaned his face closer, glaring at Ahote. They exchanged puzzled glances. I looked down, feeling helpless, craning my neck wildly around to find the Bruja, looking for Tiponi.

"Well, he is not here; he left long ago."

The man peered at Ahote with eyes so black they were like caves. "In that case, I will need the Bruja to tell me where he went."

Ahote laughed, a deep and powerful belly-laugh. "That's never going to happen. She does not want anything to do with you anymore."

Azazel smiled. Down below I could see him pressing the tips of the fingers on his right hand against each other like he was counting something. Very faintly, I could hear the crows bawling in the tree.

Ahote frowned horribly, scratching his chin. A split second passed. Then the man whipped up his odd gun and began firing off shots at Ahote while running full speed towards him. Leaping to its feet, his Rottweiler sprinted ahead, growling.

The timber wolf leapt from the porch, flew high and landed on top of the Rottweiler, crunching down on its back. Snarls erupted from both animals. Teeth flashed. The timber wolf ripped into the dog and blood sprayed high.

Ahote ducked behind the thick timber pillars on the porch, avoiding most of the silent shots until one nicked his shoulder. He winced, clutching his shoulder where only a tiny pinprick hole showed. *Very little blood*, I realized. *Thank God!*

The man jammed the weapon back in his shoulder holster. He kept moving forward, running full tilt, the air filling with electricity with every step.

*Ahote!* My mind screamed. *Watch out!*

Ahote paused, coldly eyeing the man. Suddenly, the old Indian began moving like someone 40 years younger. He grabbed a thick wooden table, held it in front of him and ran towards Azazel, screaming.

He threw the table so hard that it knocked Azazel on his back, sending his Borsalino hat flying.

Azazel snarled, drew a carbon fibre knife from a holster, jumped back on his feet and quickly shrugged his jacket off. Suddenly, he threw a hard, low kick at Ahote trying to break his leg, but Ahote quickly shifted stance, wielding his gleaming axe.

Hair and blood flew through the air as the animals fought brutally, gradually tearing each other apart.

Azazel moved forward, slashing the black blade like a skilled knife fighter. His stance was tight, keeping his knife in a stabbing grip, readying himself for close-range knife fighting, the blade protruding from the bottom of his hand.

Both men weaved skillfully from side to side, masking their attacks. In a flash, Azazel rushed forward, putting his hand on Ahote's chest followed by lightning-quick swipes to his neck.

*Whip! Whip!*

With incredible instinct, Ahote lifted the axe and blocked the knife from slicing the aorta artery on his neck while in the same motion he smashed his right fist into Azazel's face, sending him sprawling to the ground.

Azazel showed no signs of letting up. Almost in amusement he bit his bloodied lip. With superhuman strength he then jumped back on his feet, a little blood dripping from his nose.

The Indian lifted the axe and swiped it towards the man's head, but he ducked under it and sliced Ahote's stomach in an insanely swift movement.

In Ahote's face I could see his agony. Even Azazel seemed startled by its effect. The Indian moaned in pain and stumbled backwards, clutching his stomach, blood flowing through his fingers. He pointed the bloody hand toward Azazel.

*No, Ahote! No!*

Azazel licked his lips, leapt forward and with a powerful sidekick, hit Ahote so hard that he stumbled backwards, then ran towards him, his cruel blade pointing downwards, ready to make the final killing blow.

*NO, AHOTE!!! NO!!!*

Ahote rolled to his right and swung the axe, the spike lodged in the assassin's leg, and he gasped in pain and limped backwards.

The timber wolf was now on top of the Rottweiler which lay severely bleeding on the ground. It could have killed the dog, but somehow decided to let it live.

Meanwhile, Azazel yanked the axe from his leg, blood splashing to the ground, and tossed it away.

Ahote got back on his feet, still gripping his stomach, beginning to feel dizzy, his face in a feverish sweat. He staggered away to the porch with the timber wolf protecting his back, his skin pale, breathing laboured, gripping his chest as his heart pounded.

"It's not from the blood loss," Azazel shouted, taunting, patting his shoulder holster. "It's the spinning 40 calibre ice bullet laced with cyanide. Once the ice melts, there will be no trace of it. And you will die from a heart attack."

For an eternity the two men stared at each other. Shakily, Ahote nodded, gulped painfully, almost fell through the door to the cabin, fear etched on his face.

The sudden awareness of this thrilled Azazel. Nonchalantly he chuckled, started to follow, a peculiar glow in his eyes, but seeing the badly-bleeding Rottweiler by his side, he stopped to check its wounds.

His eyes straying back to Ahote, he grimly picked up the dog, took a final look and then retreated into the dark woods.

Overhead I hovered, quietly watching. A scream arose from inside the cabin. Slamming through the front door raced the Curandera, running blindly to Ahote.

Something about the forest caught her attention. For the briefest moment, her glance moved there. Her eyes fixed on Azazel's blood-spattered face, staring out of the treeline. In what seemed like minutes, they looked at each other.

Then reality set back in.

She dragged Ahote into the house, helped him onto the bed, and stuffed his mouth with riboflavin to immediately mitigate the toxic effects of the cyanide.

Ahote coughed, losing a lot of blood, his skin almost white. He choked, gasped, and clutched his chest, his eyes bulging. Suddenly his heart seemed to stop, and he lay back, limp.

Tiponi gasped and pressed both her hands into Ahote's chest, trying to restart his heart.

*C'mon, Tiponi, c'mon!!!* My mind pleaded.

At the top of her lungs with her eyes turning black and dark, she cried out into the night in the most frightening voice, "Azazel, what have you done?"

At that moment, a loud howl from the timber wolf startled me awake.

Sweating, I looked around to see where I was. *The gas station. Thank God.* Beside me in the truck, Flower was howling as well.

We looked at each other with uncertainty. In that instant, I knew the dream I'd experienced was a vision. It was real. I knew that Ahote had risked his life to save the Curandera and me. My heart was full of grief and sadness that I wasn't there to help him. After all, this assassin, Azazel was looking for me.

Flower shrieked a mournful howl. Deep inside, I knew there was a reason why Miss Tiponi had told me to leave, to find the Grays and continue my quest to discover and destroy The Seven.

"Goodbye, Ahote," I said, and sadly plunged the key in his old truck's ignition. Then reluctantly, I put the vehicle in gear, hit the gas, and chugged back onto the road.

* * *

# Thirty-Six

I decided we should find somewhere cheap to sleep for the night. I was feeling restless, still shaken and concerned about what I'd seen in my dream. But I couldn't go back, and I had no way of contacting Miss Tiponi to hear if Ahote made it, though in my heart I feared the worst.

Traffic was light. Mile after mile we drove, sometimes the only car on the road. Eventually, I saw the lights of a little motel twinkling just outside Fort Worth, Texas, with several vehicles parked. *That'll do,* I thought.

The motel boasted thirty-two rooms. Luckily, they had a few within my modest budget and were dog-friendly, so exhausted, Flower, and I camped in the tiny, dingy room which smelt of something disgusting and nasty.

As I lay my head down, my eyes examining the grimy ceiling, I wondered if I'd have any more dreams about the Curandera and Ahote. Nothing came.

Frightening thoughts kept me awake most of the night. In the early hours of the night, after finally dropping off to sleep, I was rudely awakened by a fire alarm screaming somewhere in the motel. Then I heard running feet and shouting.

My mouth dried up, my heart hammering. *Azazel. It has to be.*

I sat up. The alarm continued shrieking. Hastily I packed my things and slipped out the back door with Flower. We sneaked into the Chevy, chugged out of the parking lot, and disappeared into the night.

Lulled by the dark stars whipping past my windshield, I fell into a comfortable doze, awakening each time my wheels left the highway pavement. My eyes kept darting to the rear-view mirror, but there were no vehicles behind me, and I breathed a huge sigh of relief.

I drove. And drove. Each mile passed faster than the last. Reluctantly, I turned my eyes away from the stars, realizing that my true destiny still lay ahead of me.

I'd be travelling from Northeast Texas into Southeast America, driving through the Deep South into Florida, quite a journey.

Flower yawned, snoring peacefully beside me. I stared into space, wondering if Ahote was alright, if the Curandera's magic was strong enough to save his life.

My mind went back to our destination: the Grays. The Gulf of Mexico glinted in the distance, the sight of the water, giving me even more strength. I tore past signs for Pensacola, Tallahassee and Lake City then zipped past the turn-off for Orlando.

I was on the last leg of the journey now, feeling excited yet nervous at the same time about meeting the Grays.

As I got closer to Coconut Grove in Miami, I wondered what I would find. Why had the Curandera insisted I should see these people? What was the significance of this place, and how could they help in my quest?

Having slept so little the night before, my mind was in a fog. I was sure in time I would understand how the pieces of the puzzle came together, but right now, I needed sleep. And some answers. I couldn't keep running from Azazel, and life.

It was in the middle of the night when I pulled up to towering iron gates; an iron security fence surrounding a huge and impressive mansion, like some plantation owner's grand estate.

Ahead on my left, I saw an intercom. I cranked open the window, leaned out of the car and just as I was about to press the button, the massive gates slid open.

*That's weird.* Looking up, I could see surveillance cameras aimed at me and wondered if the Curandera had called them in advance of my arrival.

I nosed the truck slowly up the driveway, tires crunching, passing lush and well-tended maze gardens on either side of me towards a magnificent three-story villa, beautifully illuminated in the darkness.

It looked like an early 20th century home in the style of Italian Renaissance, with a lush woodland landscape and a lot of low stone outbuildings.

I parked and climbed out. "Stay, Flower." Flower groaned and sulked at being left behind. I sighed, nodded my head, and she leapt out. As we crept along, the only sound chirping crickets, the air hot and humid, the scent of flowers wafting in the air, making me a little queasy.

Shakily we walked along. As we strolled toward the mighty, ornately carved entrance doors, they swished open with a quiet hum, and there stood a butler in the sweeping hallway, the place grand and dimly lit.

He nodded without smiling. "Welcome, sir. Your room is prepared. Follow me please," and together the three of us climbed up a broad, carpeted staircase with a crest that seemed familiar—seven shooting stars crossing the sky—on both bannisters, and portraits of young children hanging on wood-panelled walls.

*Stars and children? Hmmm.* The butler watched me gaze hypnotized upon them, as if I were a precocious child. He led me along a long, shiny wood-paneled corridor, more portraits of children hanging, stopped at an elegant mahogany door, opened it and gestured for me to enter.

Stepping inside, my mind reeled. It was a stunning room with masculine brown leather furniture, dominated by a traditional wooden bed, red-painted walls, and a great view past the heavy brocade curtains along the sweeping driveway.

"Mr. and Mrs. Gray look forward to welcoming you in the morning," replied the butler, and with another nod, backed away and closed the door.

*Well now,* I thought. I peered around, eyes taking in the in-suite bathroom. Shutting the drapes, I piled the pillows atop one another. Suddenly I felt exhausted and collapsed on the bed, Flower groaning into bed beside me.

Within minutes, both of us were sound asleep. I dreamed of a timeless world, an endless hell, from which there was no escape.

* * *

# THIRTY-SEVEN

Next morning, I woke early with Flower's warn tongue licking my hand, a perky smile on her lips, eyes glittering. As she ran off out the door, I heard the giggle of a child, then running feet.

I blinked like someone awakening from a week's slumber. Feeling refreshed, I leapt from the bed, hurried across the room and peered out the door to see a little black girl in a neat school uniform running playfully with Flower by her side, giggling and disappearing down the stairs.

Smiling, I dressed and shaved quickly, startled by a knock on the door. "Hello?" I called out.

"Your breakfast, sir," the voice said, and I opened the door to see the butler with a tray and plate covered by a silver bowl, with tea, coffee, and water.

"Thanks, looks great," I said, and he marched to the table by the window, placed it down, turned to nod at me then left quietly.

I was ravenous and devoured the meal, enjoying the scrambled eggs with salmon on toasted muffins. In spite of my best efforts I couldn't stop eating.

Finishing, I left the room, strolled along the corridor then down the broad staircase, suddenly stopping dead in my tracks.

*I didn't notice that last night,* I thought. *Probably too overcome with exhaustion.*

Hung on the wall, I saw portraits of the children with their names and dates underneath. I leaned forward, fixing my eyes on the portraits.

And there they were, hung on the wall beside the children. Portraits of Tiponi, Gurung, Ahote, the Fortune Teller and Ronaldo.

*What the hell is going on here?* I asked myself, shaking my head. *Gurung...Ahote...the fortune teller.* Everything thought that came to me sounded crazy.

From outside, I heard Flower's distinctive cry. I rushed out, heart thumping.

Racing through the front doors, I nearly fell on my face. In the courtyard, I saw Flower and a bunch of children in school uniform, playing, tossing a ball between them which Flower leapt into the air to catch in her jaws, clearly enjoying herself.

I sighed, relieved. It was a beautiful, crisp, and sunny morning, and the estate looked incredible in the daylight.

Enjoying the warm sun, my anxiety vanished. At that moment, I noticed an elderly couple walking towards me, arm-in-arm, smiling and waving. Reaching me, the woman patted Flower. The man held out his hand. "Brian, I'm Harrison, and this is Madelyn," he announced and shook my hand firmly.

"Welcome to our little place," Madelyn said, holding her hand out to me and shaking mine firmly.

"Great to meet you both," I said, beaming a big smile.

I stepped back, appraising them. Madelyn was a beautiful, angelic, petite, charming and elegant woman with a commanding presence, a Southern belle, which I could hear from her accent. She was in her 90s but spritely, with long, flowing ash-white hair, a matching dress and weighed no more than 50kg. Her eyes drilled into mine with emotional intelligence and a commanding presence.

From her manners, I guessed she had been educated at a top boarding school. But I also sensed steel will.

Harrison was of similar age, tall and handsome, dressed in a smart dark suit with an open-collared white shirt. He was still agile and athletic with thick white hair which was swept back, and bright, penetrating eyes. He reminded me of the tough, grizzled, no-nonsense hard-ass Clint Eastwood in *Dirty Harry*.

"*Little* place?" I smiled, looking around us and smiling. "I'd hardly call it little."

Seems Madelyn had anticipated this. "Do your thing, darling," she said to Harrison, and his eyes twinkled as he spoke.

"Thank you, dear. The land originally consisted of 180 acres of shoreline mangrove swamps and dense inland tropical forests, Brian. The house was built with an open-air courtyard and sweeping gardens overlooking Biscayne Bay. The landscape and architecture were influenced by the Italian Renaissance, and the interior was designed in the Mediterranean style with Baroque elements."

They turned and watched as Flower suddenly leapt in the air and caught the ball in her jaws and scrambled away, the giggling children following.

"You've got a lot of great-grandchildren," I noted.

"He's onto us, Madelyn," Harrison sniggered.

"The portraits on the walls," I continued.

"Aren't they sweet?" Madelyn said, clasping her bony hands with glee.

"And you recognized some," Harrison said.

"Gurung, Tiponi, Ahote, the Fortune Teller, and Ronaldo."

"The Fortune Teller, you mean Gertrud," Madelyn smiled.

"They were all educated here," Madelyn continued, and I frowned as the children ran between us trying to catch Flower.

"What is this place?" I asked.

"This place is…very special, Brian," Madelyn continued.

The dazzling sunlight lit up her face. A bell rang, and the children stopped playing with Flower and hurried into a side entrance to the magnificent building.

Flower crept up to me, looked me in the eye, and I nodded, letting her run after the children into the building, having a great time with the kids.

"Let's go inside, Brian," Harrison said.

With mild annoyance I followed. He led the way, into the foyer, then he headed towards two huge wooden doors which he opened and in we went.

It was an impressive library, cavernous, high-ceilinged and wood-panelled with floor-to-ceiling bookshelves, books behind glass, thermostats keeping them at a particular temperature, some sitting under glass frames, pages yellowed and faded, pale blue light shining on each of them from chrome lamps.

I realized this was a book collector's Aladdin's Cave and stopped to gaze at a book, Madelyn by my side, looking at the tome with reverence.

"I'm a collector of rare books. They're all first edition, Brian," she said.

"All that man knows, is in books," I said, and she beamed at me appreciatively.

"This is *Margites,* by Homer," she continued, then pointed to other books, carefully installed in temperature-controlled viewing boxes.

"Shakespeare's *Cardenio*, Jane Austen's *Sanditon*, Robert Louis Stevenson's *The Strange Case of Dr Jekyll and Mr. Hyde* first draft…"

"Wait, these books aren't just rare; they were lost to history!"

Madelyn smiled at Harrison, who nodded knowingly, and they both exchanged a look.

"Correct, Brian. We have books from all the magnificent libraries of the ancient world that no longer exist; The Library of Ashurbanipal...The Imperial Library of Constantinople...The House of Wisdom in Baghdad…The Library of Pergamum...The Library of Alexandria...The Villa of the Papyri...The Library of Celsus…and The Libraries of Trajan's Forum…"

"This is…priceless," I said, gaping around in awe.

"We gift the children the knowledge contained in these books. And, we develop the abilities they have that already come naturally to them. Children today spend too much time on their computers and gadgets, and not enough time communicating with each other and learning to read and speak. If it continues this way, 500-1000 years from now humans will, through evolution, have huge thumbs used for texting and no longer a tongue, since it will have been ages since anyone talked to each other."

Suddenly, there was a commotion and three children appeared, two boys attacking a girl with flying kicks and spinning heel kicks. Then seeing we were watching them they all broke and ran.

"…oh, we teach them MMA, mixed martial arts too," Harrison smiled.

I chuckled. One of the girls—the young black kid who was playing with Flower earlier—suddenly stopped dead, then slowly turned as I did the same thing. We stared at each other, sharing a moment of knowing, then her friends dragged her away.

"Who is this girl?" I inquired.

"It's our beloved Destiny," Madelyn said. "She is the first of her class and a huge animal lover. Unlike the other kids who were discovered, Destiny just showed up at our gate one day with no place else to go."

"Like she was sent from heaven," Harrison added.

I grunted.

Madelyn continued, "They're star children, Brian. Destiny's one of them. They go into the world to help raise the level of humanity without fear."

I blinked, puzzled. "Star children?" I asked.

"Children who enter the world with wisdom beyond their years. They're unique, with special perceptive abilities and compassion for everything in the world, especially animals, plants, and Mother Nature. They bring magic, love, peace, and consciousness to humanity," Madelyn replied.

"They are all orphans, but very special. Almost all of them have some psychic gifts they will use to bring the world to a higher, more conscious dimension." Harrison added.

"Ronaldo scours the world identifying children with qualities like them and…you."

The blood drained from my face. "Really? Ronaldo? The Vatican's involved?"

"Ronaldo, his father, and grandfather before him have helped us since 1597 with our quest. His official role is to investigate miracles. His unofficial role is to be the Protector of the Order of The Seven Stars," Madelyn added.

"It's incredible. But why am *I* here?"

I clenched my jaw and held my breath, waiting for her reply. "Because of your special quest, Brian." Madelyn winked.

"The children will grow to become soldiers in the great battle for good," Harrison said.

Madelyn nodded. I frowned in confusion, and Harrison took me by the shoulder.

"They will help you in one extraordinary way."

Suddenly I felt the weight of his words. "What's that?"

They said nothing, sensing my anxiety. Then Madelyn took me gently by the hands. "They will help you battle The Seven."

* * *

# THIRTY-EIGHT

It took me a while to fully absorb what the Grays had told me. "But, they're just little kids."

"Like Gurung, Tiponi, Ahote, Gertrud and Ronaldo were. And you," Madelyn said with a smile.

Harrison touched my shoulder. All of a sudden, I felt my chest clench up. The Grays left me alone to gaze in wonder at the rare books, and I used the library computer to check messages. I was amazed to receive an email for an interview for a top job at one of the huge conglomerates, EYE-CORP, based out of New Jersey.

The only problem was, I had never applied for it.

I groaned. It could only be The Seven.

I squinted at the name. *EYE-CORP.* The Curandera was right. She said The Seven would reach out to me, and here it was.

Reading the email, I shuddered. Tiponi said I had to accept their offer, no matter where it might take me.

Of course, I couldn't call her to ask if it was The Seven, but I couldn't see how it could be anyone else.

*They weren't even really trying to disguise themselves.* This made me truly uneasy. Suddenly, as I was staring into the computer screen, the big mahogany doors to the library opened with a squeaking noise made by the friction of the old brass hinges.

I turned around to be confronted by a man wearing a black Cassock, long-sleeved, with his head covered in a hood. In his right hand he carried a briefcase, and as he approached me in rapid steps, he kept his gaze down.

Instantly I leapt up from my chair readying myself for anything, even combat.

Faster and faster the man approached. Two metres from me, he stopped, put down the briefcase and with both hands removed his large black hood.

"Brian?" he called out. His tone indicated we knew each other. "Brian, I am so glad to see that you made it this far in your journey, though I never doubted that you would."

I squinted, staring the man down. The voice was so familiar. *Are you kidding me?* "Ronaldo!" I suddenly shouted; my voice filled with joy, "What are you doing here?"

"I came first to update Mr. and Mrs. Gray on the killing of Bishop Cruzeria. All the evidence I've collected for the Vatican points in the direction that he didn't die of natural causes, but that instead, it was a cold-blooded assassination."

"Azazel?" I said.

Ronaldo stared as if confused that I knew that name. "Yes, unfortunately, the evidence points in his direction. Bishop Cruzeria died of acute cyanide poisoning."

I lowered my head. "I am so sorry to hear that, Ronaldo. The Bishop was so kind to me, and without him, I would not have found the Bruja."

"We all are, Brian. It is a great loss to the church, our order, and the greater cause." Pausing, he gazed around the room. "Excuse me; I need to return something."

He went over to an empty glass monitor in the middle of the library. One of those you see in the movies with impenetrable glass, a thousand alarm systems, and when someone sets off the alarm, the monitor disappears underground to a safe vault.

Ronaldo put his hand on a fingerprint scanner and then looked into an iris scanner for final access. A green light flashed, and the monitor opened. Flipping open his briefcase, Ronaldo took out a massively thick old leather-bound book and placed it inside. He pressed the bottom, and the door closed, and some sort of gas was pumped into the chamber.

"Humidity control," he said as he turned his attention to me again.

"What is this book?"

"It contains the closest kept secret of the Order of the Seven Stars."

"And what would that be?"

He hesitated for a second and briefly looked around the room to see if we were still alone. "It contains all the names, past, present and future, of the Order going back more than a thousand years. Everyone who as ever been, and ever will be, recruited for the army against The Seven and its henchmen."

"How far into the future, does it go?"

"Next year is the final year."

"But that's soon," I said.

"Yes. The final battle has begun."

All at once I felt the boil of sour acid in my stomach. Before I could open my mouth to ask another question, he looked at his watch. "Sorry, Brian, it was nice meeting you again, but the break is over, and I have to get back to teach the class. MMA."

"I never figured you for a warrior-monk, Ronaldo," I said in surprise and smiled.

"Brian, your eyes can deceive you, don't trust them," he said with a grin.

With that, he shook my hand and left.

My muscles frozen, I drew in a heavy lungful of breath. *The final battle. Great.* My mind spinning, I went back to my room. I took a long shower, then finally shaved off my long beard, and cut my hair short, making not too bad a job of it, or so I thought, then I went downstairs to see the Grays.

They were on the porch enjoying the morning sun at a big table. I pulled out a chair to join them.

For the longest time, I said nothing, my thoughts possessed by a funneling darkness. The butler approached with a tray of cold drinks, and I took a small bottle of Evian and a glass with ice and poured it.

"I just met Ronaldo, and he told me about the book," I said.

"Yes, he told us. We're very grateful that he still returns to help teach and bring recruits to us."

"More importantly, I'm *worried,* Brian," Madelyn continued.

"Worried?"

"If we'll ever see you again..." and before I could answer, she said, "alive."

I choked on my drink and gaped at them in shock. *Not see me alive?*

"Of course we will, honey butterfly," Harrison continued.

Madelyn's watery eyes told me she wasn't so sure. "Azazel has begun hunting again," she said and looked away into the distance fearfully.

Harrison learned forward, looking at his wife in concern. He turned his face back to me, and I solemnly replied, "I met him in Paris and fought him in Monte Carlo and Copenhagen."

Harrison said, "We know. And you might want to know that Ronaldo rescued him from a terrible foster father. He only spoke to birds and animals, never humans. We educated him, but his heart was black."

"Tiponi managed to reach him, and they had a brief affair, but he had no emotional skills and was cruel to her and other children, so finally, we were forced to kick him out, to ensure the safety of the other children," Madelyn added.

"For a while, it looked like Tiponi was following in his footsteps. One day, she would do the cruelest things, yet the next day, she would heal a bird with a broken wing or mentor one of the younger children. Nothing was ever grey with her. She was either very black or beautifully white."

"But we never trained him in the dark arts of poisons, bombs, and arson. He suddenly disappeared off the face of the earth. For years, no one heard anything from him. Rumour had it that he had joined the French Foreign Legion. Then one day we got word that he had been kicked out for being too brutal and enjoying killing too much. In the Legion, they don't hand out dishonourable discharge; instead, all his civilian possessions were neatly placed on the dusty road outside his base with the name we gave him when we adopted him, Azazel, and he was ordered to return his French passport. From there we lost track of him again," Harrison added, giving me a concerned look.

I steadied myself in my chair, anxious thoughts eating away at me. "What do I need to know about him?"

Harrison narrowed his eyes, lowering his brow. "That he's relentless, cruel, dangerous and will never give up."

"Can he be defeated? What's his kryptonite" I asked, suddenly more frightened, realizing that if he was kicked out of the French Foreign Legion for being too brutal, then something was seriously wrong with him.

"Gurung trained you well. I am certain you will be able to defend yourself," Harrison said, looking at me reassuringly.

"Harrison, I don't want to defend myself. I need to *defeat him*."

Madelyn turned to her husband. "Sweetheart, Azazel is a whole different beast. He is a lethal hired assassin, though we don't know his pay-master yet."

"It has to be The Seven. What else d'you know about them?"

"As you know, they're highly secretive and only interested in power and money. And they've been around as long as us," Harrison said.

"We think Azazel works for one of them, but we don't know who, or why."

Madelyn shrugged, looked at me and whispered, "Brian, you are a sweet young man, and I pray you will be a match for him. But just in case…"

She reached into her pocket and produced a card the size of a regular playing card and handed it to me.

My hand started shaking, and my heartbeat feverish as I stared down at it in disbelief. *The image on the card…where have I seen this before?* It was the winged figure of a woman wearing a faceless mask…the woman from my dreams in the desert. She was holding a sword on a chariot pulled by two giant sphinxes.

I flipped it to the other side. There a phone number was printed. I gaped from Madelyn to Harrison, terrified.

"It's the woman from my dreams! How is this possible? Why did you give me this card and what is the number for?"

Madelyn looked concerned at Harrison and back at me.

"The prophecy has begun, it is the final hour," she said with a grave expression on her face.

The solemn look in her eyes was disquieting. She leaned closer, gripping my hand, then continued. "There are no coincidences, Brian. This card was destined to fall into your hand one day. It is the most powerful card and number in the Universe," Madelyn said. "The woman on the card and from your dream is your nemesis. The Goddess of war, of sex, lust, beauty, sorcery, and death. In your Viking culture, she would be depicted as Freya."

"One day you will have to face her or one of her loyal warriors to take down The Seven, and when that day comes," she murmured and turned the card over to show the phone number, "then you may need to call this number in order to live."

"It is a number more powerful than calling any army or elite police force," Harrison added. "If you're ever in any trouble in any place in the world, call that number, day or night. No matter the circumstances, no matter who's holding you, we will get you out."

Madelyn squeezed my hand tighter. "Only seven cards were ever printed with this number. You're holding the $7^{th}$ and the last card, the fate of humanity in your hand. However, beware; things are not as they appear."

I shivered. The way they said it gave me goose bumps. It was like having a number to my army of heavenly shadow warriors, materializing out of thin air to rush to my rescue.

Now I finally understood why the Curandera had sent me to meet the Grays. Without their insight and help, I would never be able to defeat Azazel and The Seven.

My brain raced, trying to figure out who the woman could be. Suddenly a crazy thought came to my mind…*Tiponi, the Bruja and the Curandera.*

Could she have been playing me and everyone? Now that I knew that she was once in love with Azazel, it could all make perfect sense. Then again, why then did she train me and save Ahote? I tried to dismiss the thought, but it continued to rattle inside my mind. I knew that I could not afford to trust anyone. Especially not her.

"I hope I will never have to use this," I said.

"If you don't use it, Brian, it means one of two things. One: you've decided to join the darkness. Two: you haven't tried hard enough to defeat them," Harrison added sternly.

"Don't disappoint us, son," Madelyn said in the same tone of voice.

"I won't. I will fight them until my last breath."

Suddenly the immensity and weight of my responsibility swept over me like a heavy blanket. I finally understood that I would have to be willing to give up my own life in the interest of saving others.

It surprised me, but a feeling of calmness suddenly descended. I felt my part in history was predetermined, and should I have to lay down my life to help the good seven and make the world a better place, then I would not hesitate.

"They'll keep trying, Brian, looking for a way into your head until you say yes," Madelyn sniffled, tears welling.

"I don't intend to say yes to them."

"We know, Brian."

Madelyn rose from her chair and hugged me tearfully, and Harrison joined in, embracing us both in his long arms.

"Don't forget, use the number if you need to."

"I will if I have to."

*But I hope I don't have to,* my mind screamed. The Grays nodded somberly. I trudged outside, full of trepidation and sadness at leaving these lovely people.

I quickly checked Ahote's trusty old Chevy, again praying that it would manage another long drive, this one almost 18 hours and nearly 1,300 miles. When I was satisfied, I called for Flower, and she hopped onto the passenger seat.

My eyes flicked to the Grays. Madelyn, Harrison, and I stood close together, Madelyn's lips trembling. I felt like giving them one last hug, so I snatched them both up together and said, "Thank you."

As I walked to the car, my heart began to thump. After the car door was closed, Harrison came over and knocked on the window. I rolled it down.

"Brian," he whispered, "Azazel's kryptonite? It's animals. Keep Flower close to you, and you will stand a better chance of him not carrying out a sneak attack on you. He is not going to risk hurting Flower to get to you."

With that, Harrison took a few steps back and put his arm around Madelyn. *Whatever happens to these two people,* I thought, *let it be good.*

We said our farewells sadly, and with one last, long look at the star children, I drove off, the couple and their special children waving at us warmly.

Beyond the gates, out on the main road, a black car followed, keeping its distance.

I stared. *Azazel. Damn.* I gripped the wheel, driving faster.

* * *

Back in the courtyard. Brian's car has disappeared. Madelyn and Harrison look at each other, fighting distress, and hurry back into the house.

Inside their living-room, Harrison picks up a phone and speed-dials, listening and pacing anxiously, until a man answers.

"It's me. He just left," Harrison says, then he glances at Madelyn, a worried look on his craggy face. "Azazel is on his tail. On top of that, he's young, ambitious and…it's a lot of temptation."

Harrison listens as the man speaks.

"We gave him the seventh card and number. It's all we can do for now, Gurung."

Harrison finishes the call and hugs Madelyn.

She looks at him grimly, then with her face lined with worry says, "So, we wait."

* * *

# Thirty-Nine

A fog covered the highway after I had been on the road for an hour. Flower and I jolted nervously along. I drove onto US1, followed by the I-95N and then headed toward the Florida Turnpike.

The scenery overlooking the Atlantic Ocean was incredible, and for a few minutes, I wondered if I would ever see the Grays again.

I slipped further down into my seat, overcome with weariness. I was a nervous wreck thinking about the assassin and stroked Flower for reassurance.

"This Azazel doesn't scare us, girl, does he?"

Flower wagged her tail, and I smiled, wishing I was as confident. Overhead, the sky rumbled, rain ready to drench us. As I steered north, I felt my sanity sinking.

Troubled, I placed the palm of my hand against my shirt pocket, feeling the card the Grays gave me. Doubt welled up in my throat.

*I have to trust in what Gurung taught me. I have a feeling I'm about to learn what fear—real fear—is all about,* I thought, sweating nervously.

The I-95N road led past Palm Beach, the sun shining on the Atlantic Ocean, often nearly blinding me, but it was breathtakingly beautiful. The road was long and exhausting, but finally I made it to New Jersey. I parked the beat-up old Chevy among some high-end sports cars, climbed out wearily and looked at the impressive entrance to the expensive glass, chrome and concrete office with a large illuminated sign, EYE-CORP.

Above me, a high-rise tower loomed, some lights still on, some people either in very early or still working at the end of their day.

My interview wasn't until 11 AM. I needed to freshen up, so I looked for a little hotel nearby on my phone and drove there.

I got a single room, showered, shaved, dressed in my nice suit, decided against a tie, drank some horrible coffee, and checked the time then left, locking Flower in the bedroom.

I was feeling more and more nervous, partly because Google had barely any information on EYE-CORP so I didn't know what to expect, and also because of the strange circumstances; I had no recollection whatsoever of applying for this job as Global Head of Strategic Partnerships.

I parked far from their glitzy HQ so no one could see my vehicle, apologized silently to Ahote, then strolled to the block.

Stealing into the building, worry poured through my awareness. It was a beautiful morning, but my stomach churned because inside here, my gut feeling told me there were probably people working for The Seven.

* * *

Inside EYE-CORP, the reception area was minimalist, all grey and white. A fat and balding security guard glanced at me sideways. A cold chill wormed its way down my spine.

As soon as I entered, the receptionist looked up, beamed a toothpaste-commercial smile and said flirtatiously, "Mr. Frederiksen, welcome to EYE-CORP! Mr. Holt will be with you in seven minutes."

She gestured for me to sit on one of the sleek grey Roche Bobois leather couches and I smiled back. How did she know my name? And the coincidence of the exact time until 11 AM, seven minutes?

I always paid close attention to the numbers. In my life, they seemed to suddenly appear in specific sequences consistently around certain events on digital clocks and everywhere around me. To the best of my knowledge, either to encourage me or to warn me. Eleven was my birthday. Seven was the month of my birth. I felt I was on the right path.

At precisely 11 AM, a man who looked like a stylish, smooth operator advertising executive appeared from the elevator carrying an iPad. Seeing my face, he strolled up to me, beaming a smile as he offered his hand.

I smiled back and shook his hand—a warm, hard grip—so I gripped equally hard.

"Brian, what a pleasure to meet you! I've heard only good things about you," he smiled again and gestured to the elevator.

*Who did he hear things about me from?* I wondered.

The entire ride in the elevator his pink fingers plucked at messages on his phone. The lift opened at the top floor, and he escorted me toward a lush roof garden where two doors swished open, and we stepped onto the path.

As we walked, he looked over the edge where a chrome rail topped glass railings overlooking the city, many parts flooded by Hurricane Sandy which had hit just a few days before.

"Look at this devastation, Brian. Two million homes lost power, 346,000 damaged or destroyed, 37 people killed and…"

I nodded. At this height, we had a fantastic view of the area, but the destruction was evident everywhere. Trees uprooted, cars upside down, power lines hanging, electrical fires crackling, emergency services working, sirens blaring.

"…an economic loss of $30 billion."

I was surprised that he appeared more of a caring human than the usual corporate clones until he spoke again.

"Our group made more than that last financial year."

"And what exactly is your group? There's very little online."

He flashed me a calm, untroubled smile. "We like zero profile, Brian, and pay a lot of money for reputation management."

He gestured for me to go to the table and we sat, enjoying the pleasant sun.

Minutes passed. To my surprise, we talked very little about the job, or his company, or the kind of person they were looking for. After about 15 minutes, shooting the breeze on sports, cars, and fashion, he leaned forward and said, "Let me get straight to it, Brian," he growled, charming but wasting no time.

"I want you to head EYE-CORP's drive to create the biggest Artificial Intelligence healthcare partnerships in the world. You'll use AI to analyse massive amounts of data and find cures to help the human race."

My face lit up at the suggestion of helping others. There was a pause, and I kept my reply polite. "A lofty ambition. I'm tempted."

"You'll use predictive analytics to decide if someone will be warned in time and saved from an asthma attack, a cardiovascular or a diabetic event, whatever. Thousands of lives will be saved with your help and over time, many more," he continued.

My eyes widened. I gaped at him while he handed me his laptop. On the screen were the terms of my employment. Once again, my eyes grew wide at all the zeroes in the salary.

"We need to be world-beaters. That's where you come in".

"World-beaters I can do. But at what?"

He hesitated. "Brian, I'm kinda new here, like you. I want you to write the job brief yourself."

*Write the job myself? You're kidding.* He smiled and held out his hand, and before I knew it, I had a new job, a fancy job title, and a ridiculously high salary.

It was only when I was walking back to my car that I reviewed my situation.

*How had my name arrived here?* I asked myself morosely. I recalled I never applied for the job. We never discussed the details of the job brief, the CEO offered me an insane package and most important of all…

*I was now 100% certain these people worked for The Seven.*

Their fingerprints were all over it. From the minute I stepped into the glass and chrome lion's den I felt…*temptation.* It reminded me of the saying that the devil always comes disguised as everything we wish for.

Without a shadow of a doubt, I knew what forces were at work here. Still, my destiny and the next phase of my quest were here. Somewhere.

* * *

# FORTY

The office is spectacular, a cavernous place with glass picture windows in Midtown East, New York City.

The interior is fabulous; an interior designer's dream with grey dove walls, a dark grey long-haired pile rug, red pendant lights hanging from a tall ceiling and a square, glossy red desk with nothing on it.

And behind it, overlooking the magnificent view, sits the black-haired man, again in shadow.

A broad-shouldered man in his 60s with a grey suit and salt-and-pepper hair slouches at a giant shiny glass and chrome table, using his cell phone. As he speaks he keeps looking back over his shoulder at the other man.

"Of course, he accepted. He's young, ambitious and greedy, like everyone."

He glances at the black-haired man who sits without moving, just a subtle nod of his head.

"Okay, Holt. Keep me informed," the big man named Max says and ends the call.

Sweat trickles down his face. The black-haired man mutters. "Good news, Max?"

"That part, yes, but…"

"But what?"

"When he left the desert in New Mexico, he came out…different."

The other man says nothing, waiting for Max to continue.

"He's physically stronger, much stronger, running and practicing his karate every day."

Max stares at the other man, looking for acknowledgement, but nothing comes. The black-haired man stares at him sideways, waiting.

"I'm not sure he's that greedy, either."

Max glances at the man, but again, no response.

"But that's not the problem."

"Problem?"

"Mentally, emotionally, spiritually, intellectually and morally, he's...well how can I say it...he's everything we don't want him to be."

"Explain."

The man named Max grimaces. "The fucking witch taught him so much, and together with the teachings of Gurung, and his in-built thirst for personal growth, he's a new and infinitely more powerful man."

"We can use that."

"Not really, sir. His moral compass is seriously at odds with our philosophy."

The black-haired man's shoulders clench. "Then manipulate and tempt him. I know for a fact that he has greed and darkness in his nature. Tap into it, goddammit. He's been holed up on a mountain for who knows how long. Throw every temptation and honey trap at him until he cracks, and we got him," the thin man snaps, gazing out the window.

"Possible, sir. After all, we manipulate and control almost everything and everyone else in the world."

"Set up a programme that has only one target...Brian. I want that fucking boy on his knees, begging to join."

"Already underway, sir."

The man nods his approval, adding, "Now. Update Project Fear."

Max swallows. "Project Fear," he gulps. "It continues to be an outstanding success, sir. Our latest stats reveal almost 75% of people in government and the private sector have become averse to challenging the status quo, without realizing they're being manipulated."

"25% to go," the man smiles. "And the next phase?"

"Our most audacious programme yet, sir. The small matter of asserting full control of humanity. Our mind control and gene expression using sonic waves, and our DNA and healthcare data harvesting projects are all on target. Very soon, we can decide if and how well people will live, depending on your ability to pay, of course."

"And pay a lot."

Max seems happy that the other man seems pleased. He tucks the cell phone in his breast pocket.

"Do you foresee any obstacles?"

"No, sir. Although…" Max gulps.

The man leans forward. "Do not say 'Brian.' Your programme of manipulation dedicated exclusively to him must succeed."

"I certainly hope so, sir. But…he's powerful."

With a shaking hand, Max opens a slender iPad under his arm and turns it around so the black-haired man can see.

"We positioned one of our military satellites over the cabin."

The other man leans forward. The iPad shows footage of the Bruja's cabin and the fight between two men and the two dogs, sounds of a bloody battle, shouting and screaming.

"What is going on here, Max?"

"I don't know, sir."

Hot blood slams into the other man's face. He sits like a bewildered child in the shadows, watching the footage. As it finishes, he leans backward. Suddenly, he slams the table with his fist and it rattles, the loud sound making Max wince. Looking pale and wan, the man stands and hysterically peers out the huge picture window at the emergency services tidying up storm damage in the streets.

"There won't be another storm, will there, Max?"

At those words Max's head snaps back. "O-o-of course not, sir," the big man stammers, backing out of the room obsequiously, but muttering curses under his breath. "Of course there won't be, you dirty old son-of-a-bitch," he mutters—but not until he's six floors down cocooned in the elevator, all alone with his dread.

* * *

# FORTY-ONE

After the interview with EYE-CORP, I drove aimlessly, watching the clean-up in the streets, grabbling with anxiety. Leaning over the wheel, my mind pounded with dark thoughts.

*Dead. These people want me dead. Shit, what have I gotten myself into?* I desperately needed a job and money, but this job was with the enemy.

My eyes drifted to the devastation outside. A deadly silence lay over the city, broken only by the mechanical scream of garbage trucks, plucking up the rubble. As if in a dream everything moved in slow-motion. I groped for the answer. Then I remembered the proverb: *keep your friends close but your enemies even closer.*

Again, the clean-up crews caught my eye. What was left of this metropolis looked like an abandoned battleground. The dim light of the sun was blotted out by clouds. I wanted to call the Grays and tell them but was worried that their lines were tapped, or I might somehow endanger them.

And I had no way of reaching Gurung or the Curandera, so I had no one to celebrate with if you could call it that. I found myself half expecting the attorney to call and congratulate me, but that didn't happen.

I drove for a long time, my mind racing, my brain stifling bewilderment. Finally, I picked Flower up at the hotel, driving us to a nearby dog-friendly restaurant.

I was famished and ordered three courses, had a beer and some wine, toasted myself to my success, not with landing the job, but with EYE-CORP, even though it meant going into the jaws of the enemy.

"Congratulations to us!" I announced to Flower, toasting her with my wine glass as she jumped up next to me.

How long we toasted each other I don't know. All at once, I had that strange feeling of being watched again and peered outside, unable to see anyone or anything suspicious.

*It's your imagination, dumb-ass,* I scolded myself. I shrugged and continued eating my delicious steak, Flower eyeing it hungrily.

* * *

Opposite the restaurant. A third-story window. Azazel has Brian in the crosshairs of a strange-looking rifle, his gaze cupped to the eyepiece.

He aims, then hesitates. *Dammit,* he thinks. Flower is blocking his shot, licking Brian's face. He waits, gazing into the eyepiece. Beside him, a woman's voice crackles from a cheap cell phone.

"Do you see him?"

Grunting, Azazel answers, eyes fixed on the target. "Yes, he's a sitting duck."

"Then shoot him!"

Azazel feels his face grow hot.

"Shoot him, I said!!"

"I can't."

"Why not?"

"His dog is right next to him, and I might hit it."

"What? It's a *dog!* Shoot the fucking thing as well! Do you hear me?!"

Azazel sighs, stands. His eyes darken. His face twists in anger. He puts down the weapon, snatches up the phone, hissing into it.

"It's a lucky thing you're on the other end of this phone!" His voice is shaking, saliva trickling from both sides of his mouth. "If you *ever* again ask me to kill an animal, you'll be first."

There's a pause on the other end of the line. At last, the woman's voice crackles. "Then…find a way that doesn't involve the dog."

Irritation blasts across Azazel's face. He growls, hangs up the phone, turns his eyes back to the restaurant. Heat bakes into his brain from the window. Finally, he gives up, deciding to take the woman's advice. *Find a way that doesn't involve the dog.*

Azazel is satisfied with that. While he packs up his gun, a Rottweiler snarls by his side; eyes fixed on Flower.

* * *

"Eat it up, girl!" Flower licked clean a plate of blueberry pancakes, one of her favourites, then I wrapped my arms around her, and she licked my face again.

"Ready for our walk?" I asked. Suddenly, Flower stared out the window into the dark and began to growl.

"You see something?" I said, peering outside, seeing nothing.

Flower just kept staring, letting out a low growl. *What in God's name does she see?* Just then she jumped off the seat and ran to the door, weaving through other diners. In haste, I followed.

"Flower, wait!"

*That crazy dog!* I hurled opened the restaurant door, and Flower tore toward a dark car parked across the street. I sprinted after her as fast as I could.

Closer and closer, we advanced toward the car, Flower with her jaws open, teeth bared. "Get ahold of yourself, Flower!" Abruptly, the car screeched away from the curb, spewing exhaust, and at that moment, I saw him. Azazel! His dark and soulless eyes were raised at me, his vicious Rottweiler staring at Flower as they sped away.

"Flower! You were right!" I drew in a deep breath. *Now who was the crazy one?* I watched Azazel's car zoom off, wondering. *He's an assassin, sent to kill me. So why the hell didn't he?*

Not wanting to take any more chances I might be followed we called a cab. Five minutes later we arrived at our hotel.

There was no sign of Azazel outside the hotel, so Flower and I entered the lobby, checking around for any sign of him, took the elevator and hurried to our room.

Relief swept over me as I locked the door. After my big dinner, long drive and the adrenalin from the encounter with the assassin, exhaustion overtook me, and I collapsed on the bed and quickly began to fall asleep.

Dark thoughts continued to assault me. They raced around my head, and I reached to stroke Flower. My naiveté suddenly seemed foolish. *These people aren't playing, yet they could have murdered me just now, in an instant. What stopped them?* Like a thunderbolt, the answer hit me.

"It was *you,* Flower! That fucker Azazel saved you after the crash. He didn't want to shoot in case he hit *you.*"

My eyes moved across the ceiling, my brain playing the events over and over, thinking. A dizzying burst of excitement ran through me. I lay back and began to doze off, mumbling to myself, "Animals. His kryptonite. Just like Harrison said."

* * *

I fell asleep with my clothes on. Early the next morning, my cell phone rang. Groping for it on the nightstand I answered.

"Good morning, Mr. Frederiksen. This is Pandora from Mr. Holt's office."

I frowned and spoke with a croak, "Um…uh, hello Pandora."

"Would you be free to view an apartment this morning?"

"Apartment?" I said, surprised.

"Mr. Holt likes to take care of his special colleagues. 8 AM, Mr. Frederiksen?"

For a long, meditative moment I pondered. Finally, I yawned and stretched and agreed to meet at EYE-CORP's offices at eight.

Quickly I dressed in my only suit, shaved, grabbed some coffee then strode to the office.

As I stepped inside, I gaped at the receptionist in confusion. It turned out that Pandora was the executive receptionist at EYE-CORP.

She beamed a wide smile, dangling car keys. "Ready?" *Ready for what?* I wondered, as we jumped into her smart little Mercedes roadster and headed to view the apartment.

"The storm wiped out most of the available rentals, but we managed to find you something…suitable."

Incredibly, she weaved through traffic like a veteran NASCAR driver. Ten minutes later, we stopped outside a cool apartment block, ultra-modern and sleek, a top architect's finest work and right on the main square in Morristown.

I whistled, impressed, and Pandora looked pleased.

"Shall we?" she gestured.

Inside, the house was equally impressive; penthouse floor, the walls whitewashed, the furniture minimalistic, and all appliances hidden out of sight. I immediately liked it and felt at home.

"How come you managed to find somewhere like this, still available?"

"Working for EYE-CORP has its perks," she said with a flirtatious wink.

I thought about this, then spun circles, eyes wide, eyebrows raised, taking in the apartment. "I love this place, Pandora. So, what's next?"

"Electricity," she replied.

For a fleeting second, I thought she meant between us, and I flushed with embarrassment. Then she went to the wall, flipped the switch, and muted mood lighting came on.

She laughed, and I understood what she meant now; the building had working electricity, a rarity after the storm, most people being forced to live in the dark and to eat cold meals and take cold showers.

As I turned to Pandora, she was still looking at me with that flirtatious smile. Suddenly, there was a timid knock on the door. Pandora opened it.

Outside stood a stooped-over, older woman, carrying cleaning equipment and bucket and wearing cheap maid's clothes. She followed Pandora into the room, gimping along on a bad leg with her teeth gritted.

"Ah, Brian, this is Lilith. I'm leaving shortly, so start with the bedroom," Pandora snapped dismissively, and the woman barely glanced at me, shuffling into the bathroom to start cleaning.

Pandora dropped the keys to the apartment into my open hand and beaming her beautiful smile, left me there. "Enjoy," she announced.

*Enjoy, indeed!* I thought. Somehow, I realized, it seems they knew I'd love the place. *They've done their research on me.* In the bathroom, the cleaning lady produced a silver object from her apron pocket, flipped up the lid, and lit the droopy cigarette between her lips with the flame. Puffing deeply, she threw a thumbs-up in my direction, then shuffled off to mop the floor.

Reverting to my sense of paranoia, I quickly shut the bathroom door. Once again, I was grimly reminded that I was under surveillance, being watched. I was also fairly certain that the apartment would be full of audio and video bugging devices. However, I could use that to my advantage by pretending to be happy and utterly clueless.

I explored the apartment, and then I took a walkabout around the facilities.

There was a gym, sauna, small pool, showers, and smart changing rooms. Excellent, I thought. I was keyed up for my next steps, feeling my paranoia crank even tighter.

Murmurs of laughter greeted my return to the apartment. It was the cleaning maid, whom I startled whispering on her cell phone. Apologizing, she snatched up her mop and bucket, and gimped back out the door, a smile oozing out from between her teeth.

*No more need to prove your point,* I silently announced to the unseen bugging devices. The same week, I would learn precisely why the Curandera thought I had to accept this offer at EYE-CORP.

* * *

# Forty-Two

It was a cold morning. I arrived at the EYE-CORP headquarters just after 8 AM, and there she was, Pandora, seated at her desk. Time to pretend I was a regular employee.

She gave me a huge smile, we said our good mornings, and she handed me a steaming Styrofoam cup of green tea. I sipped it—just like I prefer. *Hmmm.*

Pandora sashayed down the hall, led me to the elevator, and we rose to the top floor, the views amazing, apart from the storm damage created by Hurricane Sandy.

Strolling down a long hall, the few people we passed smiled welcomes, and I grinned and nodded back, looking at every one intently. Keeping my gaze focused for so long made my eyes water.

"You're examining people," Pandora said.

"I study their body language, their smile, and the tone of their voice."

"What for?"

"To see into their hearts. People usually transfer their attitude to life to their workplace."

"Really? Let's see you prove it," Pandora said, giving me a strange look.

We walked into a vast office where people sat working, some at the water-cooler, and others deep in conversation. All heads turned to look at Pandora and the new guy.

Some nodded, some smiled, some said, "Welcome!" and some turned away.

Bolts of intuition whistled through my head. I whispered to Pandora. "She's very caring," as I gazed at a middle-aged woman, then a young man, "and he's pleased to see me, doesn't feel threatened." I continued.

"That woman remembers her first day, it was bad," I whispered as a woman waved at me, then I looked at a man at his computer, saying,

"He thinks he deserves a higher position in the business," and the man gave me a cursory glance then resumed working.

A well-dressed older-looking gentleman walked by, and the minute I reached out to say hello, he reciprocated and continued walking.

"A *quid-pro-quo*'er," I whispered, "more in his head than in his heart. He will always repay a favour and remember when it's his turn to get the check because it's written down in a small notebook. Not because his heart compels him to, but instead because he doesn't want to be in debt to anyone. To him, it's a math exercise; the joy of just giving for the sake of giving is lost on him."

Pandora smiled and shook her head from side to side, appraising me with a long, searching look.

We strolled past a big meeting room with glass walls, employees in suits around a table, some acknowledging me, but no smiles.

I stopped and watched them, experiencing more intense shots of intuition.

"They're the legacy people, as I call them. The new guy will never be allowed to get in their way," and Pandora raised a shaped eyebrow.

I continued. "They reject a change to maintain the status quo. They're a huge impediment to progress, and ridicule new ideas."

My eyes flashed back to the meeting. "New guys with ideas worry them because they lack ideas themselves, relying on outdated corporate politics. They stick new ideas in glue, demand countless meetings, create doubt, and demand proof of success. Of course, when you plan to change the world, there's no proof, and they know that."

I could see Pandora was taken aback. We walked into a spacious restaurant, and she led me to a table by the window, set for two, with a magnificent view of the city. We sat, reading a menu. Pandora swallowed a gulp of sparkling water and curiously eyed me.

"What makes them think and act like that?" she asked.

"They're insecure about their abilities because of fear."

"Some of them are board members," Pandora said, eyeing me over the menu.

"They, unfortunately, too often reach the top of the ladder because they don't rock the boat. They never hurt the business, and CEOs know they're loyal, counting the days to pension time.

"Hmm," Pandora said as a waiter approached.

"But that's the past, where the size and strength of business were defined by how many buildings they had."

The waiter took our order, and we continued our conversation.

"Only 12% of Fortune 500 companies that existed in 1955 remain."

"So, do we have a chance?" Pandora asked.

Gazing into her eyes I elaborated. "Look at today's disruption of traditional business models. The founder of Spotify didn't know much about the music business before creating Spotify; Airbnb, owns no hotels and knew very little about the hotel business before disrupting it; to the best of my knowledge; Uber, owns no cars; and the world's biggest retailer; Alibaba, carries little to no inventory, and I'll bet you that the fastest-growing future healthcare company isn't going to be a healthcare company. Legacy companies keep hiring and promoting people that seems right on paper, when in fact they need to hire the wrong faces, the people that bring in new blood, aren't stuck in the ways things used to be and instead can bring innovation and disruption based on new thinking. But it takes courage to hire the faces that don't fit because it is so counterintuitive. Often, when someone says they have ten years of experience in something, what it means is one-year experience ten times, since they keep doing the same thing over and over again even when they change jobs."

"That's a good point, I never really thought of that," she replied.

The waiter arrived with soft drinks, and I poured for us both, toasting Pandora.

In my mind's eye I could see exactly what she was thinking. An uncomfortable feeling shot through me.

*She sees right through me,* I thought, my mind conflicted. *Or maybe it's just my paranoia.* I was on a different mission—but while there, I would offer my contribution and pretend to be a good employee.

We finished lunch, Pandora leaning so close at times that I could smell her perfume. At the end she led me along another long corridor and opened a large white door.

"I hope you like your office...sir," she said, flirting unashamedly again.

She escorted me inside a stunning office; a corner site with superb views through two picture windows, a sweeping curved desk with a huge white Apple Mac monitor, and stylish grey leather and steel chair.

"It's great, Pandora. And it's also *Brian,* not sir."

"Of course, Brian," she winked.

Suddenly my paranoia cranked even tighter. *Get a grip,* I told myself. "Thanks for everything," I said, and she bowed gracefully then backed out, leaving me to gaze around my new working environment.

I raised an eyebrow at the room, then shook my head. The next stage of my quest has arrived. Meantime, I need a new car to go with my fancy new job.

I went for a short walk to Bank of America, since it was closest, but they flatly refused to give me a credit card since I didn't have a good enough credit, even though I was getting a seriously fat paycheck. *Bastards,* I grumbled.

Next, I went to Audi to try to lease a car. They also declined to lease me a car and politely explained that their finance department was unfortunately not able to approve me since my credit score was too low. In other words, I thought, we don't want undesirable customers like you with your low credit and social score.

*Screw it,* I told myself, strolling out, *I'm gonna raise the stakes and try to climb the highest fence instead.*

I went to a shiny Mercedes Benz dealer and *surprise surprise*, they approved me, and I got a brand-new SUV.

There's no greater feeling of freedom than driving a new car. With the keys in my hand, I immediately drove by the Audi dealer. The sales manager was in the car lot showing cars to new prospects. As I drove by, I rolled down the window and gave him the finger without even looking at him. I knew that was seriously beneath me and would probably have disappointed the Curandera, Gurung and the Grays.

But man, it felt *good!*

Fuck it, I'm just human, and once in a while, I have to give in to my basest instincts.

Basking in my new independence, I proudly drove the Mercedes back to the office and climbed out, striding in the back entrance to my building.

The janitor was just finishing cleaning my office. *What, again?* I wondered. Escorting him from the office, I lay back in my luxurious office chair, my face cracking with a huge smile. Ten minutes later, there was a knock on the door. There a young kid stood, looked about 18, tall, gangly and geeky, with a headful of puffy hair.

"Mr. Frederiksen? I am Oleksii, here to give you the guided tour?"

*Guided tour? What next?* The kid held out a skinny hand, and I shook it gently in case I broke it.

I sighed, wanting to just chill in my new office. But he was a nice person, with a goofy smile, taking me into every department; management, research and development, order processing, finance and marketing, introducing me to everyone.

I discovered he was a junior member of the internet security department. This gave me an idea.

"So, Oleksii. You've told me everything good about the place. Now, the bad points."

Oleksii gave me a quizzical look. He ran a hand through his sleep-corkscrewed hair. Weighing me up, then with a conspiratorial look around, he gave me the lowdown, sharing all the juicy details with that same goofy lopsided grin.

Listening, my eyes lighted with pleasure. I liked Oleksii, and it turned out that he lived near me, so we started walking to the office together. Besides the occasional work talk, he was very forthcoming about his private life, always mentioning what he called a special girl. However, he never gave me her name.

* * *

# FORTY-THREE

It was Friday. Five days after beginning my first hectic week at EYE-CORP, I dragged myself home, nervous with perspiration.

I felt a heaviness in my whole body; then, a stinging, searing pain drove through my eyeballs. I plopped on the couch and shut my dizzy eyes.

*God, what's happening to me?* Soon, my eyes felt heavy, the room was swirling in slow-motion, and I dozed off.

It wasn't long before I felt my entire body twitch, as I was plunged back into the dream.

It was the desert again, blazing hot, heat shimmering, sand blinding white, and there I was again, walking across the sand towards the woman who had her back to me.

The woman was stooped over, busy doing something I couldn't see. Desert sunlight blinded me. As I crept nearer, she sensed I was there and half-turned to face me. Pausing. Waiting.

*Who are you?* Suddenly, a gust of wind blew sand everywhere, and I shielded my face and couldn't see her. *Where is she?* I shielded my burning eyes, then held my hands out, clawing at the air.

Desperately my fingers ripped at the air. I felt the wind whipping me in circles. The wind died down just as suddenly as it started, and I looked to see the woman had vanished.

Hysteria swept through me. I stepped over to where she had been and saw a stick lying in the sand; something was written there.

Two letters. It looked like *DN*. What the hell does *DN* mean?

The woman must have been trying to tell me something, but what?

An explosion of wind slammed my face, the impact arching me backward. I looked around for her again, eyes desperately scanning the dunes, the desert, and the sky. My eyes swept everywhere. Suddenly, thunder rumbled from the sky. The wind whipped up, blowing rocks and sand; a blinding hot blizzard. I shielded my eyes again. Choked coughs erupted from my throat. I opened my cracked lips. I bellowed in fright.

Abruptly the storm stopped. I peered down, looking for the letters in the sand.

They had been blown away.

*Did I imagine it?* A voice in my mind whispered. I ran my tongue around my cracked lips and waited for an answer. There was none.

* * *

Rays of the desert sun broke through. The air became cooler. My eyes continued to search the desert, but saw nothing, and my ears heard nothing. My face stung with sand. I wiped my mouth off, then noticed that in my panic, I'd bitten through my tongue.

Suddenly I heard a strange, persistent sound and jumped awake.

It was my cell phone.

I rubbed my eyes, staring. The caller ID said MOM and I answered immediately.

"Brian? Is that you, son?" I lay back and sighed, then leaned my chin on my hand, and groaned. "You sound tired."

"I just woke up after another one of my crazy dreams."

"You work too hard," she said, then, "What was it about?"

"Nothing important. How are you? I've got some big news. I…I'm going to accept the attorney's offer."

Her pause worried me. "Your…inheritance?"

"That's right. I couldn't say no to the incredible package."

"I hope it's the right decision, Brian."

*Me too,* I thought. "I guess the magic runestone you gave me as a child brought me luck, finally."

"Son, the only thing that's magic is you. The runestone is just a stone, meant to remind you of me and where you came from."

I grunted. "So, I've been carrying a rock in my pocket for years with no special powers or anything?"

"Well, who knows if it truly has powers? My mom gave it to me, and she swore by it—nevertheless, you already have all the powers you need to succeed in life, son."

"You're right, Mom. Everything I wanted, I got. And I believe anyone could. The only obstacle is the fear of failure. Once fear grips people, we become afraid to live and afraid to die."

Mom sighed, long and hard, and through the phone, I could hear the moan of wind and loud whistling.

"Mom, where are you? What's that noise?"

"I'm in the attic. There's a storm coming."

I should've paid attention to those words.

"What you doing up there, with all the spiders and cobwebs and dust?"

"I know, it is pitch black, kind of spooky. I'm using a Maglite."

"But *why* are you up there?"

"I was tidying up the attic and found my parents' old suitcase. There were some yellowed letters inside."

"Okay, and…?"

"My paternal great-grandmother Laura gave them to her son, my Father Poul, to…you know, explain things."

"Please, Mom, tell me what she said, I'm desperate to know."

At that, her voice became tight. A sheen of sweat broke on my forehead. "She felt terrible putting my father into care. And he never met his father once. Laura had met him one stormy night outside her office. He was smitten with her beauty. She was young, fell for the expensive car and his huge mansion and the great job he offered as his PA with a fat salary in the big company his family owned for such a long time…"

I listened, imagining my great-grandmother meeting this rich guy and being young and impressed by his attention.

"The letter says they had their first dinner one night in his mansion and he seduced her. She was only seventeen, Brian."

"Poor girl. So young."

"After she discovered she was pregnant, she went to the house, but no one was there. She went around the back and peeked inside. The fancy, expensive furniture was all gone. A neighbour said no one had lived there for over 25 years."

I stared at the phone, taking a deep breath. "What a bastard! But...the house wasn't lived in?"

No reply. Mom went on, "…and when she went to his offices, all the signs were different, and they denied that a person like she described had ever worked there."

"My God, Mom! This is a nightmare, for you too."

"She wrote that she had tried jumping from the kitchen table to dislodge and abort the baby…"

"Poor grandad," I said in horror. "And poor us, because if she had lost the baby, none of us would be here."

"Thank God, son…anyway, then, World War II started and it was like the man she met never existed."

*Of course he didn't,* I thought grimly "All of this must have been a terrible shock for your father and great-grandma."

She sighed hard, and her voice shook. "She said he was not just cruel and callous, but pure evil."

At that moment, I felt great-grandmother's pain physically. *How brave for her to have lived with that!* Seconds later, I heard Mom catch her breathe.

"Wait…what's this?" she said, and my ears pricked up.

"What is what, Mom?"

"A business card just dropped out of the envelope. Let me see…"

I waited impatiently, desperate to discover whose card it was. I tapped the arm of my chair, my lungs tight.

"Damn flashlight keeps going on and off."

"Maybe take it downstairs?"

I kept tapping the chair. Waiting. Finally, Mom's voice came back on the line. "So…it's just a phone number, and on the back…a fancy logo."

"What's the logo, Mom?" I asked, my excitement and nerves gnawing.

My lips tightened as I awaited her answer. "It says…THE SEVEN."

"THE SEVEN?!" I gasped and jumped to my feet in surprise.

"You've heard of it?"

"Mom, The Seven are the people, the group Mr. Swanson, the attorney, represents!"

With a shrieking heart I listened as the truth collided with her. "Oh my God...*my grandfather was also part of The Seven!* That explains his inexplicable disappearance and heartlessness to care for my grandmother and his new-born son."

"Does the letter say anything else, Mom?"

Over the phone, I heard her moan. "Your great–grandad was part of this group of terrible people that you're about to accept your inheritance from."

"My...God."

"She never saw him again, and the letter to my father says how sorry she was that she didn't know any more about his own father. But she remembered one particular thing."

"What was that?"

"He wasn't very handsome or anything, tiny, bird-like, a bit ratty really, but enigmatic and…his eyes."

"What about them, Mom?"

"One was brown and the other, blue."

There was a moment of silence between us. I heard her lips working. "Like…the attorney," she suddenly gasped.

Before I could answer, the truth hit me. "It can't be," I choked out. "So…Swanson is my great-grandfather?!" I spluttered in amazement, my brain spinning.

*Swanson. It can't be. It can't…!* Suddenly, Mom screamed.

"What is it, Mom, what happened?!"

"A rat, a big one!" she shouted. "I've never seen one up here before."

"Careful it doesn't bite," I said, but my mind was in a whirl at the news about Swanson.

"Wait a minute," Mom gasped and blurted out. "Swanson, the attorney…he came to our house, kept phoning, went to see you, and all along, he's the one who seduced great-grandmother."

Mom could hardly speak, fighting emotion and tears, like me. At the same time, I could hear her fiddling with the letter.

"There's more," she said.

"What is it?"

"She says, they were in bed, intimate, when she asked him, 'Who are you really?' He whispered in her ear a name…' Norburg. Daemon Norburg.'"

Hearing the name gigantic bolts of pain slashed into me. "So…Swanson's mysterious deceased client doesn't exist. It's him; he's the client. He's the leader of The Seven. He's called Norburg. And he's my great-grandfather?!"

Mom screamed again.

"Mom? What is it?"

There was silence.

"Mom!?"

"Sorry, Brian. Dropped the damn Maglite, it's broken."

I heard her struggling for air then, obviously in turmoil, like me, struggling to absorb everything we'd just learned. Or so I thought.

"Brian, son. Crows have gotten in now."

*Crows.* I knew what she was saying. Crows are a symbol of evil. I sat back, my mind frozen. Then she screamed again, and I was in a panic.

"Jeez, Mom! Are you alright?"

"A crow flew into my face! I don't like this, son!"

"Mom, this Norburg is my great-grandfather, the evilest man in the world. No one outside of The Seven knows his real name except us, and that he's alive and well!"

"Don't take it, darling! Don't take his damned inheritance; it's from the devil's wallet. Oh God please don't—"

Suddenly she let out an immense wail and hung up.

I sat there, stunned, not knowing what to do. I re-dialed Mom's number; no answer. I swallowed the last of my drink and paced up and down the room. I looked squarely into all the news I'd just learned. I twisted my hands through my hair, trying to understand.

That's when another thought leapt into my mind; the dream — the two letters.

*DN.*

*No. Dear God, no, it can't be.*

"DN in the sand is…Daemon Norburg!"

My stomach lurched, and I collapsed onto the couch. I shook my head. *This is madness. It's all a damn riddle.* My fingernails gripped the couch arms, my lungs laboring to catch my breath. Confusion filled me like a blinding white light.

*What does the dream mean? Is it a warning?*

My brain replied with only silence. Snarling, I searched my brain for any other clues. Nothing. My eyes narrowing into slits, I made a snap decision. I grabbed my cell phone, punching in a number. It rang and rang. Seven times. *Answer, dammit!* Finally…

"Hello?"

"Mr. Holt? It's Brian. How are you? I need you to fix an urgent meeting with Mr. Swanson."

"Mr. Swanson? Who's that?"

*Who's that?* I struggled against losing my temper. "He's my great-grandfather, but let's cut the crap Mr. Holt, we both know who you're working for."

The line went eerily silent.

Pulsing alarms went off in my temple. For a split second, I cursed myself for this obsession. A tear formed, then dribbled down my face and made me blink. I didn't say anything. I had a feeling that not even Mr. Holt knew that Swanson's real name was Daemon Norburg and that he was the head of The Seven. He was like the mysterious Keyser Soze in *The Usual Suspects;* a rarely-seen, nearly mythical crime kingpin involved in cybercrime, financial crime, drugs, murder, and possibly international terrorism.

Thinking of this, my whole body stiffened. Then his voice came back, with a slight tremble. "I'm going to ask you to hold the line for a sec," he said, and the line went silent again.

I sat in a shocked hush. I thought of Gurung, the Bruja, Ahote, my training. My mind spoke in a soft, wondering voice. *Well, Brian, I guess you're finally getting what you wanted. The truth.*

I wasn't sure I still wanted it.

* * *

I stared hard at the floor. Waiting, wondering. A minute later, Mr. Holt was back.

"Brian? Sorry for the delay. Mr. Swanson said…"

*Yes, yes, get on with it!* For a few long seconds, I thought he was going to tell me he flatly refused.

"…that if you are ready to accept your inheritance, he will meet you."

There was dead silence for a moment. I held the cell phone to my chest, breathless, then pressed it to my lips. "Tell him…I accept…but…I also have conditions."

"What conditions?"

"He arranges for me to meet all of The Seven."

I waited, feeling sweat trickle down my neck. After another long moment of silence, he came back on the line.

"Then he says…welcome to the family," and I gulped. It worked, dammit.

"Expect to be picked-up within one hour," he said, then hung up.

* * *

# FORTY-FOUR

Less than an hour later, a stretch limo pulled up outside my apartment, and a hulking driver sounded the horn like Mr. Holt said he would.

I stood there, staring out the window of my apartment, letting the horn blare. I was as nervous as hell. *Get your ass down there,* my mind screamed. When the horn blasted again, the thought vanished like a dream upon waking, and I rushed down to the limo.

We drove at a leisurely pace downtown into the heart of top-dollar Midtown Manhattan, then onto Fifth Avenue.

At 725 Fifth Avenue, between 56th and 57th Streets, the vehicle stopped, the driver opened the door for me, and a familiar face waved at me from outside the most plush, high-rise office block I'd ever seen.

"Welcome, sir," Pandora said, her voice breathy. She extended a hand and nodded, welcoming me in, all smiles.

She escorted me to a blacked-out elevator, which she explained only the board used, and up we went.

In the elevator we stood in total silence. *Let's get this bullshit over with,* I thought. The lift stopped, and Pandora led me to a massive reception area, also in black, matte-black glass doors swishing open.

Inside, the room was plunged in darkness, but I could see the silhouette of someone sitting at the head of a large boardroom table, three seats on either side, a seventh seat at the top.

In the seventh chair sat a small black-haired man in the shadows. In the darkness, his eyes gleamed.

I looked at the man, my palms sweating, hands quivering. *Time to act...*I gulped hard, inhaled sharply and hurried over to him, holding both arms out. My throat felt tight, too tight for words. *Obliterate your fear*, I told myself. *Wipe it away. Fear doesn't exist anymore.*

Pain shot through my head. I wiped it away. The lights came on, and for the first time, I saw The Seven.

Pandora motioned me forward. *Relax, Brian,* I told myself, giving the group eye contact. They were all power dressed, looking wealthy, smug, and arrogant.

One was a big, chunky man about 60 with salt-and-pepper hair; another a skeletal, ill-looking man with sallow skin in his 70s; then a man who looked like a snake, 80-something, bent double with thick glasses; across from him a short bald man, about 30, with a ruddy alcoholic face; beside him a flawless-looking woman who'd obviously undergone a lot of plastic surgery, her age indeterminate, big diamonds sparkling; across from her a stunning female in her 40s who looked like a femme fatale; then finally, the old man himself.

My eyes snapped to the seventh man. My voice came out heavily as if I were sleep-talking. "Good to see you again...*great-grandad.*"

Behind me, I heard Pandora gasp in shock at my familiarity with one of the world's most powerful men. As her shock faded, the doors behind me swished shut.

The old man straightened up. He looked completely taken aback at my words and gasped aloud when I hugged his scrawny body.

"Brian," he croaked. "Good to see you too." He grasped my hand with a bloodless fist.

"Let's cut the fucking crap," I said, and by the way he jerked back I could tell he had never been spoken to like that before. "I know everything."

"Everything?"

"How you seduced my great-grandma."

He smiled contemptuously.

"I'm impressed," he said.

His head moved out of the shadows. I let a half-smile cross my lips. "Why did you keep up this Swanson shit act, Pops? You wasted time when we could've been making lots of more money together!"

His small intent eyes became round holes in his face. For the first time, he flashed a real smile, trying hard to pretend that there was something warm inside his soulless old heart.

"Well, Brian, I had to be certain you wanted to join our beautiful family."

*Beautiful family?* I got the sudden urge to throw up but managed to compose myself. Lilith my house cleaner appeared, carrying a tray with a teapot and snacks. She placed it on the table and left. I nodded at her as she passed by me, a bit puzzled to see her here as well. *Why should I be surprised at anything anymore?*

Norburg looked at me, studying me like an exhibit in a zoo.

"Green tea, Brian?" He poured, slid the fine-bone china cup over to me. I toyed with it. "What made you change your mind?"

"Oh, I can think of 470 million reasons, for a start."

He stared at me with intense longing. "Good boy, but unfortunately, I'm going to have to disappoint you." He pressed another button under his desk, and within seconds, the doors swished open again, and Pandora appeared, carrying a glittering golden box shaped like an oversized briefcase.

She placed it in front of Norburg, and he nodded, then Pandora opened the box, her face bathed in bright light. She peered inside, let out a little laugh like a child, and then turned the case to me. As she slid away, the old man patted her butt.

"Ready for your inheritance, Brian?" Norburg asked.

I tried to meet his burning stare, jerking my eyes away as if I'd been slapped. I sucked in air, trying to catch my breath. I was horrified by the thought of what my inheritance may be. I could sense every eye in the room on me, waiting. Sweat rolling down my neck, my eyes shifted to the box, then I peered inside.

My jaw dropped as I stared at what was inside the box.

"Surprised?" he asked me.

I was fucking astonished.

* * *

# Forty-Five

Norburg pushed the box closer. He watched my dazed eyes crawl over it.

"What do you think?" he asked, starting to smile.

For several minutes I stared, my eyes wide and fascinated. *Oh, God. Oh, dear God.* It was a slim computer with a 3D image emerging. Hundreds of applications glittered on the screen, working at lightning speed.

My reaction seemed to satisfy Norburg. He inched closer, his lips moving as if he were silently speaking to the machine.

"Once the algorithms have finished, you will know absolutely *everything.*"

"Wha…what's *happening?*"

Norburg leaned back, widening one eye in triumph. "This is a genome, Brian," he whispered, twisting his long-nailed fingers together. "Your …*inheritance.*"

Norburg sat, looking at me with eager curiosity. My throat tightened. *My inheritance? How could this possibly be?* "What the fuck *is* this?" flew out of my mouth.

At that moment, the computer flashed. The 3D image emerged, slowly taking shape. It was my picture, but in digital form, and only partially complete. Norburg sat back, watching me.

"I'm totally confused," I said, in a quivering voice.

Norburg smiled and cocked his head. "From birth, each of our unique DNA holds incredible potential to change the world. Your inheritance was never about money—that was just a test designed to bring out the worst, I mean the best, in you. Your inheritance is actually...*my DNA*. Incredible power comes with it."

"So, if I had signed the papers in Florida and you'd pressed the button for a transfer to the Swiss account, I wouldn't have received the money?"

"Not a fucking penny," he said, laughing sadistically.

I tried to tear my eyes away from the image, but couldn't, still in shock at Norburg's surprising news.

"I need you for...something... very special."

"For what? And how did you get my DNA?" I gasped.

"Easily. We hacked the DNSB, the Danish Neonatal Screenings Biobank, who kept the blood samples of every child born in Denmark, including you."

"But...*why?*"

"I'll come to that, but meantime..."

The image began to pulse faster. My eyes grew wide, filling with its blinding light.

"For the first time in history," Norburg said, "there's a perfect storm of the volume of data, an explosion in sensors, cell phones, internet usage, and social media, with 90% of all data in the world created in the last few years; meeting enough computing power needed to run AI algorithms that need mountains of data to learn and powerful computers to analyze that amount of data."

*This is insane,* I thought, the air in the room growing thick. I inhaled deeply, feeling The Seven draw in closer around me, my mind struggling to take it all in.

"It once cost $100 million to sequence a human genome. Today it's $1000 and getting cheaper daily."

At that, Norburg whirled the computer around. His fingers danced across the keys. Suddenly, my image began to morph slowly into...something else. Something twisted. Something ancient. Something inhuman.

Into *Norburg's.*

*This is ridiculous!* I tried to clamp my eyes shut but couldn't. It's as if they were nailed open.

"What the hell is happening?" I whispered out.

"*Hell* is the right word," Norburg grinned, his face glowing as a digital version of his genetic blueprint appeared in front of my eyes.

Again, the computer flashed. The next phase happened instantly. Inside the computer there was an indented palm—some scanner, I figured—and Norburg placed his bony hand on it.

A word popped onscreen—PERSPIRATION—and to my horror, the machine started to analyse the sweat from the palm of Norburg's hand.

*It's to authenticate his unique DNA,* I realised.

Now Norburg's eyes weren't just gleaming; they were blazing. "Brian," he said, gesturing for me to also put my hand on the scanner.

I hesitated, my heart thumping, my head thudding. *What the hell was this old man going to do? What does this mean? If I authenticate my DNA, then what? This man is evil personified—but he's still my blood, and I wouldn't be here if it weren't for him.*

"Brian?" the old man repeated, his voice cracked and urgent. "It's your turn."

My eyes shifted back and forth wildly, from Norburg to the computer., then back again. After what felt like minutes, sweating profusely and wilting under Norburg's beady glare, I reluctantly, hesitantly placed my hand onto the scanner.

The machine flashed through hundreds of applications, then whirred to a stop. I closed my eyes until the feeling of vertigo went away. Then cautiously I opened them.

Once more, my jaw fell.

On the screen, in brilliant 3D, words began to appear. A metallic voice spoke. "*Hello, Brian. Welcome to the family.*"

*The family. My God.* Breath caught in my throat. I felt close to tears. Suddenly, 3D pictures of my life flashed across the screen. My birth, my brother, my mother and father, my first baby steps, school, selling flowers, being beaten by bullies, Gurung, fighting the bullies, karate lessons, competing in the tournament, university, studying, failing, getting my degree, and now today, this…

"It…it knows everything about me," I gasped, in horror.

"Almost," Norburg said proudly.

His cold hand crept over mine. Again, I felt like throwing up, not sure how much longer I could keep up the act.

"Brian," he continued meditatively, "those algorithms you've been applying were never developed for healthcare. I'm planning to use them for something… *different.*"

*Something different? I don't like the sound of that.* Tugging weakly at my shirt collar I stared, our faces inches away from each other. Could *this* be the reason why the Curandera wanted me to accept the offer from Norburg?

*Could it?*

That's when it hit me.

"It's about everyone's most valuable asset, their DNA," I realised, shivering.

"Quite correct, Brian," said Norburg, casting his eyes over mine. "It's part of it."

His eyes seemed almost blurred with tears. Fear as explosive as flames flashed through me. My gazed locked on the old man I studied him. *Time to push the act further.* "I hope you're planning something truly devious that makes us mountains of money?"

For a moment I felt his trickle of pleasure. "Beyond your wildest dreams, Brian."

I wondered what he meant. His blurry eyes weren't giving him away. Finally, he said, "Would you like a little…appetizer?"

I smiled and nodded, my gut churning with hate.

"I could select a target from one of our 4.7 billion healthcare records…that *you* helped collect from around the world."

He gave me a chilling stare. I shivered at the thought that I'd contributed to their database of innocent lives they could target. *Dear God, I helped create this!*

Norburg leaned forward. My knees wobbled. Then suddenly he picked a target, and everyone in the room gasped.

* * *

BBC
AUGUST 4, 2019

I GAVE MY DNA AWAY. CAN I GET IT BACK?

A growing number of people are willingly handing over their DNA to corporations in return for learning about their ancestry or to get health reports. And what happens if you want your data back?

It is estimated that by the start of 2019, 26 million people had added their DNA to four leading databases, operated by Ancestry, 23andMe, MyHeritage and Gene by Gene.

USA TODAY
JUNE 8, 2019. 3:00 PM

DNA SITE'S HACK IS REMINDER TO THINK TWICE ABOUT ANCESTRY TESTING

DNA testing packages are becoming increasingly popular, especially as gifts, but the sensitivity of the genetic information they collect has raised privacy alarms. Add hacking to that list of concerns.

DNA testing site MyHeritage.com said this week that more than 92 million users' email addresses and passwords had been stolen. The data had been sitting for months on a private server until an outside security researcher alerted the Israel-based company. MyHeritage stated the breach didn't contain sensitive data, such as DNA and individuals' family trees.

But that personal data, such as users' medical histories and biological relationships, can also be accessed through legal means, the site confirms...

# PATH / DAY SIX

## THE PUPPET MASTERS –
## ESCAPING THE MATRIX

*Everything you want is on the other side of fear.*

*— JACK CANFIELD*

# Forty-Six

Norburg pressed a button under his desk, flashed me a chilling stare, and then strolled to gaze across the New York skyline. Far off, Park Avenue was bathed in golden rays of warm sunlight. Norburg cocked his head, blotting out the light, lurking in the deepest shadows of his office.

"Did you get your flu shot like everyone else, my boy?"

His question confused me. "What does that have to do with anything?"

Turning his eyes from the bright sunlight, Norburg grinned a peculiar one-sided grin. "You'll find out soon. Not that it will save anyone," he whispered.

Ignoring me, he ran his fingers through his iron-grey short-cut hair, staring sombrely out the window at the world far beneath. Suddenly, the air seemed to change. The walls to his right parted with whirring sounds, opening to reveal an enormous dome, almost like a giant IMAX sky theatre. From inside, thousands of human voices competed, filling the room, millions of computer servers all over the planet working in concert. I stared, breathless and awestruck. *These are the voices of anguish and terror from my dream!*

I took a step back. My pulse pounded in my throat. I was actually *inside* Norburg's AI super-brain!

It was incredible—a swirling array of colours, people, countries, and computers flashing past and spinning all around me, making me dizzy. *Is this happening? Really happening?*

The throb of voices grew, becoming louder, so loud it made me dizzy. Beneath my feet, the room rumbled. My eyes continued to scan everything, my ears ringing with the pulsating voices, trying to keep up.

"Impressive, right?" Norburg grinned.

I gasped, still trying to catch my breath, the voices roaring in my head like a 747 engine. "A master of understatement, Pops. It's fucking *spectacular*."

"The voices are from billions of people around the world whose genome we've sequenced. We monitor them constantly through global surveillance, even turning on their cellphones, laptop cameras, and their TVs to monitor and listen to them. And they think the devices are turned off!"

"How do you plan to get governments to continue to allow you to track so many people?"

"Simple my boy," he said, the corners of his mouth rising. "A virus."

"A virus? What do you mean, Pops? A computer virus?"

He shook his head. "A live cell hacking virus that will infect the world, precisely thirty days from now."

My hands trembled uncontrollably as I stared into his cold dead eyes.

"Explain?" I said, terrified to hear the answer.

Norburg crept further into the room. "The virus hijacks the person's cells to translate its RNA into new copies of the virus. In just hours, a single cell will produce tens of thousands of new virions, and its game fucking over. Each person will in average infect three people and when each of these three infect three others in just ten layers, fifty-nine thousand people will have been infected by that one person."

I couldn't believe it. I was terrified, but needed to hear the rest.

Stepping closer, Norburg's eyes glowed fiercely, threatening to drown me in their dazzle. "What happens during a pandemic of epic proportions?"

Waiting for my answer, he rubbed his hands together with glee and giggled psychotically.

"Well, people need to be isolated and vaccinated," I said, trying my best to play his game, but with every fiber in my body fighting the urge to throw up.

"Good," he said, smiling wide. "In other words, tracking people to ensure only those not infected can move around freely, is simply a necessary public health measure."

I breathed deep, risking a smile. "Brilliant," I replied. My mind was racing since I now understood his terrible plan was to release a virus into the population and create a global pandemic, that would lead to governments being forced to track every citizen in order to control the spread of the virus. Of course, once those systems were in place, things would never go back to the way they were before. To a time when our faces weren't being scanned at every corner and our phones tracked, monitoring every step we took. It meant that no one would ever have any privacy again. And who knows? They would probably start using these tracking devices to influence the population to buy certain products, vote a certain way, and to think and live a certain way. No one would have free will because the people in charge would control their thoughts and every move.

"What's even better," he continued, "is this virus mutates so fast that even if you've been infected once, you can be infected again. Which means that no one will ever be able to claim that they don't need to be tracked. And this, my boy," he said, pointing at the briefcase.

"What?" I asked, fearful of the answer.

"*This,* my son, is the super-brain that will connect and track everyone. It connects to massive volumes of our servers all over the world. It can be carried like the nuclear football US Presidents talk about. And it can only be activated by someone with my DNA."

I whistled, alarmed but still impressed at the ingenuity.

Surveying my dumbstruck expression, Norburg appeared satisfied. "That lets you see the importance of your inheritance. I'm the administrator and control it now; you're the guest. But soon, *you* will be the only one who can activate and control it and everyone in the world. No one on earth has my DNA, which means no one else could ever activate or control the machine."

I made no response. I turned my gaze helplessly back to the New York skyline. My mind flashed back to Norburg's comment. *How much of this does the old son-of-a-bitch own?* I heard a cough. Out of the corner of my eye, I saw Norburg allow himself a brief smile.

"What does this machine do?" I asked, trying to sound innocent.

Norburg's skinny chest puffed up with pride. "The potential is endless. It monitors data from everyone, like their usage of social media, what they buy at the grocery store, what movies they watch, where they travel to, who they talk to and what they talk about, and it has sequenced their DNA. That gives us ultimate control and ability to exploit and monetize weaknesses in their DNA."

"Exploit? How?" *I was right about them controlling every decision, every thought.*

"First of all, we know who will be immune to the virus and instead needs to be infected by something else. Once we have everyone tagged like cows, for the sake of 'public health measures,' we can monetize the data, track people for governments, info for insurance companies and employers, while offering to pay for genetic upgrades, money from scoring citizens and monitoring them under our new social control program, and get them to pay for our vaccines."

His cracked lips twisted into a power-drunk sneer. "Of course, the wealthy can also make donations to increase their score, pay fines to get bad scores erased or buy social score credits. This money comes to us since our companies run the social scoring systems for governments like we run the prisons we put people in if they don't follow our rules under the new social control programs."

"What about the people who can't afford that?" I asked naively.

"Poor people? Well…if they can't afford to pay to improve their scores, they will continue to have low social scores indefinitely. Finally, they will become an underclass, because with a low score they can't get access to fast Internet. They'll be used for labor, mostly. We will block their access to decent jobs, we will refuse loans, deny them access to libraries, reject their travel visas, prevent access to credit cards, remove the ability to rent a car and stop online purchases. And most important of all, their babies won't be able to get genetic enhancements like increased memory, intelligence, speed, strength, ability to sustain cold, longevity, access to the best private schools and so much more." Norburg smiled like a mad man.

"You've really thought this through," I said.

"This is only the beginning," he said, seeming to study the insane plan in his mind. "We've already developed a genetic calculation that predicts a person's odds of reaching a certain income."

"Well, that's not so bad, is it? I wouldn't mind knowing that," I replied.

"Be careful what you wish for, son. There are a million opportunities for us to monetize and weaponize it, to increase existing inequalities or create new ones."

"Like what?"

"Well, social programs might use it as disqualifying criteria for receiving social benefits. Your employers could ask you to submit your genetic income score as part of a job application and based on that, they could determine your salary. Insurance companies could use it to calculate your premiums. Social and dating apps could allow you only to pair up with those genetically inclined toward success. Fertility clinics could incorporate it into their genetic screening procedures so parents can choose the highest-earning embryos."

This was truly terrifying. My heart thudded faster. At the same time, I noticed the sky over New York growing darker. I wanted to ask the question in my heart but was afraid of what the answer would be.

"So...what happens when AI meets cutting-edge genomics coupled with people's social media data and other digital footprints, including facial recognition?"

Norburg looked at me like a proud psychotic father and grinned. "That is the trillion-dollar business question, Brian."

My heart boomed and thudded. Norburg glared at me with one widened eye. "We're the major financial backers of companies overseas who are far ahead of the USA in creating a 'digital DNA avatar,' or in other words, a digital version of each of the billions of people we have in our system. The AI then monitors their entire genetic blueprint as it evolves day by day. The avatar knows everything about the person as it keeps tracking interactions between a person's genes."

Norburg continued. "The work at EYE-CORP is to exploit it to its fullest—the combination of AI and genomics data to drive precision medicine since we can understand why any of our subjects' bodies react to different viruses in the environment and types of chemicals. Then, we can recommend the best medicines and treatments."

*We...we...we.* That one word kept screaming in my head. It now began to make sense to me. And even though EYE-CORP's work sounded like something positive, something with the potential to save lives, I was sure there was an evil angle to it. Controlling people was taking away their own free will.

Norburg continued. "We will own key patents to, for instance, Alzheimer or cancer diagnostics and therapeutics. That's billions and billions of potential revenue, son, as we hold and control the crystal ball into the future health of each of our subjects."

"Precision medicine, Pops."

"Exactly."

"Is no one challenging your right to use all that personal data?"

"You're too young and naive," he replied. "Do you think we're asking for permission? Did you read about the hacking of health insurer Anthem in 2015? Or about the bold 2016 ransomware attacks targeting U.S. hospitals across New York, Florida, California, Kentucky and Washington D.C., where we forced the health systems to shut their IT programs and only restart them after we'd managed to get access to the patient data we needed? Industrial espionage on a massive scale, son. We hack not only hospitals' electronic databases but also online medical devices and health applications used by patients around the world. Remember ReQuest Diagnostics, which uses IBM Watson's Genomics platform?"

"Of course, I do."

"We hacked them also in December 2015, and robbed their 134,000 patients of their data."

I struggled to understand. "What did you get out of that?"

He laughed sharply. "Son, stealing people's most sensitive genetic data allows us to exploit it for insurance fraud or identity theft. We will profit in every way from all of our subjects' health information. We are the equivalent in the medical world of Facebook and its ability to exploit and monetize your social media data without asking for your permission.

"In fact," he gloated, "Facebook is a choirboy compared to what we can do now. Combing the world's most powerful AI with your genomics data, your physical footprint in the world through facial recognition, your entire digital footprint including social media that we stream live from Facebook, Twitter, dating platforms, your phone calls, emails, et cetera, we'll fucking *own* you and do whatever we want to you. Hell, we can even hack in and stop your pacemaker or change the dosage on your insulin pump. No one in human history has ever had that much power and knowledge about an individual."

"Pure evil genius," I replied, feeling sick to my stomach at the thought. Norburg licked the tip of his cracked upper lip. "So, what happens when someone doesn't want to comply or protests the use of their health or social media data?"

"What do you *think* happens? We know everything about them. We know which genes can kill them, we know what viruses can cripple them, we know what medication they're allergic to, their darkest secrets on the Internet, we read all their emails, have cloned their voices...we fucking *control* them and from a scale from 1-10 can decide on how badly we want to hurt them."

*Control them, and hurt them.* I drew in a sharp breath. I felt my right hand dangling at my side, and realized I was clenching and unclenching the fingers without noticing. "OK," I shuddered, "what is one, then?"

He smiled. "One is a warning. We embarrass you online, or we lower your social score, which won't allow you to get a loan or the ability to get health insurance or get into the best schools."

*This man is more of a lunatic than I realized,* I thought. "And what is 10?"

"Thank you for asking. 10 is my favourite," he said, with a sick smile. "We can locate a person and armed with their genetic information, AI knows which genes can be expressed and how to kill the billions we control. It raises the temperature and transmits a sound over a cell phone, and warms a patch of skin to the exact temperature needed for a killer gene to produce a protein that will kill. It only takes a few seconds."

*Dear God. The old man is truly out of his fucking mind. I have to find a way to stop them. I need your help, Lord!*

"Brilliantly evil," I said, my heart suddenly pounding out of control with fear. "But how do you make them pick up the phone call?"

"The AI can clone anyone's voice in less than 3 seconds, which we, in fact, have already done for the billions of people from whom we hold the DNA and monitor their phone calls. So it imitates their voices, and the call will be from a family member, a loved one or their boss, to make sure they answer. Before they suspect anything, it's too late. They all die differently, based on what genes are activated.

"Precision medicine for ya," he laughed, his face glistening with sweat.

I nodded. Suddenly, a large 3D image in the globe-like ceiling changed to a map of the world, spinning faster, then faster again, finally zeroing in on the USA, then zooming in on the East Coast, then New York and finally, JKF International Airport.

My eyebrows went up. *What is going on here?* From there, the image zoomed in on the tarmac, the image finally coming to rest on a heavyset man with grey hair, power-dressed, about to climb the steps of a small private Beechcraft King Air 100 jet.

"Let me show you what happens a few months from now when someone breaks the virus quarantine, or tries to evade our tracking of them," he said.

The image continued zooming in on the grey-haired man at his jet.

"Who's *he*?" I asked, trying not to sound anxious, hearing the plane's engines warming up in the background.

Norburg just smiled.

"AI, initiate the sequence," he instructed.

Breathless, I waited. Millions of numbers scrolled on another part of the massive screen. It suddenly stopped and selected a number.

It dialed.

There was a murmur of assent from Norburg. As we watched, the man froze on the jet's steps as his phone rang. *Don't answer,* I thought. *Dear God. Don't!* I pleaded. The man stared surprised, reached inside his left suit pocket, fumbling around, took out his cell phone, looked at the screen, and pressed it to his ear.

At that moment, another part of the screen monitored the man's body temperature rising fast. 33 degrees Celcius. …34 degrees…35…

"The sonic attack is underway, and he doesn't even know it," Norburg snorted.

The man on the screen pressed the phone tighter to his ear, listening. He rolled his shoulders and adjusted his tie, then loosened his collar. Suddenly, he turned around and looked back. For the first time, I saw his face and recognised him.

*The Secretary-General of the United Nations. Holy shit.*

My eyes scanned the man's face. *Oh my God,* I whispered. The screen registered 37 degrees now. Then 38. I panicked.

"What d'you want with *him?*" I blurted out, trying my best to appear composed.

Norburg's tongue flicked across his mouth. "He refused to join us and began interfering in our plans. And he's the former President of Socialist International…"

The target temperature flashed on the screen: 41 degrees, and rising.

"When it hits 42 degrees Celcius..." Norburg said, pleased with himself. He didn't finish his sentence. My tension was accentuated by his silence. The screen flashed from 41 to 42…Suddenly…

*"Wait!"* I shouted, and Norburg spun to look at me.

"Abort," he ordered.

On the screen, I could see the Secretary-General gasp a huge breath, then stare in wonder at the terminated call.

Norburg looked at me with a twinkle. "Are you out of your fucking minds?" I snarled.

Norburg dropped his head, bitter disappointment turning to rage. "He's the Secretary-General! You can't kill him!" I screamed.

Leaning back, Norburg turned with polite deference, tapping his crossed arms with his long fingers. *Tap, tap.* He gazed at me, eyes full of hurt. He glanced over at two of his giant goons hovering nearby.

"And why not, Brian?"

I gave him a sweet smile, gulping. *Have to think. Think fast.* My fingers trembled. "Because…we can *use* him!"

My voice quivered a little, the words coming out quickly. Suddenly, great-grandad's face transformed, and he stared at me hopefully.

"We can *manipulate* him!" I added. "He's a socialist who wants equality, better living standards, an end to hunger, and organized society, right? We can offer him unparalleled social control and growth and an end to disease because we can eradicate it with gene editing. He can help us herd the sheep where we want them!"

As I watched Norburg, a shiver crept up his old spine. "Son, that is pure genius."

I blinked, a drop of sweat sliding down my cheek. "It's in my genes, Pops. Give me a day."

Great-grandad looked at me with unbridled joy and pride, then applauded.

"You remind me of myself at your age, Brian. I love this."

His affectionate stare gave me a creepy feeling. I smiled faintly. "You can arrange a meeting with him, right? Make me a Senior Government Advisor to one of the Nordic countries, maybe Finland, then I take him by surprise."

He winked, delighted, and flashed a smile that looked ready to burst. Leaving the shadows, he embraced me, his sharp nails digging into my back. Sweat trickled down my chest. As we hugged, I looked up at the vastness of New York outside Norburg's window, dark storm clouds blotting the sky. Then the heavens opened up, and the rain began to fall, battering the city in biblical torrents.

* * *

# Forty-Seven

The address of the headquarters of the UN is 760, United Nations Plaza in the Turtle Bay neighbourhood of Manhattan, New York. It's bordered by First Avenue, East 42nd Street, East 48th Street, and the East River, housed inside an iconic building with flags of every nationality flapping in the wind.

Ironically, it reminded me of one of the Twin Towers.

I walked there, rather than take a cab in the traffic madness that is Manhattan, even in the pouring rain, to give myself time to think. To ponder. To come up with a plan.

This was going to be a challenging meeting, and I had to bring my A-game.

I arrived on time for our two o'clock meeting and was met in the reception area by a short, squat, stern little woman with a knife-sharp smile. She introduced herself, showing teeth as big as a horse's, gave me a visitor's badge, then kept silent as we took the elevator to the top floor.

On the ride, my nerves felt shattered. I felt like the world's biggest fool. *You aided and abetted all this madness, your entire lifetime, without ever suspecting!* The elevator stopped, the woman gestured for me to exit, then walked swiftly past me toward gargantuan wooden double-doors where a muscular security guard sat at a desk. He nodded at me, checked his computer, eyed my face closely, and then escorted me down a long, twisting corridor to meet the Secretary-General.

Immediately, I recognized the man. He sat in a spacious office behind a massive wooden desk that dwarfed him. *You have no idea how close you came to dying, my friend,* my mind whispered.

"Nice to meet you, Brian," he said, offering me a firm handshake. "Although I can't imagine why you want to meet me."

*There are a lot of things you can't imagine,* I thought. *All right, Brian. Time to fire away.*

"You turned us down, threatened us."

The Secretary-General sat back, stared at me, perplexed.

"No, Mr. Secretary-General. I don't mean Finland," I said, squinting down at my Senior Government Advisor badge, "I'm talking about The Seven."

The smile immediately dropped from his face, and his stare became laser-like, his words spitting out in a nervous, staccato beat.

"I…I…I won't change my mind!"

I looked around, eyes narrowing at him. "Remember that call you received at JFK yesterday, on the stairs to your jet? Spoiler alert: you weren't talking to the President of the United States."

He looked momentarily shocked, and shifted in his seat.

"What do you mean?"

"It was the world's most sophisticated AI computer emulating his voice. Would you like me to repeat every word of your conversation?"

He surveyed me in a panic. He raised his hand to stop me. Then his hand fiddled with a button under his desk, and he muttered, "Nice to meet you, Brian. Now, if you'll just…"

"You better listen to me."

He pressed the button. Again. And again. Abruptly the muscled security guy barged inside and glared at me. The Secretary-General paused. I could almost hear his breath catch.

"Why should I listen to you?" he said, his voice tight.

I gave him my best stony look. "Because I saved your fucking life yesterday. You were half a degree away from suffering a massive brain haemorrhage and dying on that staircase."

We stared hard at each other. After a moment, his eyes didn't seem to see me at all.

"Sir?" the guard interrupted.

The Secretary-General looked rattled. He looked back at me then waved the guard away. He leaned forward, listening intently, his expression settled into a puzzled mask.

"How did you do that? And why save my life?

I started talking, and he leaned further forward, visibly trembling.

* * *

# Forty-Eight

YOUR APPOINTMENT IS FOR ONE O'CLOCK, read the text message on my phone.

It was the day following my meeting with the Secretary-General, a rainy and windswept Wednesday. I left my apartment building briskly, ready to reveal the first part of my plan.

Strolling up 5th Ave, I turned left onto East 40th Street and up 8th Avenue. The rain splashed down, harder and harder, but I had my coat on and walked again instead of taking a cab, my old, brown leather handbag by my side.

Kids pushing clothes on metal rails dashed and darted about. I was close to the Garment District, and I watched the amazing building opposite, all glass and steel with people busily working at glowing computers at hundreds of desks. The huge sign on the side of the office block read THE NEW YORK GLOBAL PRESS.

A nervous twitch stabbed my gut. I was here to see my friend, Louise, an investigative journalist at the paper, to hand over the hard-copy and thumb drive of my book, *UNIVERSO-i.*

I had spent the past four months frantically writing the book that was going to reveal everything I had discovered on my journey. A book that was going to rip away the curtain and expose all the secrets behind The Seven. There was no more time left.

This was not my first book. I had written some historical fiction for young adults set in the Vikings age, and the first book in the series had been published in several countries in Europe. But this book was a whole different beast—what it revealed would rock the world, what it uncovered was frightening, shocking, scandalous, a content of epic proportions, and a matter of life and death for me and for hundreds of millions of others.

I needed to open people's eyes to what was happening, why they're so fearful, and how The Seven had orchestrated this.

I only had one hard copy of the book since I worked on it offline, conscious that The Seven could hack my computer and destroy the files. As I reached the New York Global Press' security station, a guard mumbled, "Empty your pockets, sir," and I put my thumb drive and keys in my satchel, placing the bag gently in the basket.

I gazed around. There was a long line of people trying to get through security. When I finally stepped through the metal detector and looked around for my satchel, my heart missed a beat.

My satchel was gone. So was the thumb drive, and the only paper copy of my book inside.

*No! This can't be happening, not now!*

"Fuck!" I hissed, clenching my hands into fists, the people around me staring.

At the back of the security a crowd was gathered. I dashed back and forth, scanning the crowd, then the corridor. Speechless, I stared everybody passing me up and down, hoping to find the culprit clutching my satchel. *Who has it?* I noticed one of the security guys rushing towards a back door, glancing suspiciously over his shoulder.

"Hey, you! Stop that man!" I shouted and ran back through security with guards roughly reaching out, grasping my arms, my legs, trying to stop me.

The thief raced outside, shoving pedestrians aside, hopped on a motorcycle, kick-starting it. I tore away from security, sprinted toward the man, reaching him as he gunned the motor, trying frantically to wrestle my bag away from him.

"Give me that bag!" I shrieked. I tried to break his fingers. In the struggle, the man slugged me hard in the face. Disoriented, I lurched backward, then hit the ground. This managed to free him from my grip, and he roared away on the bike, clinging onto my ripped-open leather bag.

I stumbled back to my feet, knees wobbling, clutching the ache on my jaw. I watched him speed around the block. Cursing my luck, I hustled back inside the lobby where my friend, Louise the journalist, was waiting.

Taking Louise aside, I announced, "The Seven must have bribed one of your security guards to steal my book."

Louise stared in shock. "I can't believe you didn't keep another copy or put it in the cloud."

"They could hack into that, Louise," I groaned, licking my wounds. "They're on to me."

She shrugged, grunted, shook her head slowly and then walked off. I looked at my watch — s*hit, running out of time.* Rubbing my aching jaw, I bolted outside to catch a taxi, praying I still had one very big ace up my sleeve.

* * *

Eighth Avenue. Later that morning. A petite 11-year-old black girl is sucking a lollipop on the corner. As she strolls the boulevard, her candy dripping, she notices something glinting brightly on the sidewalk.

She stops. Bends. Looks down. *A thumb-drive.*

Curious, she picks it up, looks around, and then heads off down the sidewalk again to visit her aunt on school holiday. Ready for another happy reunion, she plugs the thumb drive into her MacBook.

There, she finds a file marked *Confidential NYGP Louise Schwarzman – UNIVERSO-i.*

The girl stares, puzzled, then googles *Louise Schwarzman* and sees she is a journalist at a major New York newspaper. *Interesting.*

After lunch with her aunt, the girl goes straight to the newspaper, lollipop still in her mouth. At the front desk, a friendly receptionist smiles at the little black girl and makes a call.

"Louise, there's a school-girl asking for you at reception."

"Tell her I'm busy. I have a copy deadline."

The receptionist looks down at the girl and smiles. "Miss Schwarzman is a very busy lady," she advises the little girl. "Can I take a message?"

"That's alright, I'll wait," and the girl plops into a chair, producing a pocketbook, *The Prophet* by Kahlil Gibran. The receptionist eyes her, impressed as the girl sits, slurping her Popsicle, patiently reading.

Ten minutes later, the receptionist—impressed with the little girl's determination—picks up the phone and calls again.

"Um…Louise? Sorry to pester, but that little girl is still here, and she's not leaving until she sees you." And she winks at the girl.

Minutes later, the journalist arrives looking harassed.

"Hello, little girl. I'm Louise Schwarzman. How can I help?"

The girl puts down her book, rises, shakes the woman's hand. "I'm Destiny, a pleasure to meet you, Louise," she replies like a grown-up. "By the way, I think it's me that's helping *you.*"

She reaches in her pocket, digs deeply, emptying that pocket then emptying the other, while exasperation crawls up the journalist's spine. Finally, the girl smiles, hands Louise the thumb drive, telling her, "I found it in the street."

Louise takes the thumb drive. Studies it. Immediately she realizes what it is.

"My God, *Brian's file!*"

She beams at the little girl, noticing her school uniform and the school crest depicting a cluster of seven shooting stars soaring across the night sky.

"That's a beautiful uniform. Where do you go to school?"

"Florida," the girl replies.

"Well, you tell your parents for me that they have an incredibly special girl."

"I don't have any parents. I live in an orphanage."

The answer takes Louise by surprise.

"Don't worry, it's a little more than an orphanage," the girl whispers and winks at the journalist.

At that moment a phone call buzzes through on the little girl's Apple wristwatch. Encrypted binary codes stream across the small monitor on her wrist.

"OK, gotta go now, lives to save," she says, and shoves a new lollipop in her mouth.

"Right," Louise says, smiling sardonically at the little girl. "Go save the world."

They hug. Quickly the girl vanishes out the door into the rain and the crowd of pedestrians and New York cabs.

Louise ponders a moment about this remarkable little girl, her watch with encrypted codes, the strange orphanage, *The Prophet.* She scrambles to pull out her phone, speed-dials and says excitedly, "Brian, it's Louise...you'll never guess!"

* * *

# Forty-Nine

Sure enough, the next morning, published on The Global Press website, Louise had posted her article:

*THE RISE OF THE SEVEN*
*By Louise Schwarzman*
*Part one of an investigative series revealing an evil shadow group.*

*Every time you buy a house, a car, jewelery, soft drinks, alcohol, gas—anything—your dollars drop into the pockets of The Seven. They're the ruthless, secretive group that owns most of the world's biggest brands. You've not heard of them. But they've heard of you. When you put your money in the bank, some goes to funding wars and other illegal criminal activities. And if you think you're giving them a lot of your cash now, wait till you hear about their plans for your DNA. Even more terrifying are their plans to release a virus so infectious that it will create a global pandemic, forcing all governments to implement protocols to track its citizens to control the spread.*

My cell phone dinged, and a text appeared.

*'Hope you like the article. I'm nailing these bastards. And good luck at the UN...Louise.'*

I checked my watch. *Already 9:15.* I smiled and went back to preparing my speech. As I grabbed my phone to call Louise and thank her, I heard a strange whimpering sound I'd never heard before. I stopped, drew in a breath. Listening. *There it is again.* With a glance toward the kitchen I froze.

It was coming from Flower.

"Hey, girl, what..."

Around the corner I could hear Flower, whimpering, mewling, gasping. I dropped my phone and raced over to find her lying on the kitchen floor, her lips pale white and curled back from her teeth, eyes red and woozy from vomiting, and a dark chocolate wrapper by her face. Raspy sounds gurgled from her heaving white chest.

*What the hell? But I hadn't given her chocolate!*

I dropped to the floor and hugged her. Flower's muscles were tense, her body rippling and writhing with pain. "Flower! Hey girl! Who gave you the chocolate, girl?"

Flower moaned, her eyes flooding with tears, her head sagging. I cursed aloud, listening to her heartbeat. As I did, my teeth ground together. Her heart rate had increased, she was panting excessively, muscle spasms spreading across her back, her legs trembling, her head convulsing.

*Oh my God! She's been poisoned! Dark chocolate will kill a dog!* I had to do something. I knew that she wouldn't be able to metabolize the theobromine in the chocolate as fast as I would and as a result, her heart, kidneys, and central nervous system would soon shut down. She could die any minute.

"Dammit, Flower, don't die!" Hastily, I picked her up in my arms. I searched around, fumbled in my pocket, grabbed my phone, and made a call.

"Animal Hospital," a voice said, and I anxiously replied, "Dr. Winton, please!"

"He's in surgery right now, sir. Can I take a message?"

*In surgery? Now? Bloody hell!!* My mind raced as I tried to recall any other vets I'd taken Flower to in the past, drawing a blank.

"Listen," I pleaded, "it's an emergency!"

The other end of the line was silent. "I understand, sir. If you give me your number…" but I was too anxious and hung up.

"Dammit to hell!!" I stared around the room, eyes scanning, heart thumping, mind spinning, trying to gather my wits. Louise's article seemed to stare back in my mind's eye. All at once, I knew who had done this to my precious dog.

*The Seven! Those fuckers!!!*

All at once my phone rang, and I answered, half expecting one of The Seven to be on the line, gloating.

"Your taxi is outside, sir," a voice said, then hung up.

*My taxi?!* I cursed aloud again, shoving my phone in my pocket, not knowing what to do. In my arms, I could feel more spasms rock

Flower's body, her head lolling, going limp. I hugged my beloved pet closer, watching the flicker of her eyes slowly fade, her eyes closing.

"Flower?"

At my voice, Flower opened her eyes wide.

"Don't die, Flower! Not after all my pain we've been through together!"

Flower peered up at me, her eyelids fluttering. She whimpered pitifully. Tears filled my eyes.

"Stay with me, my best friend!" I cried, wrapping my arms tight around her, kissing her head, stroking her ears. Wisps of hair fluttered down in her eyes.

I choked, struggling to speak. Flower's eyes closed. Her body spasmed, went limp, then spasmed again, in pain. *"Flower!! Stay with me, girl!"*

For a moment her eyes snapped open again, then the eyelids dropped. Together we laid our heads down on the cool kitchen floor. *Dammit, she can't die!* Suddenly, I remembered something. I dragged myself off the floor, picked Flower up and carried her gently to my bed, then ran to my bookshelf, grabbed a thick book and frantically flipped pages.

*Where is it? Where is it, dammit?!*

I flipped more and more pages, in a panic. It was Tiponi's book, and I searched for herbs that could help combat poison.

*C'mon, Brian, think! Where is it? Where the hell IS IT??*

*There!* At last, I found it. Quickly I read the entry for *PCHM,* Poisonous Chinese Herbal Medicine, ran to my shelves where I stored hundreds of bottles, scanned them alphabetically, and then hastily grabbed a bottle of Arsenicum album and some food-grade activated granular charcoal to absorb any remaining toxins inside her body.

I ran back to Flower and opened the bottles, pouring the Arsenicum album liquid down her throat and the active charcoal into her drinking water, her eyes giving me an imploring look, breaking my heart. *C'mon, Flower, you can make it, girl!* I lifted her head and forced her to drink the water.

I looked at my watch, hearing a car horn blare outside, rifled my pockets for notes marked *UN Speech* and fought back the tears. *Not now…dear God, why now??*

"My beautiful Flower, please get better. And please…forgive me."

I kissed her again, praying she'd be alright, peeled my trembling hands away from her, then with one long look at her, raced out. As I hit the streets, the rain pummeled me, and I realized the great storm over New York had arrived.

* * *

# Fifty

The taxi swerved and careened through the streets, screeching to hard stops on the rainy pavement, whipping around corners. I sat in the back seat, jolted around, my breathing suspended, fighting like hell to blot out my feelings. It was impossible.

I was leaving my precious Flower alone, not knowing if I'd see her alive again. It was only the thought of helping humanity with my speech at the UN that kept me going.

Guilt and worry poured through me, creasing my face. The driver kept asking, "Are you alright, man?"

I waved him off. After a while, the outside world blurred, out of focus. *I'm not sure how my address at the UN will turn out,* I pondered, *as I'll be thinking about poor Flower all the time.*

I hoped and prayed that everything would go as planned. This was my end-game.

There was a sudden slackening of speed and a sharp hiss of brakes as we hit downtown traffic. I pressed my eyes to the window. *C'mon, shit!* The cabbie barked and snarled at other drivers. With a thundering howl our car took off down a side street. Two minutes later the taxi screamed to a stop. The driver hurled my door open to let me out, and I hustled up 3rd Avenue, covering my head from the rainstorm, turning right on East 42nd Street. Soon I was standing in front of the United Nations headquarters.

Bright flags from 193 countries flapped in the breeze, making a fluttering sound, like a flock of angry birds. The rain had soaked and transformed each of the 193 flags a darker hue, some blood-red, some almost black.

I hurried up the UN steps. They were packed with crowds, hundreds of protestors waving and shouting slogans written on placards that read: *UNeed to ACT*, *UNeed to LISTEN* and *UNeed to HELP*. Countless press reporters interviewed angry demonstrators as dozens of TV cameras pointed at the mob, screaming as the colourful foreign dignitaries arrived.

There was also a huge police presence, including SWAT teams, snipers on roofs overlooking the building and police helicopters buzzing above.

I showed my credentials, got through security, two guards leading me into the massive, impressive General Assembly Hall, in virtual darkness now. Then the guards turned on the bright lights and left.

I gazed around at all the empty seats. I closed my eyes and drank in the silence. The silence I heard was more intense than any I'd ever felt. *Don't fuck this up, Brian,* my mind pleaded. I stepped up to the podium and took a deep breath for my rehearsal speech.

"Excellences, distinguished delegates, ladies and gentlemen…"

I looked over the enormous hall, imagining it full.

"…it's my privilege to speak in the UN, created to make our world a safer, better place."

Behind me, the screen showed the UN logo, then captions: *Rising to the Challenges of International Security and the Emergence of Artificial Intelligence, 70th Session of the UN General Assembly.* Then below, *The United Nations Interregional Crime and Justice Research Institute (UNICRI).*

I blinked several times, shook my head, and then continued, "I've been on a quest, a voyage of discovery."

The big screen behind me flashed an image, white on a black background, *UNIVERSO-i.*

"You don't know my name. That's unimportant. But my message, what I have discovered...*is*."

I closed my eyes. I imagined people exchanging confused glances.

"Human civilization started around 12,000 years ago. We went from zero to the Declaration of Human Rights, Michelangelo's Pietà, Shakespeare and Mozart, to modern advancements like the telephone, flight, moon landings, gene-editing, artificial intelligence, and quantum computers…in less than 500 generations."

I fixed my gaze on all the empty seats and smiled.

"That progress is astounding, but it didn't happen by chance. Generation after generation, every soul born had to conquer their fears of failure, the unknown and of disappointing others."

I paused for effect, hoping my message would be heard.

"Fear prevented people from following their dreams and exploring their passions and unbelievable talents."

"But those who overcame fear unleashed powers granted to everyone at birth; greatness with unimaginable potential to shape their lives and control their destiny, leaving a path for others to follow."

I imagined people nodding their heads in recognition.

"It's said that long ago, human lives were full of magic."

The screen behind me showed film of stunning woodlands, rivers and lakes, a couple holding hands, childbirth, a baby chuckling, smiling elders watching in delight.

"As time passed, people obsessed on things that were less real than magic; money, power, owning things, dominating other people, other life forms, and utilizing the earth's resources to increase wealth. Our reality is our perception, and so these things became dominant in our lives, and we slowly forgot about our magic."

The film changed to images of human hands greedily grasping cash, money fluttering in the air, followed by awful scenes of slaughter of indigenous tribes around the world.

"We drowned out the voices of our ancestors and stopped conversing with swaying trees. Our lives became to-do lists and money worries. Money ruled us. And slowly, without us noticing, materialism became our reality. We lost our ability to see the magic inherent in all creation and lost the abundance of the magical earth."

The footage behind me showed images of people in swarms hurrying, rushing, shoving, anxious, in a panic, flashing cash, buying things, screaming.

"Now, people only hear about magic in old songs and stories or Hollywood, and they think it's make-believe, fiction, nothing else. We've forgotten the magic and how to pass it to the new generation. Our children grow up on computers instead of outside. We don't hear the beautiful voices of nature. And we forget that there's magic in plants and herbs with which we can heal ourselves."

The filmed images showed native tribes all over the world, gathering herbs and treating people.

"But the magic still surrounds us, even when we can't see it, like stars burning in the daytime. There are clues everywhere if we take the time to look."

The footage over my shoulder revealed a beautiful sunny day, darkening to a skyfull of twinkling stars. I imagined the delegates gazing up in wonder.

"We used to live in harmony with earth. Today, we trample all over it. Our obsession for material wealth overwhelms everything, including war and peace and all the glorious things humans *should* be interested in."

The film behind displays a family walking in the forest, a lake sparkling, fish leaping, horses galloping.

"We've failed to solve our individual and social problems, which reveals a tragic deficiency in the true understanding of the basic nature of the human race, and the true purpose of life…

"Each year, 50,000 women are killed at the hands of intimate partners or family members…that works out to nearly six women every single hour of the day."

Video zooms in on a cobbled street in Italy, the front of a courthouse, with 137 pairs of red women's shoes displayed for the number of women killed each day in the world, together with some white shoes for the children who died alongside their loving mothers.

In my mind, I could hear the entire assembly gasp in shock from the powerful effect of seeing all these empty women's and children's shoes on the street.

I continued.

"There are approximately 20 to 30 million slaves in the world today. According to the U.S. State Department, up to 2 million people are trafficked across international borders every year, of which 80% are female, and half are children.

"For all of them," I shouted, "fear is *damn real!*

"This evil abomination of how humans exploit and treat each other cannot and will not stand. A terrible storm is gathering, ready to detonate. It will wreck universal disaster until we change our behaviours…but it's not inevitable."

In my mind, the delegates and audiences across the world watched and waited for what I had to say next. I paused. I let my words sink in.

"We're guilty of collective amnesia. We've forgotten something incredible; the magic within us. How we're part of everything, and everything is part of us."

The image on the screen showed plants, forests, insects, fish, coral, mammals, and humans of every race.

"Instead of living *with* the earth, today we destroy it in the name of material wealth. Everyone with vested interest thinks they fight for right. Instead, they've caused terrible wars and bathed our society in bloody conflict."

The image flashed to show environmental damage: polar icecaps melting, machines digging up diamond mines, and Amazon rainforests being destroyed.

"Why have we forgotten the real meaning of life?"

I paused, imagining the audience thinking about that.

"The reason is simple: there are gigantic power and money at stake for people and organizations that can make us forget that we were born with amazing abilities to shape our lives.

"These people call themselves The Seven. They are the puppet masters behind the scenes, pulling strings. They call it Project Fear. But that's only the first phase."

I paused again, picturing delegates fidgeting in their seats, the watching world waiting, on edge, full of trepidation.

"First, Project Fear learns everything about you. It knows more about you than someone looking through your window or rifling through your drawers."

The large image behind me changed to a colour-coded pie-chart titled *What people do online every minute.*

"Every 60 seconds, there are one million logins on Facebook, 18 million texts and 188 million emails sent, 3.8 million Google searches, 4.5 million views on YouTube, 1.4 million Tinder swipes, over 154,000 Skype calls, over ½ million photos shared on Snapchat, 456,000 Tweets, 46,740 photos posted on Instagram…and the data is exploding. It reveals everyone's lives in intimate detail. Imagine what they know about you from analysing that data every second, every day. Simply, they know more about you...than *you.*"

I could almost hear people in the room gasp in surprise.

"Then, using predictive analytics, they forecast if you'll commit a crime, if you'll buy a steak or a cheeseburger, the music you'll listen to, the TV programmes you'll watch, where you'll be any time and crucially, what disease you might get, based on your genetic makeup."

I imagined people everywhere holding their breath.

"For their next step, The Seven collect people's DNA. They set up companies offering info on ancestry or disease prevention. When people send their DNA, they believe it's safe. The Seven also launched cyber-attacks on biobanks and healthcare companies which hold citizens most vital personal healthcare information, as well as their DNA. Billions of records."

Screens showed millions upon millions of images of medical and ancestry records.

"People insure possessions, but they're so careless with their most priceless asset…their *DNA.*"

I paused again, imagining shouts from the audience around the world, getting angrier and angrier.

"There's no such thing as anonymous DNA. Corporations claim removing names anonymizes it. Lies. From one drop of blood, they can accurately reconstruct anyone's face using DNA Phenotyping, creating physical features from your genetic data. They've built models that predict 3D facial structure, voice, biological age, height, weight, body mass index and eye, and skin colour. And once they know your face, using their global surveillance technology, they can find anyone, anytime, anywhere in the world. You think turning off your cell phone, computer or TV makes you safe? Wrong. Every device can be activated remotely and turned into a camera and a listening device…

"To ensure tracking of every citizen on the planet, a few weeks from now a terrifying virus will be released from an unknown location in the world that will create a pandemic of epic proportions. Thousands and thousands will die. To control the spread of the disease governments will be forced to track all of its citizens. Perhaps they will create a chip to be inserted into vaccines and perhaps they will make the vaccines mandatory. That's how they can monitor everyone's behavior. Naturally, lies will be spread about how and from where it started, to make us believe this was an accident.

"This isn't science-fiction—it's happening right now. Google it. Previous pandemics like the DNA Avatars, CRISPR gene-editing delivered by a gel, sonic devices that can activate a gene through heat to release a lethal protein, social control programs being introduced to replace the older credit score system, reconstruction of someone's face from a drop of their blood then using that sketch to locate them on global surveillance, AI identification of genetic disorders by the shape of someone's face—three seconds is all it takes for AI to clone your voice. Meanwhile, researchers working on linking your genes to determine your future income..."

I opened my mouth to say more. Erupting from the shadows, loud clapping interrupted, a bright light shining in my face.

Shocked, blinded, I put up my hand to try to see where it was coming from. Tension rippled through me. Stepping to the side of the podium, I squinted, peering deeper, my eyes narrowed. "Who's there?"

A long silence. Out of the empty seats, a voice echoed.

"Brilliant, almost made me cry," a man with a cultured accent said patronizingly.

My blood froze. *I know that voice. It's...*

"Almost," the voice repeated gravely.

*Azazel.*

Out of the shadows he approached, keeping his gaze on me. Sweat rolled down my face, stinging my eyes. Quickly I scanned the room for an escape. I saw an exit but would never make it. *Too far. Now what?*

Closer and closer Azazel prowled. In one impressive lunge he jumped on stage, swept off his hat and his long coat and laid both carefully on the floor, revealing all black underneath. For the first time, I studied his face: clean-shaven, his short dark hair slicked to the side, even the hairs of his brow curated. *Very polished.* He grinned, without showing any teeth.

"You've spent too much time with those old sentimental folks at the orphanage," he said, standing 10 metres away, continuing to stroll until he'd blocked my exit.

His hand flashed to his hip. He produced his 3D ghost gun. I held my place, unmoving.

This was the moment to talk. Get him thinking, arouse his curiousity, try to confuse him. "You were once one of them, Azazel. They still love you like a son," I lied.

Some of the tension went out of his face. For a moment, he just looked at me, then smiled.

"Emotional intelligence won't save you. They know what I am now."

"We're not that different. We love animals, and they love us back. They give us unconditional love and friendship rarely found in humans."

He paused. He let the gun drop an inch. Slowly he put the weapon back in his holster. He stared at me thoughtfully. "You and I are on a collision course," he snapped, "and no cute animal stories will save you."

"Well, you do know that the virus will infect animals as well, right?" I said, trying my best to stall him."

"Yes, cats will be infected. But not dogs," he said and smiled with pride of his insider knowledge.

My bluff hadn't worked. Was it worth wasting my breath feeding him more lies? His mind seemed impregnable. He stepped towards the podium, then halted. I could see thoughts race across his face. He reached into his shirt pocket.

"They gave me this when I was young when they still believed in me."

He showed me a card, then flipped it over. On the back was the number SIX, and the phone number I recognized with an image: *Death.*

For a moment, I could see Azazel's mind working. I wondered if his thoughts were drifting back to the past.

"I've never called the number," he said. "No one would show up to help me."

I nodded and pulled out my card.

"Number SEVEN, Azazel. The final card in the deck."

At first, he looked puzzled, breath whistling through his teeth. This his eyes flickered, and a grim smile spread slowly across his face.

"And so here we are…destined to meet for a final battle here at the UN, the representation of all nations on the earth," Azazel replied quietly. "Let it be man-to-man, then."

As if in slow motion, both cards dropped and fluttered to the ground. Azazel's eyes went black.

I took a deep breath as the smell of rot filled my nostrils.

We ran towards each other with full force.

I leapt high in the air. *This is for Flower and Ahote, you bastard.*

I exploded upward with a flying kick hard in his face. He stumbled backwards and landed on his back, blood gushing out of his nose.

As I hit the ground, I spun around with a high heel kick, hoping to pummel his face before he recovered. But he rolled aside, and my foot pounded the ground with a loud thump. A sudden gush of pain jolted throughout my body. My stomach ached and my legs began to weaken.

"You've improved," Azazel muttered. With a vile smirk, he took his hand and smeared the blood across his face as he tried to wipe it off. Then he pulled out what looked like a composite knife from his shirt. "I could forgive you for the kick, but not for ruining my favourite shirt."

He circled me, twisting the knife in his hand through the air.

I rose from the floor, knees wobbling with pain. *God, it hurt!* Focusing my eyes on Azazel's knife, I quickly removed my jacket to use as a defence from the blade.

Hissing like a viper, he stepped towards me, waving the knife back and forth, faster, faster, then pointed it at my stomach. He lunged at me with a mighty cry. He wasn't as fast as I was. I dodged to the side in one fluid move. Then Azazel swiveled in my direction.

"*Oh, you bastard!*" he spat. He took two steps left, and I carefully moved backwards toward the wall, keeping my eyes on him.

Azazel swiped at me again and I dodged but this time, I felt his blade slice into my right side. I felt no pain; my adrenalin pumped fast and fierce.

He jabbed again. He lunged forward, cursing and screaming and slashing in downward strokes. I held out my jacket in front of me and managed to catch his left hand and wrap my jacket around it. Together, we writhed in a blur of kicks and punches… slashing, shrieking, and biting at each other.

At that point, rage overwhelmed Azazel. He moved backwards, dragging me in towards him so close that our noses almost touched. Then he reared back and slammed me in the temple with his right elbow. A sudden gush of pain jolted throughout my body. My tongue was soaked in the taste of blood. My stomach ached, my arms lost tension and my legs began to weaken.

I slumped to the ground.

"*Yes!*" Azazel wailed. "Say hello to death, Brian!" The roar from his shriek of triumph was ear-splitting.

Azazel pounced, his knife held high, as he got ready to stab his knife into my throat.

Suddenly, a voice from the empty seats shouted. "Hey! Security's on the way!"

The grip on me slackened and I fell backwards.

Filling my lungs with air, I tried crawling away. Azazel shoved the knife between his teeth, pulled me backward, then dragged me offstage to a room behind the curtain. He cursed, then snapping my head back he bashed me on the skull with the butt of his knife, and the whole world went black.

* * *

I couldn't breathe. There was a plastic bag over my head and in my mouth. *Oh, God! I'm going to suffocate!*

My head lolled at my chest. I opened my eyes a tiny slit. I was alone. I opened my mouth to suck in air, but no air came in. Only more of the plastic bag. I tried to move my hands, but they were fastened with duct tape.

My eyes widened in fear. I peered left, then right. The world beyond them was foggy and blurred. I realized that I was lying in a tiny storage room and this plastic bag was going to suffocate me.

My lungs screamed for air. I tried to stay calm so I wouldn't hyperventilate but found it impossible. *I need air—now—or I'll pass out and die.*

My hands struggled, then fell limp. If only I could dial the number on the card.

I heaved forward, a string of obscenities launching out from my clenched teeth. The plastic bag was like fire around my head. I looked up through the blurry material to see cameras recording everything. Azazel could come back at any moment.

Frantically, I struggled to free my hands, finally rolling onto my side. I strained and dug into my back pocket for my phone.

*Where is it, dammit? If it's gone or off, I'm dead. I won't have time to switch it on and punch in the code.*

My lungs were beyond screaming, and I desperately sucked in for air, but the plastic bag was deep in my mouth and throat.

I was about to pass out when inexplicably, a sense of peace washed over me. This was it. Death was here. I knew I'd made my share of mistakes in life but also that I had done my best to correct them and give to others every day. I was not afraid of dying but knowing that Flower may still need me made my instincts pull back from letting go.

*I can't die as long as Flower is out there, needing my help.*

In one last desperate effort, I dug deeper, felt my fingers scrape the phone, then touch the screen. I knew the phone app was in the corner of my screen. I pressed my index finger against the corner where the number one was.

The speed dial was set for the number on the card.

I pressed. And pressed again. Finally, my fingers went numb from pressing, and without knowing if I had dialed the number or not, everything in my vision faded to black, and my head dropped.

I'd just taken my last breath on this earth.

* * *

There was a loud click. Suddenly the storage room door opened with a squeak. I was vaguely aware of a tiny figure entering, sucking on a lollipop, wearing a baseball cap. The figure rushed to me and looked up, aware of the cameras recording. Then with a shrug the figure took the lollipop out of her mouth and used the stick-end to tear a hole in the plastic covering my mouth.

I breathed in. Deeply. Agonizingly. The Elixir of Life. The fresh air stung my lungs. *God, it feels good!*

I felt like I was dragged from the jaws of death as air re-entered my body. I coughed and choked. My lungs ached. *Air. Need more air! More—*

At that moment the plastic bag was ripped from my face. For a precious moment I breathed in more air. I opened my eyes. I couldn't believe what I saw.

"Destiny?" I spluttered as the young girl put the candy back in her mouth.

"In the flesh," she announced nonchalantly. "Here, let me untie you."

"I thought I was dead…"

At that her lips gave me the most angelic smile.

Cool air raced through my lungs. I looked up, seeing a faint luminosity around this young girl. Probably the overhead lights in the storage room. I lifted a hand up to my eyes. "Thank you, Destiny…"

There was no reply. The luminosity grew brighter. Then I blinked my eyes and she was gone.

*Bloody hell,* I grunted. I climbed dizzily to my feet and staggered forward, out into the hallway, bruised, bloody and half-dead.

A guard saw me, stared in shock, whirled around, and then ran to support me as sirens screamed. He hauled me outside and into the arms of two paramedics who gently laid me on a stretcher.

Searing pain shot through my body. I made a vague movement with my mouth but couldn't speak. The place was swarming with armed cops and SWAT teams in tactical gear in front of the building, while more breached the perimeter and rushed inside.

I clenched my teeth in pain, struggling with my memory of the little girl. *How the hell did she find me?* Suddenly, gunfire blasted from the roof. Everybody took cover.

Seconds later, a SWAT commander strode past my stretcher with his hand-held radio crackling.

"You got him?" the commander snapped into the radio.

A scrambled voice responded, "Yes, sir. Two pops in the chest, then he fell off the roof into the river."

"Roger that," the commander responded and raced into the UN.

I lay on the stretcher, stunned. I felt my pain slacken. *Azazel's dead, finally. We won the final battle,* my brain registered as the paramedics loaded me into the ambulance. The doors slammed, and I was rushed to NYU Medical Centre.

As we sped through the rainy streets, I heard multiple booms rumble overhead. *Thunder.* In my mind, it sounded like doom.

* * *

Later, as I lay in my hospital room and watched TV, I saw Azazel's death reported all over the news.

"…The U.S. Coast Guard says the tidal strait often changes its flow direction and is subject to strong current fluctuations, worsened by the narrow East River with its different depths, so the body was likely carried away. In other news…"

I clicked off the TV and twisted onto my back, thinking. A nurse arrived, and I struggled to sit up. "I need to get to the UN…"

She gently pushed me back. "Not anytime soon, sir. Your health is important."

I flopped back on the pillows and groaned, "Okay, but listen, I need to see if my dog is alright."

The nurse appraised me curiously. "Is there someone you could call about that?"

I thought hard. "D'you have my phone?"

Rifling through my possessions, she produced my jacket, prodded the pockets, and shook her head. "No, sir." My eyes welled up with worry about Flower, with haunting memories of our happy lives together—the quick patter of her paws on green grass, her fur flashing in the sunlight, nose thrust into my hand. Dear old Flower!

* * *

# Fifty-One

I begged and begged, until they released me from the hospital. Immediately I hailed a cab to get back to my house.

My body aching, I hurried into my building and tore into my apartment.

"Flower?" No reply. "Flower, I'm home!" I shouted. But there was no sign of her.

"Where are you, girl?" I called out, fighting fear. I paused, waiting for the shock to die down. She always scrambled up to me as soon as I arrived home. Not this time. The creeping reality suddenly hit me.

I raced to the bedroom.

"Flower!"

Instantly my heart sank. There she was, my lovely Flower, lying on the same spot on the bed where I'd left her. Crying uncontrollably, I rushed to her, kneeling with extra care, shaking her.

"Flower!" I whispered, running my hands through her fur. I flexed my fingers and took a firmer grip, holding tight.

"Flower! Please be alive!"

Fighting tears, I caressed her gently, stroking her head. A moment later, I noticed she was breathing as her sides heaved up and down. Up and down. Up and—

"Flower?" I gasped. Slowly her eyelids opened, and she looked at me with big beautiful brown eyes.

"Flower! You're alright!" I cried out, my voice breaking with joy. She shook her head sharply and focused her eyes. I hugged her and then lay beside her.

We lay close together for a while; her strength seemed to return.

For the longest time I didn't dare leave her. I cursed Azazel for poisoning my beloved dog. *At least he got what was coming.*

Softly, half-hypnotized, another thought came to mind. Then again, I wasn't so sure it was Azazel—he loved animals as much as I did. However, if not Azazel, then who?

* * *

# FIFTY-TWO

After a long hot bath, I sat on the couch with my laptop, recounting all that had happened. My phone dinged—a text from Louise, with an online link.

I opened the link, and my jaw hit the floor.

It seems a young Costa Rican intern at the UN named Gabriel had been in the Assembly Hall that day, seated in the back row, eating his lunch. He recorded my rehearsal speech, and the fight with Azazel, on his smartphone, then uploaded the footage to the Internet, realizing someone tried to kill me to stop me from making the speech.

In the hours since then, the views of Gabriel's post started climbing…1 million…1.3 million…2 million…then 5 million, 8 million, 12 million and climbing fast.

The talk went viral.

I gasped in surprise and delight.

The press went ballistic. My email was jammed with media demanding interviews, sound-bytes, and succinct wisdom, so I made a snap decision.

I'd launch my own YouTube channel, to try and reach as many people as possible, all around the world.

Without hesitating, I immediately hired a local private studio with top-quality audio and lighting, along with a green-screen. Then I plopped myself in a comfortable, fat brown leather armchair, and spoke without notes.

I broadcast my message. Live. To people around the world.

* * *

# Fifty-Three

The streets were crowded, jammed with pedestrians and automobiles, and policemen screaming at taxis. Strolling the next morning to Equinox Fitness Club on Broadway for a quick workout, I tried to focus my mind on absolutely nothing, freeing my thoughts to absorb the energy of the city. *Had I imagined my message would go viral? Seen by millions? No way!* Finally reaching the gym, and feeling a huge sense of triumph and relief, I lifted some weights and began my usual routines in the upstairs boxing studio, which was usually empty at this early hour.

With my wireless AirPods blasting music in my ears, I punched the bag from every angle. Sweat dripping down my face, and for a moment, I closed my eyes and imagined Azazel's face, the way martial artists do to motivate them.

Adrenaline pounded through me. I snarled, and immediately, my heart rate rose, as I intensified my punches and kicks to the bag. I slammed home a vicious left-right-left combination; the second left snapping the bag as I'd imagined snapping Azazel's neck. I let out all the rage I had in me against this madman who had caused me and others so much pain and fear. In a roar I counted my punches.

"NINE!" *Slam!*

"TEN!" *Slam!*

Even though Azazel was dead, the technological dangers in the world were not eliminated. I still needed to find a way to stop the virus from being released.

"ELEVEN!" *Slam!* "TWELVE!"

Suddenly, my fury was interrupted by an incoming call. I picked it up, saw *Number Withheld,* so I answered tentatively.

"Hello?"

"Brian, it's Gurung." My ears pricked up. His familiar voice made me smile, though I noticed I was still grinding my teeth in rage.

"Gurung! How are you?"

"I'm doing great, Brian. Hey, did I catch you at the wrong time? You sound out of breath."

"Not at all, old friend, just doing my morning workout," I said, kicking the punching bag brusquely away. "What is it?"

"You should know Interpol arrested The Seven. All their assets have been seized, but…"

I straightened up. "But what?"

"Norburg escaped."

*Shit!* Deep furrows cut across my brow. "But at least the others were captured. Right?"

There was a pause. "Would you mind doing a Skype video call right now?"

His Skype address pinged on my phone, and within seconds, I saw Gurung's familiar face beaming at me. That wise, old Gurung smile always made me feel as though things were going to be alright.

At that same instant, Madelyn from the orphanage suddenly blinked on my screen. "Madelyn? What…?"

"Brian! Watch this…the UN General Assembly and UNICRI in The Hague are condemning in the strongest terms possible what's been going on."

Over her shoulder, a giant TV screen flashed footage from the UN and The Hague. At that moment, Harrison appeared by Madelyn's side, grinned and said, "There's been a ban on facial recognition after Gabriel's post, and amazingly, the U.S. Democrats and Republicans in a rare move of solidarity are also against it."

The TV behind them revealed the politicians together, nodding collectively, indeed a rare occurrence.

*Incredible,* my brain whispered.

Next, Ronaldo and Gertrud joined them onscreen. "You've done well, Brian," announced Ronaldo.

"Thank you, we've all done well," I said, my senses overwhelmed. Again, my Skype screen blinked. "Wait, who else is there?" I asked.

The image flashed. Ahote's face joined them. He waved.

"Ahote! I am so glad to see you're alive." Tears stung my eyes.

"People are reconnecting with nature, Brian," Madelyn said.

As she spoke, behind her the TV displayed footage of people walking in forests and along rivers, appreciating wildlife and trees. "We're discovering the magic again, Brian."

"And *The Unplugging from Technology Movement* has been launched," Harrison added excitedly.

"People are joining in record numbers, disconnecting from tech, connecting with loved ones. Google and Apple are even helping the movement along," Madelyn added.

"Special pouches were issued to shield us from spying technology. There are already hundreds of thousands of people zipping their cell phones in them," Harrison continued.

Hearing this news, I smiled. *Thank God!* People were finally getting it.

Madelyn added, "A 4th Industrial Revolution has begun, Brian. Countries around the world are experimenting with UBI—Universal Basic Income. It gives every citizen the right to a basic monthly income paid for by the productivity created and the taxation of AI and technologies that would replace the human workforce. Working for humans instead of spying on them."

*Holy Moses! And governments were getting it, too?* This was mindblowing!

Madelyn added, "And here's someone very special, Brian. The one who saved your life."

I waited with bated breath, narrowing my eyes at the screen. *Who could it be?* The screen blinked and flashed. The little black girl with a lollipop in her mouth appeared, smiling bashfully.

"Destiny! How can I begin to thank you?!"

"By taking her under your wing," Gurung said with a big smile.

"Be her mentor, "Harrison added.

I caressed the back of my neck, overwhelmed. Finally, I saluted him. "Yes sir! Absolutely!"

Destiny smiled and waved at me, and I waved back. We both started laughing.

"When I saw you at the Grays, Destiny, I had a feeling this day would come," I said. "When I see you again, I have something special to give you that my Mom gave to me when I was a little boy," I added, putting my hand in my tracksuit pocket and feeling the stone with the powerful Algiz rune inscribed on it. *Ah, yes, there you are, precious stone.* I always carried it with me, my greatest treasure.

"I can't wait, Brian," she replied.

For a long moment the screen went silent. "We're *The Order of The Seven Stars...*" Madelyn started, then added, "The *Good Seven.*" She looked at everyone around her. "Thank God that Destiny has replaced me! I'm getting too old for this running around!"

I took a quick head-count—Harrison, Gurung, Ahote, Ronaldo, Gertrud, and Destiny—then cocked my head. "Wait…hold on." I frowned. Something was off. "Where's Tiponi?"

Every face on my screen stared tight-lipped. "I'm not sure and I'm gravely concerned," Ahote answered. "She saved my life at her cabin, but I haven't seen or heard from her since. We'll find her...I hope."

*You hope?* "She was the only one who knew I was planning to go to the UN and to release my book, *UNIVERSO-i.* I sent her a letter telling her of my progress within EYE-CORP, and my plans," I said. "I know this is perhaps not the right time, but any chance she hooked up with Azazel, and they fell in love again?"

There was silence. "It is possible. However, the good Curandera side has been stronger than her dark Bruja side ever since their romance in the orphanage," Ahote answered.

"What about the virus? Did the WHO or anyone else manage to find out who will release the virus and when?"

Madelyn responded, "Nothing has been found, Brian. Actually, we suspect it was yet another lie designed to confuse you and make you seem unreliable."

My eyes flashed to Gurung, then Madelyn, seeking confirmation. Both nodded. With every cell in my body, I hoped that was true, yet deep inside, something told me it was not true and that the worst was yet to come.

"Everyone, I can't thank you enough for everything you've done for me," I said. I wanted to change the sudden dark mood on the call.

"You're welcome, Brian," Gurung said. "And now, the next phase of your quest begins. With everything you've learned, you must help people overcome their fears, and begin living the exact lives they want to live."

*The next phase?*

*Won't this ever end?* My head down, I felt fears of defeat coming. *How much further would I have to go?* Through my tears, I saw on the screen in front of me all of my friends, gathered around, waiting for my reply. Trusting. Believing in me.

"That's great," I said, "when do I start?"

"You start immediately, of course," Madelyn replied.

*Of course,* I thought. Everything was suddenly clear…clear and inevitable.

After everyone said goodbye and good luck, I disconnected the call, gave the bag one last ferocious punch and left the gym, turning right on Broadway and disappearing into the morning traffic, toward home, toward Flower, and toward an unknown and unexplored future.

* * *

THE WALL STREET JOURNAL
APRIL 15, 2020 11:03 AM ET

TECHNOLOGY TO TRACK AND MONITOR INDIVIDUALS AIMS TO SLOW PANDEMIC, BUT RAISES CONCERNS ABOUT GOVERNMENT OVERREACH

In South Korea, investigators scan smartphone data to find within 10 minutes people who might have caught the coronavirus from someone they met. Israel has tapped its Shin Bet Intelligence unit, usually focused on terrorism, to track down potential coronavirus patients through telecom data. One U.K. police force uses drones to monitor public areas, shaming residents who go out for a stroll.

The Covid-19 pandemic is ushering in a new era of digital surveillance and rewiring the world's sensibilities about data privacy. The first global pandemic in an age of ubiquitous smartphones has meant governments now have surveillance capabilities unimaginable during prior outbreaks. Data flowing from the world's 5.2 billion smart-phones can help identify who, where and how people get infected.

In Western Australia, lawmakers approved a bill last month to install surveillance gadgets in people's homes to monitor those placed under quarantine. Authorities in Hong Kong and India are using geofencing that draws virtual fences around quarantine zones. They monitor digital signals from smartphone or wristbands to deter rule breakers and nab offenders, who can be sent to jail. Japan's most popular messaging app beams health-status questions to its users on behalf of the government.

Security professionals say the coronavirus crisis could become a watershed moment similar to the Sept. 11, 2001, terrorist attacks, which ushered in new government surveillance powers around the world in the name of protecting public safety.

FORBES MAGAZINE
MAY 6, 2019

ARTIFICIAL INTELLIGENCE CAN NOW COPY YOUR VOICE: WHAT DOES THAT MEAN FOR HUMANS?

It takes just 3.7 seconds of audio to clone a voice.

In just a short time, the capabilities of AI voice generation have expanded and become more realistic, which makes it easier for the technology to be misused. When you listen to several cloning examples, it's easier to appreciate the breadth of what the technology can do including being able to switch the gender of the voice as well as alter accents and styles of speech...

SMITHSONIAN MAGAZINE
MAY 4, 2018

HOW ACCURATELY CAN SCIENTISTS RECONSTRUCT A PERSON'S FACE FROM DNA?

This is the world of 'DNA phenotyping' – reconstructing physical features from genetic data. Research studies and companies like 23andMe sometimes share genetic data that has been 'anonymized' by removing names.

But can we ensure its privacy if we can predict the face of its owner? Last year, researchers from geneticist Craig Venter's company Human Longevity, made detailed measurements of the physical attributes of around 1,000 people. Whole genomes (our complete genetic code) were sequenced and the data combined to make models that predict 3D facial structure, voice, biological age, height, weight, body mass index, eye colour, and skin colour.

Not only can the machine sequence an anonymous genome it can then reconstruct the fact of the person and find the person on global surveillance but from the face, it can also identify certain genetic disorders already and put you in low score category...

NEW SCIENTIST
JANUARY 7, 2019

AI CAN IDENTIFY RARE GENETIC DISORDERS BY THE SHAPE OF SOMEONE'S FACE.

People with genetic syndromes sometimes have tell-tale facial features but using them to make a quick and cheap diagnosis can be tricky given there are hundreds of possible conditions they may have. A new neural network that analyses photographs of faces can help doctors narrow down the possibilities.

Yaron Gurovich at biotechnology firm FDNA in Boston and his team built a neural network to look at the gestalt – or overall impression – of faces and return a list of the ten genetic syndromes a person is most likely to have.

They trained the neural network, called DeepGestalt, on 17,000 images correctly labelled to correspond to more than 200 genetic syndromes. The team then asked the AI to identify potential genetic disorders from a further 502 photographs of people with such conditions. It included the correct answer among its list of 10 responses 91 per cent of the time.

The fact that the diagnosis is based on a simple photograph raises questions of privacy. If faces can reveal details about genetics, then employers and insurance providers could, in principle, surreptitiously use such techniques to discriminate against people with a high probability of having certain disorders...

WIRED MAGAZINE
APRIL 12, 2019

A PUSH TO CALCULATE A "GENETIC INCOME SCORE" USING GIANT DNA DATABASES RAISES A RAFT OF ETHICAL QUESTIONS.

The UK Biobank is the single largest public genetic repository in the world, with samples of the genetic blueprints of half a million Brits.

Prospective employers could ask you to submit your genetic income score as part of a job application.

Health and life insurers could use it to calculate your premiums. Social programs might use it as disqualifying criteria for receiving benefits.

Apps like the ones that prevent you from accidentally dating a relative could help you pair up with those genetically inclined toward prosperity.

IVF clinics could incorporate it into their genetic screening procedures so parents can choose the highest-earning embryos in addition to the healthiest ones.

# **Path / Day Seven**

## Love and Family

*Too many people are thinking of security instead of opportunity.*
*They seem to be more afraid of life than death.*

*— JAMES F. BYRNES*

# Fifty-Four

One day, months later, it hit me. The grim and fierce will it had taken to defeat The Seven I still carried with me like a sword. Yet there was one major thing missing in my life, the single-most-important thing of all.

*Love.*

Only one woman in my entire life had ever touched my heart in that way. Thoughts of her thrust me into agony.

I kept seeing her at Central Station in New York in those days—elegant, full of grace, stylishly dressed with lovely long dark hair, a mesmerizing face, skin like honey and heart-shaped eyes that I could gaze into forever and ever.

I was hooked, no doubt about that. But she never made eye contact with anyone. Least of all me.

One day, I figured, *What the hell, what do I have to lose, other than my self-esteem? What if I just plucked up my courage and walked up and spoke to her?*

I almost did on many occasions. But my plans always fell through.

It was very easy, being an introvert, to convince myself not to walk up and talk to a stranger—especially an intoxicatingly-beautiful stranger like her. I realized how powerful the fear of being rejected was inside of me—even though I knew very well that the rejection I imagined was only fiction, making me suffer more in mind than in reality.

By now, I found I was dreaming about her, day and night, so unearthly in her beauty that it obsessed me, and drove me to tears. *I'll approach her the next time I see her. Then she can tell me where to go, or she can come for a drink with me.*

It was a sunny but cold morning when I saw her next. She was wrapped up in a sweater and coat, waiting for a train in Central Station. Steeling myself, I sauntered up to her, trying to look casual, pulling out the universal conversation opener.

"Cold day, huh?"

She turned and looked at me like I was a leper. Still, her gorgeous lips twitched, she smiled like sunshine, and her open mouth flashed brilliant white teeth.

"That's it? That's the best you can come up with?" she asked. She sounded Italian.

I was dumbstruck, unable to think of a single sensible thing to say. That's when she laughed.

"I noticed you noticing me weeks ago."

"Um…yeah. I love your accent," I managed, and she smiled again.

"Yours isn't terrible," she beamed.

I winced. I couldn't believe my luck; she hadn't told me to go and throw myself under a train. Buoyed with a burst of confidence, I asked her out on a date.

To some surprise and my greatest delight, she agreed. We walked off together for conversation over the usual glass of wine. My mind twisted into knots. *If she hates me, she can finish her drink quickly and ride off into the sunset.*

She didn't hate me.

She liked me—a *lot*—and I liked her back. *A lot.*

The wine quickly became dinner, which became overnights away on business, then weekends away together, which were heavenly.

After sharing some intimate details about my family over dinner one night—including the story of how Norburg seduced Laura, my great-grandmother—it turned out we had some unusual things in common.

"My Aunt is Danish," she confessed, "and I used to spend all my summers in Denmark with my cousins."

"Really? That's amazing!" I replied, thrilled.

"Even more amazing is that I went to school in Denmark, and the school was located on the same road in Christianshavn where your grandad grew up and where Norburg seduced your great-grandmother!"

"What? No, it's not possible!"

She laughed. "And my old apartment was right next to the church where your grandad was buried. The Church of Our Saviour, famous for its helix spire with an external staircase you can climb for beautiful views over central Copenhagen."

"What an unbelievable coincidence," I said, "*if* you believe in coincidence."

She smiled. "I don't."

I laughed, an unexpected laugh. "Then we were made for each other," I said, staring into her amazing eyes.

As the dessert arrived, I said, "Nothing surprises me anymore. I'm being watched over and guided towards my destiny, even if I made a few detours chasing what I thought it was."

"I love hearing your stories of love and how you help people overcome fear to live the lives they want."

My cheeks and forehead burned with thoughts of the life we could have together. Wisps of her dark hair fluttered as she offered me a slice of dessert. "I…I love you," I blurted out, praying she felt the same.

"And you are the first soulmate I've ever had," she replied.

We clinked glasses. That was it. Our mutual love was confirmed.

We were married at New York City Hall, our witness a realtor who helped us, even snapping our wedding photos from his iPhone. We both loved the Hamptons, and after househunting, we found our dream home, though it needed a ton of renovation.

There, with the magical miracle of love and life, our son was born.

Over time, as our love matured and deepened, and our son grew, I began to notice a transformation in the world.

People were consuming less, reconnecting with nature and loved ones, suicide rates dropped, and people were beginning to feel happier.

The new dawn I longed for was happening, slowly but surely.

More news stories appeared about The Seven, chronicled by my journalist friend Louise. Books were released by other authors about their murderous past. Their secrets weren't secrets anymore. My wife and I continued to press forward. We decided we'd do what we could for people less fortunate—especially the elderly, women, children, and animals.

We connected with Keely, the amazing founder of a non-profit charity called Sierra House in New Jersey, helping young, under-privileged mostly African-American homeless women like Destiny had once been, some out of the foster-care system, some runaways and many abused, offering them food, safe shelter, community services, and education to help integrate them so they could live independently.

Life was an amazing miracle, full of love and joy, sharing every hour possible with my wonderful wife and son in our lovely home.

I felt like a completely new man, totally changed, reborn, free of thoughts of chasing riches, enlightened, and desperate to continue helping my brothers and sisters around the world. As I helped, it quickly became apparent that there were more good people in this world than bad.

We later teamed up with some incredible people at ONE SPIRIT, a non-profit organization that needed firewood for the cold winters and baby clothes, strollers and other necessities for families with single moms, as well as the elderly ones caring for their grand-children, all living at the Oglala Lakota Native American reservation in the state of South Dakota, originally included within the territory of the Great Sioux Reservation.

We could hear the faint cries of a new world being born. The struggles of the poor and the innocent were always close to our hearts. Yet every now and then, my thoughts went back to Miss Tiponi, the Bruja, and what had happened to her. Questions arose without answer. After awhile, and no word from her, those thoughts went silent, and I learned to ignore the questions.

* * *

# Fifty-Five

"It's a beautiful morning," my wife said to me as we ate a light breakfast. "Why don't you guys take a walk on the beach?"

"That's a wonderful idea!"

I took my son for a walk along the ocean. The morning breeze feathered the deep waters. The golden sand glistened. The warm surf lapped at our feet as we held hands, high above his head.

I watched our two resident white swans swimming and recalled that swans only love once. I connected with that.

I looked back at the house to wave at my wife who smiled and waved back. The sound of the birds taking flight close to us broke my thoughts, and as I reached down to take my son's hand again, my cell phone rang. *Unknown Caller,* the screen read. Flexing my finger over the ANSWER button, I hesitated for one sweet moment, then pressed it.

"Mr. Frederiksen?" a monotone voice asked.

I sighed. "Yes, who's this?"

"This is the police, sir. Detective Kelly. We found a body here in Queens, and forensic analysis of his cell phone revealed your number."

"A body?" My throat tightened. "Who is it? And how come my number's on his phone?"

"His name is Oleksii, sir. Do you know someone by that name?"

"Oleksii? I…well, yes, I do." *Oleksii, dear Lord!* My lips started to tremble. "What happened to him?"

"He was found dead in an alley. We're awaiting the post-mortem to establish the cause of death, but it appears to be a drug-related incident."

"You're sure?" I asked. "My God, poor Oleksii."

"What was your relationship with him, sir?"

"We were work colleagues, and friends."

"Would you mind identifying the body, sir?"

"Yes, of course. Just text the address."

I hung up. Instantly a chill ran down my spine. Feeling my son grip my hand, I gently caressed the back of his head.

"Azazel?" I whispered to myself. Hearing the name, my son looked up at me, then quickly raced off to paddle in the water.

*No. It's not possible.*

I gazed off at the horizon, in silence. I felt my lips form the words of the real answer. I quickly leaped into the crashing surf, gathered my son up in my arms, and carried him back to the house.

"Something's come up," I said to my wife, as she pulled our giggling son close to her.

"Where are you going?"

As I raced from the house, my wife gave me a worried look. *She knows something bad has happened.* I kissed her forehead, then my son's, and hurried off, speeding away in my car, not knowing what I was in for.

* * *

At the New York City Medical Examiner's Office in Queens, I asked for Detective Kelly. A small, unshaven, unkempt man appeared, eyeing me up and down.

"Appreciate you coming, sir. Please follow me." He limped away, me trailing behind.

Grimly we took the elevator down. Thoughts of Oleksii tugged at my brain. We entered the freezing-cold basement, and the medical examiner's assistant led us towards a stainless-steel wall where the bodies were stored.

The assistant scanned the nameplates, shuffled to one, and slid the drawer open.

I stared. Grunted. *That's Oleksii.*

"Is it him, sir?" asked Kelly, and I nodded, examining Oleksii's partially-naked body for any signs of attack or violence.

"You looking for something in particular?" the detective asked.

"No, no. It's just…a shock."

Kelly nodded, the assistant slid the drawer shut, and the detective led the way back upstairs to his office.

Kelly produced Oleksii's phone. "D'you know any of these numbers?" he asked and handed the call list to me.

I studied them. "None of them look familiar."

"He called this one a lot before he died," Kelly noted, then tapped a number on the phone's screen.

I looked at it and shrugged.

"Let's try calling it," the detective muttered, and punched in the number.

We waited. I held my breath. But no one answered, and it went to voicemail.

I sighed in relief. As I did, a cold-sounding woman's voice crackled from the voice message.

The voice was Pandora's.

*Oleksii knew Pandora? How could that be?*

I trembled, and ran my hand over my hair, in shock.

Kelly saw that I'd recognized the voice. "You know her?"

I hesitated. I squinted at my feet, then at the detective. "Pandora, another work colleague."

"What's her connection to Oleksii?"

*That's what I'm wondering.* "We all worked together, but I never saw them speak or even refer to one another," I said.

"Any idea why Oleksii would be calling her so much?"

"I have no idea."

Kelly seemed troubled by my answer. He grunted and said, "I checked his text messages, too."

"Did you find anything?" I wondered what he was getting at.

Kelly cocked an eyebrow at me. "You were the guy at the UN shooting, right?"

"Correct."

"Well, it seems Oleksii told this Pandora you were making a speech at the UN."

*What?* My stony face betrayed my shock.

"That means something to you, sir?"

"Um...no...yes, I mean. I thought...someone else gave that away."

*Oleksii told Pandora?* I felt like I was losing my mind. I never told Oleksii about the UN, so the only way he could know was if he had access to my computer. *That rat must have placed spyware on my laptop.*

Kelly raised his eyebrows. "And who would that be?"

"What?"

"You said someone else gave that information away."

"A woman named Tiponi. It's a long story. She's a Curandera..."

"A *what?*"

"A healer. But sometimes she's also a Bruja, a witch."

Kelly looked at me like I had two heads. I caught his eyes looking puzzled. Then he nodded, putting Oleksii's phone away, our conversation over.

Outside the police station, I regretted concealing the truth. I drove home in a daze, my mind rattling with questions about Oleksii betraying me to Pandora. And why.

*Oleksii, you stupid kid, what the hell...Talk to me! Were you in love with Pandora?* I kept thinking about Oleksii, all the way home, wishing he'd reached out to me, wishing he'd confided in me, wishing I could raise his body from the dead.

* * *

# Fifty-Six

I cruised home in the dark, Oleksii still on my mind.

At home, I found my wife and son sound asleep, so I kissed their cheeks and ambled to the kitchen, rooted around the fridge, but found nothing that interested me. All I wanted were answers. All I found were more questions.

I gulped a large glass of red wine, then feeling weary, fell asleep on the couch.

That's when the dream returned, sparked by the day's revelation about Oleksii.

I plunged deep into the madness. It was her again, the woman in the desert, the one with the bland, faceless white mask.

I tossed and turned on the couch, seeing her writing in the sand again.

She wrote two letters. *DN*. But this time, she continued.

She added the letter *A*.

I peered closer. Together, the letters read *DNA*.

Then she removed her mask, and to my greatest shock, it was a face I recognized, the face of...

*Pandora.*

I woke with a start, sweating. I sat up and stared around. *Where am I?* I rubbed the back of my neck. Everything seemed normal. But the image of the woman removing her mask and seeing Pandora's face was still fresh in my mind.

*Was Pandora behind all of this? My nemesis, the woman on the card? Did she work with Norburg? Or Azazel?*

Suddenly I felt eyes in the room, watching me. I was bewildered. This made no sense at all. And why write *DNA*? Unless she was warning me about Daemon Norburg being my DNA, and their plot around controlling people's genomes. *But hell, I already knew that.*

* * *

After a sleepless night, I rose early, quietly made some tea so as not to wake my wife and son, then grabbed my free-diving gear and spear-fishing gun and took my small Boston Whaler boat out to sea to shoot some fish.

There was nothing like feeling the salty spray of the sea on my face to clear my head. I raced the boat out to my favourite spot below the Ponquogue Bridge, a 2,812-foot-long passage over Shinnecock Bay in the hamlet of Hampton Bays, close to our house.

I dropped anchor, put my mask on, and tipped over the edge.

I hurtled downward, the sunlight above me growing dimmer. The blue ocean around me shimmered. After only fifteen minutes, from beneath the surface, I heard the sound of a boat approaching and pulling up next to mine.

*Who in the world could that be?*

I frowned, pushed off the bottom of the seabed and with my large free-diving flippers, swam upwards, blasting out the last air in my lungs through the tip of my snorkel as I breached the surface of the water.

Through my mask, I peered, looking patiently around until I saw a figure. A man.

*It can't be. There is no fucking way.* My body instantly shivered—not from the cold, but from staring right into the face of my assassin.

Azazel.

He sat in my boat, staring down at me, only a metre away. His Rottweiler scrambled around the boat, snarling and snapping its mighty jaws.

My fingers clenched in agony. I removed my mask and held myself up by resting my arms on the edge of the boat. For a moment, Azazel ignored me.

"Will you ever fucking die?" I asked.

Azazel laughed, leaning closer.

"I thought you were dead and The Seven were all arrested, except Norburg."

"The Seven were never my bosses, fool. It was always Pandora."

"I know." I sighed.

He smiled, impressed. "But did you know that your cleaning lady is her Mom, who she planted in your home to spy on everyone? Or that Pandora is also a great-grandchild of—"

Azazel let his sentence hang in the air. He glanced up, into the darkening sky. Instantly I knew who he meant.

"Norburg," I said.

Azazel started clapping his hands slowly.

"Which means she's your distant cousin."

For a moment, I took long slow deep breaths, letting that thought register. I wanted to vomit. Suddenly the last dream made sense. Seeing Pandora's face and the dream about DNA meant that my arch-nemesis—Pandora herself—came from my bloodline, my DNA.

"She kept it a secret from everyone," Azazel chuckled. "Together with her mom, they plotted to remove you, to make her the last and sole heir of Norburg and The Seven Empire."

I flexed my fingers tight again. My mind quivered. A wave from a boat passing by splashed me and almost pushed me under my boat. But I bounced back, staring Azazel down, exhausted with each revelation.

"Not even Norburg knew who she was, or that a fling with a woman in St. Petersburg 70 years ago with her great-grandmother produced a second heir. Her mom groomed and prepared Pandora from birth for this," Azazel gloated.

"Like mother, like daughter," I said, horrified that it had bypassed my usual strong instincts.

"Don't feel bad about that. Pandora and her mom are as evil as they come. I should know."

Hearing this made my skin crawl. Staring at Azazel and the Rottweiler, I realized Pandora might succeed in her plans, as I had no way of escaping now. Even if I dived back under the water again, I'd need to surface in a few minutes to breathe. Azazel knew that. He'd thought of everything.

"You killed Oleksii and Murphy," I said, trying to stall the inevitable.

"I did," he smiled in triumph. "But I didn't poison your beautiful dog."

"Then who did?"

"Pandora's mom. She poisoned her to stop you from going to the UN—and if you did, to make sure your dog didn't come with you so that I could kill you."

"Where is Pandora and her fucking mom?" I spluttered, full of rage.

"I have no idea. But when I find them, they won't like what's waiting for them; I told them not to touch the dog."

My face strained toward the horizon. Sluggishly my mind puzzled. "One more thing, since I am going to die anyway, tell me, is it true that a pandemic virus going to be released on the world?"

"Who knows? Even if it was true, how would you locate the first person in the world to be infected in order to spread the disease? I mean, it could be your wife, for instance. A quick stab from a syringe would do the trick."

I felt sick. An uncontrollable fury roared within me.

"You stay the hell away from my family, you motherfucker!" I screamed from the side of the boat.

My voice shattered the calm sea. I looked into Azazel's face, searching for any tiny facial expression that would reveal if he was lying. I found nothing. Only a smugness.

"Yes, what a great family you have, starting with your great-grandfather," he hissed. "I thought you might ask where Tiponi was." He grinned, clearly playing with me.

"What d'you mean?"

His grin widened. "She's safe with me, and no one will find her, not even Ahote—who I hear she saved, although he looked pretty dead when I stepped over his body on the porch." He cackled like a hyena.

I felt even sicker, wondering what I could do next.

"The Bruja is mine, in case you're wondering, and together, no one can stop us. Two fallen angels." He was psychotic. Unhinged. Crazy.

My heart pounded as a wild sense of blinding rage surged through me. Ocean waves slapped the side of the boat. Carefully my eyes explored Azazel's.

"Hey, Azazel have you ever dreamt that you were being dragged off to hell, with burning flames licking your ugly face? Then you woke up with a nurse leaning over you holding a defibrillator saying, *'Glad to have you back, we thought you were gone, we lost you for almost three minutes?'*"

Azazel's white teeth glinted. He gave me a look that could kill. Then without warning, he lunged forward, locked me in his arms, and wrapped the boat line around my neck, placing the other end in the mouth of his Rottweiler. He turned the ignition and started the boat.

"Time to die now," he shouted while the Rottweiler pulled on the rope, its fierce jaws tightening it further around my neck.

The boat thundered off, dragging me through the water, into the channel separating Southampton from Hampton Bays towards the Atlantic Ocean.

I choked, windpipe cut off, hands desperately trying to untangle the rope, almost slamming into the cement pilings of the bridge.

I snorted for air. *I'm about to drown!*

I scrambled for my dive knife, hidden on my right ankle. *Yes, by God, there it is!* Gripping it, I sawed back and forth on the rope, frantically slashing and cutting until I'd managed to sever it loose.

I floated in the water facedown, with my snorkel above the waterline, allowing me to breathe.

*Breathe, Brian, just breathe,* my brain quietly commanded.

My eyes flashed to the surface. Suddenly, I could hear underwater that Azazel had swung the boat around and returned to my body floating lifelessly in the water.

He made one critical mistake, though. He should have checked what I was holding on to between my legs while resting my arms on the side of the boat listening to him gloating about the evil deeds of him and Pandora, his paymaster.

Just as I heard the boat stop next to me, I rolled around, aiming my spear-gun. I fired, the spear whistling, hitting him right in the chest, and he stumbled overboard, writhing and jerking.

*"Die now, motherfucker!"* I shouted with indescribable relief.

I peered through my mask underwater and watched his body drift slowly to the bottom, blood swirling, his eyes turned to the fading light. *May the sharks find you, asshole.*

My troubles weren't over. On deck, the Rottweiler went berserk, biting and snapping at me as I tried to hold onto the boat. I rocked the boat back and forth, and amazingly, the dog tumbled out and into the sea. Immediately, she dove down to save her master, into the ocean blackness, but was unable to reach him.

All at once a grave thought hit me. *I was still gripping the spear gun connecting me to Azazel on the other end,* I thought, suddenly faced with the biggest decision of my life.

If I saved him—the man who had brought so much fear and destruction into my life—he would kill me one day.

However, there was still the matter of Tiponi. She was missing, and I'd promised to save her, like she saved me. Only Azazel seemed to know her whereabouts. *Bloody hell!* So, it seemed like I had to save Azazel, even if I believed in my heart he was lying.

*Damn. No other choice.* I flipped around in the water and dove down, swimming toward the bottom, yanking and pulling on the rope to my spear-gun. Peering deeper, I could see him, hovering above the coral bed, bleeding profusely with a blank stare on his pale white face.

I dove down. With immense strain and effort I hauled him to the surface. *Come on, asshole, don't make me regret this.* At the same time, his Rottweiler surfaced, gasping for air.

With a massive grunt, I managed to pull his limp body onto the boat. The spear had gone right through his chest, protruding from the other side.

Stubbornly I went about my business. I tied him up and left him in the front of the boat. I threw a line for his dog to bite onto and dragged her back to the beach.

As I tied up my boat at our dock, I grabbed my phone and dialed 911.

"I need a doctor," I spat into it.

I hung up, then noticed another caller was waiting. *My wife.*

I looked to see the Rottweiler licking Azazel's face. Taking a deep breath I answered her call.

"Are you OK, sweetheart? I've been out everywhere, looking for you!" she blurted out.

I stared at Azazel on the dock. "I just got back. I'll tell you everything when I get home."

With a sigh I began to hang up. Abruptly I had this strange feeling, a sixth sense that something was wrong.

I spun around and looked up toward the house.

"Brian, what is it?"

At the kitchen window, I spied two shapes. My eyes focused. *That's my wife, holding our son in her arms.* Seeing me, they both waved like everything was fine.

A moment later, my stomach melted in tension. Something was nagging at my mind. In a split second, I realized what was wrong. *That wasn't my wife who called me.*

*Dammit!* I swallowed hard, my thoughts stunned. *The AI machine had survived. And it had called me, mimicking her voice.*

I stared up at the sky, eyes burning. I instantly threw the phone into the sea, realizing the machine was keeping me talking while launching a sonic attack I couldn't hear, but would instantly kill me.

In desperation I waved back at my wife. "Hey, hey!" I screamed. She gazed at me long and thoughtfully and kept waving. That's when I heard a beep from inside my house. *Dear God. My home alarm system.*

Now everything made sense. I squinted up at the house and saw my giant flat screen TV flash on in the living room.

And on the TV screen?

My great-grandfather's face.

*This can't be!* I felt my senses drifting, my hands and feet going numb. I raced to the house, sprinted up the stairs, snatched my little son in my arms and my wife by the hand. What I heard before I could unplug the Internet and cable routers chilled me to the bone.

"Welcome to the family!" said a metallic voice, calling my little boy's name. "When the time is right, I will find you, and we can discuss your inheritance…"

With blazing speed, I ripped the TV cord out of the wall. Horrified, I wrapped my son tightly in my arms, hugging my wife, clutching them both in a fierce embrace.

"Brian, what is it?"

I froze. I clutched them tighter, not sure what to say. My eyes drifted through the kitchen window out to the boat, moored at the dock.

"Brian? What—?"

My heart stopped.

My chest heaved.

*Oh, God.*

*Oh, God, no.*

In a hypnotized gaze I stared. The boat was empty. Azazel and the dog were gone, leaving a bloody trail on the dock.

As I embraced my family, holding on for dear life, I felt my brain growing dizzy, the world beyond my eyes beginning to sway back and forth, like a pendulum.

*What a fool you are, Brian,* I thought. *It's not over. It's never going to be over. I thought I could rest, begin a new life. But I'm being dragged back in again. The final battle has yet to come. Until Norburg, Pandora, her Mom, and Azazel are captured—or better yet, dead—no one will be safe. No one.*

Clutching my family, I was heaving with sobs, nearly bent over, purging from deep inside my belly. All of a sudden, my deepest fears seemed to crumble. A decision swirled through my brain. Putting my arm around my wife's waist, I kissed her cheek, then the cheek of my dear sweet son. As I strode off, with my wife's phone in hand, my body language left no space for misinterpretation—it was obvious what I planned to do.

I knelt beside the kitchen cabinet.

From the hidden safe inside, I retrieved the card I'd received from the Grays. *It's time,* I thought. Then I headed outside to get a good cell signal, racing across the wet beach, my chest pounding, waves crashing onto the sand as I stared out at the dark horizon.

For the second time, I punched in the phone number.

"This is Brian," I said, gripping the phone fiercely, my eyes focused on the black skies and the thin shaft of light far in the distance. "We've got to get everyone back together again," I said, picking my words painfully. "The fight's not over."

~ THE END ~

CNN
JUNE 9, 2020

IBM IS CANCELING ITS FACIAL RECOGNITION PROGRAMS

IBM is canceling its facial recognition programs and calling for an urgent public debate on whether the technology should be used, officials announced.

In a letter to Congress, IBM's CEO stated the company aims to work with lawmakers to advance justice and racial equity through the responsible use of technology.

"IBM firmly opposes and will not condone uses of any facial recognition technology for mass surveillance, racial profiling, violations of basic human rights and freedoms, or any purpose which is not consistent with our values," the company's statement went on to say…

## EU SHOULD BAN AI-POWERED CITIZEN SCORING AND MASS SURVEILLANCE, SAY EXPERTS.

A group of policy experts assembled by the EU has recommended that it ban the use of AI for mass surveillance and mass 'scoring of individuals'; a practice that potentially involves collecting varied data about citizens — everything from criminal records to their behaviour on social media — and then using it to assess their moral or ethical integrity.

Experts have also noted that similar systems of surveillance and punishment already exist in the West, but instead of being overseen by governments they're run by private companies. With this additional context, it's not clear what an EU-wide ban on 'mass scoring' would constitute.

# Awaken

How can one awaken from the feeling of being a prisoner of one's life, suffering torment at the hands of unseen puppet masters, time and time again?

This is the question *UNIVERSO-i* asks you to ponder.

In your answer is the path to your life's true purpose. In your answer is the door to freedom from the puppet masters.

This is my call to action to you, the reader.

There's enormous power and money at stake for people and organizations that can make us forget we were born with wings and dreams—with amazing abilities to shape our own lives. Instead, these forces maintain control over us by keeping our lives in a constant state of panic—working long hours, monitoring our digital and physical footprints, and distracting us from what's really important.

We stop living in the moment, while our minds create purely fictional present and future scenarios. These scenarios make us afraid to live, just as we are afraid of dying.

But the trappings of The Seven, the small and powerful puppet masters who pull strings in our lives, can be escaped.

To do so, you will need to make important and drastic life changes that will free you from debt, the insatiable appetite for things you don't need, eating unhealthy food, watching the news that was purposely planted in your life to distract and frighten you. Anything that benefits these powers through your fear is attempting to destroy you.

Refuse to be manipulated into acting against your self-interests, and find the ability to appreciate what you already have, instead of constantly chasing what you want.

In the end, your escape from a life based on fear to one of purpose and peace depends on who is in control of your life—you, or someone else?

Everything you need for your new journey, you already have.

Rise now and clear a new path—one for others to follow. Be brave, take risks, experiment, be curious, be bold, challenge the status quo, and be entrepreneurial, because the world needs you.

After everything is said and done, you will discover that life is always and only about one thing: *love*. Love is your original North Star and the most important thing you're here to give and to receive.

Discover your true destiny by loving and giving, rather than in taking and consuming.

If you live your life with courage, fairness, integrity, dignity, being of service to others and pursue love as your path, your life will be a success, as you've accomplished the two most important goals in life:

*'To love and be loved.'*

# 7-Day Exercise

**Path / Day 1 (Childhood)**

Think back to your childhood.

*What are your happiest and saddest memories of growing up?*

*Do you recall something that someone told you that either encouraged or saddened you?*

*How do you think it affected you later in life?*

Remember that when people criticize or intentionally hurt other people, even their own children, either physically or with cruel words, it is ALWAYS because the person feels bad about their own lives. In their own pain, insecurities and self-loathing, they project that pain onto other people and animals and strike out to share their pain with others.

So, name the person, then receive the message and wisdom that, whatever was said or done, it was not about you. The wisdom to be drawn from that experience is that you are not to blame and that you can do anything you choose in your life. Nothing anyone ever said or did to you can prevent you from freeing yourself, right now. Nothing can prevent you from making a conscious choice to work towards the life you want for yourself. Let it go and use that adversity and the strength it took to overcome it, to propel you even faster towards the life of your dreams. How can anyone who has never faced adversity compete with you? You're stronger, more determined to change your life, better equipped to overcome fear and anxiety and better prepared to live the life of your dreams.

**Path / Day 2 (Growth to Young Adulthood)**

*Growing from a child into a young adult isn't easy.*

*Think about your young adulthood and write down the memories good and bad.*

Again, do you recall something that someone told you growing up that either encouraged or saddened you? An example could be someone telling you that you're not beautiful enough, not good enough, that you're never going to make it. Or someone telling you what they want you to become in life because that's what everyone else in the family did.

*How do you think it affected your choices in life?*

Always remember that when someone says something to you that is not encouraging, the only intention of this is to hold you back from realizing your dreams and to sadden you. It says everything about that person and NOTHING about you. The reality here is that they wish they had the courage you have to do things. So that, in their pettiness and on account of the regrets they themselves have about their own lives, they try to ensure that you fail as miserably as they did. DON'T LET THEM INFLUENCE YOUR LIFE, use their negativity as a motivation for yourself, to do even better.

**Path / Day 3 (Money, Power and Temptations)**

*We all want and need money, enjoy or want power and fall for temptation. Jot down your personal experiences of all three.*

*Do you remember times in your life where you knew in your heart that you had made a promise, but the temptation to not keep your word was too great?*

*Do you think you would have been better off in the longer term by keeping your word, even if it meant less money or power in the near future?*

Have you ever heard of anyone who never kept their word, who simply took advantage of other people at any available opportunity, actually living a long and peaceful life? I have never seen it. I have seen people who briefly prospered from taking advantage of other people, but sooner or later their bad deeds caught up with them. Nothing good can come from things that came from something bad.

Are you ready to make a change and trust that if you do the right thing, eventually money and influence will come your way as a consequence of your decisions? It takes courage because the temptations to get ahead, to take what is not rightly yours and to go back on your word can be great, but I promise you that if you resist, then good things will come your way and people will trust and respect you.

Remember that just being poor does not guarantee you virtue and honour. Just as being incredibly successful and prosperous doesn't automatically make you a sinner either. It is the content of your heart that matters.

If you asked me what is the most powerful thing I can do to change my life, to achieve anything I want and to live the life of my dreams, the answer would be: - to love people and use things, not to love things and use people to acquire more things. The game of destiny is only won by loving and giving, not by attempting to be constantly loved and adored in life, through for instance social media, or by trying to win responses, favors and things from others in any way. Take a chance on love and your world will change. Trust me!

**Path / Day 4 (Searching for a Balance - a Spiritual Path)**

In my life I always tried to control everything, until that fateful day everything fell apart. I lost all my money and became homeless. At that point I realized that if everything hadn't been wrestled away from me, I would never have trusted in anyone or anything else to shape events in my life. In hindsight, it was almost the most loving thing that could have been done to me.

Letting go, believing that you're loved and cared for and that everything will be fine is very powerful. Most children don't worry about their next meal or being clothed. They innately believe that they are safe and will be provided for. As we grow older, somewhere along the way we forget that feeling.

I have found life to be like going to school, we meet certain people and encounter events that are all designed to teach us the lessons we are meant to learn. If we try to avoid them, or we keep repeating our mistakes, those events and people will keep on re-emerging in our lives until we've learned our lessons.

I've found that the more I worry, the more I think I'm the only one who can influence my destiny, the more I hold on to money, the fewer the opportunities are that come my way and the lower the resulting income. When I trust in something bigger than myself, trust that my creator and the universe have a plan for me, I let go of my worries and freely spend money, time and energy on good things. Then, miraculously, more money and opportunities come my way. It works, trust me!

*Do you believe in a higher power or something other than yourself?*

*Are you ready to give to trust that you are not alone, that you will be cared for, if only you follow the right path and give as much love and help as you can to others?*

*Get your notepad and write down your thoughts and feelings.*

**Path / Day 5 (Corporate and Betrayals)**

I was born to be a change agent, doing things differently and breaking down silos to foster collaboration and innovation. I found that corporations are designed to encourage longevity, providing compensations and rewards to encourage people to stay longer. As a consequence, people begin designing their careers at an early stage, planning for promotions and retirement packages.

The result is that they become very averse to any type of change or disruption, since that influences their carefully planned careers. In an attempt to avoid disturbances to their plans, they will do anything to get rid of any person or new idea that challenges their status quo. It brings out the worst in people and stifles innovation.

However, I have learned that in most cases it is not because people are evil. When people oppose you it is often due to fear and insecurity about their careers and plans. Understand that resistance to change often comes from a level of personal insecurity. Avoid fighting them if you can, have them join you so you have one less battle to fight.

That's not to say that there are no bad people out there, there are of course absolutely terrible human beings around who will do anything to get to the top. I've had close encounters with a number of them. I even had one as my boss. The best thing you can do is to leave the job or arrange a transfer away from them. Don't spend one moment with an abusive person, at work or in your personal life.

One of the most valuable lessons I learned in life was this: what people do to you is their karma, how you respond is yours. I have carried that with me through challenging times in relationships, ventures and corporate jobs. I've not reached the spiritual level of turning the other cheek, but I have learned to find compassion where there could easily be anger and a temptation to seek revenge. This doesn't mean that you shouldn't protect yourself, shouldn't defend your idea or space, or shouldn't litigate if necessary. But you should act righteously, your actions should come from a place of fairness, balance and proportionality. Remember, "Weak people revenge. Strong people forgive. Intelligent people ignore" – Albert Einstein.

The other lesson I learned later in life is to surround yourself with good people in business and in life of course. Your life will be so much easier. It seems obvious, yet time and time again we allow people into our circle of trust who we know instinctively aren't quite trustworthy. This is because we think they can bring us something or because they are very talented, so we decide to keep them. Don't do it - get rid of them and hold on to those you know you can really trust and care for in your inner circle.

*Write down the good and bad things that happened to you. What do you learn and how would you handle situations and people differently a next time?*

**Path / Day 6 (The Puppet Masters - Escaping the Matrix)**

The easiest way to control people is to straddle them with debt. When you face the risk of your car being repossessed, of losing your home and your job, you're very unlikely to protest to demand changes.

Fear is about certain danger, anxiety is 'an experience of uncertainty.'

And uncertainty is what fear-mongers play on. So, if people are persuaded to feel anxious about their families, finance or homes, and the other side wants to influence our thinking, and our actions, they offer certainty or the illusion of it. They combine uncertainty with the concept of a growing threat to your day-to-day routines or your entire existence.

There's enormous power and money at stake for people and organizations that can make us forget we were born with wings and dreams—with amazing abilities to shape our own lives. Instead, these forces maintain control over us by keeping our lives in a constant state of panic—working long hours, monitoring our digital and physical footprints, and distracting us from what's really important.

We stop living in the moment, while our minds create purely fictional present and future scenarios. These scenarios make us afraid to live, just as we are afraid of dying.

The puppet masters in the background convince us that we need to keep up with trends, making us buy things we don't need, eat the wrong food and watch tv that makes us anxious so that eventually we're out of balance and feel insecure and anxious to the point where we are willing to give control of our lives to people who say they can keep us safe."

*Have you ever felt that someone or something unseen is pulling the strings?*

*You're right, they are. The question is, what are going to do to take back control of your life?*

*Get that notebook and take note of your thoughts on this, plan concrete steps to take back control of your life and ensure that you are no longer being manipulated.*

**Path / Day 7 (Love and Family)**

Allowing love to dawn in your life leads to a reduction of self, for yourself and others. Love and Life need to be harmonious, like a growing, tended garden. Where there is life there is love. However, human love is too often surrounded by infatuation, greed, lust, anger and jealousy. Pure love is the blossom of spiritual fulfilment.

I've also discovered that there are many versions of love. Some are needy, some conditional, some are restrictive, some are an illusion, and some are insecure. Of all of them, there is only one kind that is truly love; and that is the unconditional kind of love, which gives you the strength, if you love someone, to set them free. And the courage to trust that if they come back, they're yours. If they don't return, they were never there.

I have found that some people are terrified of love, even when it's right in front of them. They will push it away, since past happiness and love were followed by deep trauma, so that all future love is associated with the potential risk of more pain, right around the corner. Therefore, they feel it is better to never love again, to prevent that pain from happening again.

That is why people keep dating and are unable to commit to getting married, you will not be the one standing at the altar. How many times have I not heard of couples dating for 2-3 years. I've even heard of people dating for 10 years. After breaking up, you will hear that the person met someone else and proposed within a few weeks or months. They may have loved you, but were never in love with you.

That is what happens when you constantly try to save someone you recently met. Then you usually end up having to save yourself, or needing to be rescued by friends or family - sooner rather than later. Beware of the behavioral pattern of trying to save others. You may quickly become the one who needs saving.

*Try to think of things you've done while being in love. Do you know a happy family that grew from being insecure?*

*If you love someone, remember not to do anything to restrict them, or make their lives worse than being alone. That is not love, it's something else, but surely not love.*

*If you know you're trapped in an unhealthy relationship that prevents you from living the life you want and should be experiencing, what's your plan to free yourself?*

*If you know your insecurity is making your partner or family miserable, do you have enough courage and faith to believe that if they truly love you, they will stay with you?*

*You cannot find happiness and love, if you don't offer happiness and love. What are going to do differently now, to bring love into your life?*

*What could be more important, right?*

*We all want a family and hopefully, love.*

*Write down your experiences of love and family, good and bad.*

Congratulations on having completed the 7 days of exercises. But remember there is no trying, there is only doing.

Now rise and use the work you've done and the lessons you've learned to take back control.

Believe that fear and anxiety only exist in your mind. Have faith, start moving towards the job, relationship, home, you wish for…the life of your dreams.

This is my call to action.

**Rise.**
**Speak.**
**Act.**
**Give.**
**Love.**
**Risk.**
**Discover.**
**AWAKEN.**

# ACKNOWLEDGEMENTS

**ROBERT BEEDHAM**, you're an inspiration and a pleasant and kind human being. Thank you for breathing magic into my book. I'm forever grateful for your friendship, wisdom, and support in helping me help others overcome their fear and unleash God-like powers to live the lives they were always meant to live.

**SAM SEVERN**, anyone who has the fortune to meet you in their lifetime will become a better person—and in my case, also a better writer. Your guidance, your kindness, your encouragement, and your amazing ability to breathe life into a sentence was invaluable.

I feel so blessed that you both agreed to help me on this most important journey in my life.

Many blessings,

*Brian Frederiksen.*

# Connect With The Author

**Website**
brianfrederiksen.com

**Amazon**
amazon.com/author/brianfrederiksen

**Goodreads**
goodreads.com/brianfrederiksen

**LinkedIn**
linkedin.com/in/brianfrederiksen

Signup for the author's New Releases mailing list and get a free copy of *The 10 Principles to Unleash Your God-Like Powers to Achieve Anything You Want.*

https://brianfrederiksen.com/free-book

Printed in Great Britain
by Amazon

41736629R00205